THE HILLWALKER'S
GUIDE TO SCOTLAND

For Ann, my companion along the way

THE HILLWALKER'S GUIDE TO SCOTLAND

Bruce Sandison

Unwin Hyman

London   Sydney   Wellington

First published in Great Britain by the Trade Division of Unwin Hyman
Limited, 1988.

UNWIN HYMAN LIMITED
15–17 Broadwick Street
London W1V 1FP

Allen & Unwin Australia Pty Ltd
8 Napier Street, North Sydney, NSW 2060, Australia

Allen & Unwin New Zealand Pty Ltd with the Port Nicholson Press
60 Cambridge Terrace, Wellington, New Zealand

British Library Cataloguing in Publication Data

Sandison, Bruce
  The hillwalker's guide to Scotland.
  1. Scotland. Hill walking. Visitor's guides
  I. Title
  796.5'22

  ISBN 0–04–440025–X

Designed by Julian Holland

Line illustrations by Martin Smillie

Typeset in 11 on 12 point Bembo
by Nene Phototypesetters Ltd, Northampton

Printed in Great Britain
by Biddles, Guildford

Contents

Introduction

The baby weighed 5 lb 12 oz. I know, because I carried him to the kitchen, where my wife Ann put him on the scales. There were four hundred and sixty pages of script, maps and illustrations and I was sad it was done, but father and child had survived delivery and the rest of the family were delighted. A huge sigh of relief resounded throughout Ruther House. Peace at last.

This book marks my half-century and I am thankful to have arrived at that milestone more or less intact – thanks to Ann, who has kept me fit for the hills and encouraged my efforts to describe some of our favourite walks. I have written about them warts and all, for not everything always goes according to plan. We have our disasters like everyone else, but, somehow or other, Ann turns mishap into adventure and a walk with her is full of surprises. I know of no other person with whom I would rather share that special magic of our Scottish hills and moorlands.

Apart that is, than with my son Blair. We have walked many miles together, Blair and I, over the wet, desolate, distant places – fishing, talking and generally getting lost. Frequently, a case of the blind leading the blind. Blair knows and loves the Uists and Benbecula and kindly refreshed my Outer Hebrides memory. As he explained, at my great age memory begins to fade and bits of the revered personage tend to fall off. That's the last time I lend him my compass and whistle.

The other members of Clan Sandison were also most helpful. Daughter Lewis-Ann pointed out where I had gone wrong, as she has been doing for the past twenty-five years. Artist Charles groaned a lot over my childish attempts to produce reasonable illustrations. Thoughtful Jean got it most right; she just kept telling me that it was wonderful. But this book is as much theirs as it is mine, because some of our most splendid walks have been together, as a family. Some of our most memorable days were the days we spent together and I treasure them all.

The book makes no pretence to be anything other than a personal account of a number of Scottish hill and coastal walks. If my experiences of these walks differ from your own then I apologize for any errors or omissions. If some seem less interesting than others, then remember that beauty lies in the feet of the beholder and one man's pleasure is another's pain. Some of the walks described are exhausting but most can be managed by anyone who is reasonably well preserved. Provided you follow the hillwalker's code and pay due regard to safety measures, then you should come to little harm.

I have made every effort to ensure that the information given and the routes described are accurate and up to date but, obviously, things change, so you should make your own assessment before setting out. Nor do I imply that there are guaranteed legal rights of way. Most landowners will allow public access and it is up to us all to ensure that we respect that privilege and do nothing to damage property. Always seek advice from the estate, particularly during autumn months when stalking or shooting parties may be active in the hills.

A number of kind people helped me in my work and I would like to thank them. Sustenance and sympathy along the way were provided by Mrs Sandison senior of Edinburgh, my mother, who put up with my presence and tantrums for weeks on end as I checked details of Borders, Lothian and Fife walks. Suppose after all these years she is used to it, but without her support I could never have finished my task. Similarly, in the West of Scotland, I have to thank Messrs George and Bruce Reynolds of Killearn for giving me bed and board. Sorry, Uncle George, for dripping all over the house every day but I can't really be held responsible for Trossachs weather.

In the far north, Harry Mulford of the Orkney Field and Arts Centre at Birsay was wonderfully supportive. His knowledge and love of Orcadian landscape and wildlife are outstanding and his guests and clients are fortunate to have such a guide. I wish to thank Tony Henderson at the Garvault Hotel, Kinbrace, Sutherland, for his advice and I am grateful also to the Scottish Arts Council for making my life easier by the award of a travel and research grant. Finally, may I thank my publisher, Merlin Unwin, for his encouragement, courtesy and endless patience.

I very much hope you enjoy reading the book and that it will draw you out into the wilderness wonderland of the Scotland I love. Without our land we are nothing.

Ruther House
January 1988

Location of Walks

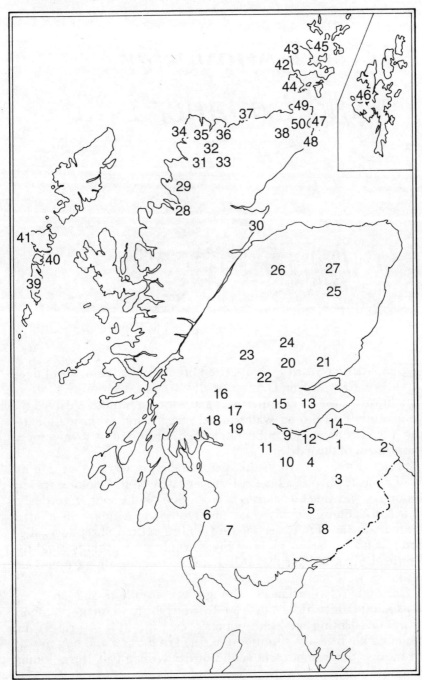

1

Longyester
and Lammer Law

FOR THE first year of our married life my wife, Ann, and I lived in a cottage at Fala Dam, a small village sixteen miles south of Edinburgh, close to Lammermuir and Moorfoot hills. We lived the simple life: no running water, no electricity and no inside toilet – just a bucket in an old timber-built shed, disguised by a yew tree at the bottom of the garden.

From October until April, paraffin lamps were lit at 2 p.m. Water was fetched in a bucket from a nearby well. Cooking was by Calor gas. Heating – coal fires and running on the spot, vigorously. Our companions were two kittens, Dolly and Mima, named after mothers-in-law for easier cursing, and a retired sheepdog called Spud, who had spent most of his working life dashing round the Pentland Hills and yet was still game as ever for a long moorland walk.

Changing circumstances, thoughtless ambition and an ever-expanding family moved us from Fala but the fond memory lingers – smoke drifting in cold winter's air, the riot of roses and honeysuckle that was summer, the smell of heather and bog myrtle on moors, the ever-present sound of trout-filled Fala Burn 'loupin ower its linns'.

So it was like visiting an old friend when I passed the village again, on my way to Gifford and Longyester, intent on walking the majestic Lammermuirs. I parked by twitching curtains at Longyester Farm cottages and surveyed the soft shoulder of Lammer Law, rising 1,765 feet before me, grey, blue and green against the horizon. The buzz of busy combine harvesters and barking dogs followed me up the road to Blinkbonny Wood. Rose-hip and raspberry bobbed and danced in mounting wind. My brother, Ian, and I used to make itching powder from rose-hip berries. Drove the girls wild with pretended anger – red hands tussling with long hair and jumper collars.

Squared banks of conifers line the fields, wind-breaks against Lammer storms and welcome shelter for sheep and cattle. To the left of the road are the remains of something intensive – probably a pig-breeding unit. The empty pens are overhung by tall, light-less security lamp-posts, like a Lilliputian greyhound racing track.

Clearing the shelter of the woods, I catch the full force of the wind howling downhill into my face. Butterflies and moths are keeping a low profile this morning. Scabious, tormentil and buttercup toss and bob in the gale. An enigmatic notice warns: 'Danger, Range. Do not pass this point when red flag is flying.'

Should I want shot? I search carefully for evidence of red flags. Higher up the hill, I look back into an old quarry. It must have been used as a Sten-gun range, hence the notice. The sand-backed target and firing point are so close together it could hardly have been anything else. I remember that unless you were actually sticking the muzzle of the gun directly into the middle of the target it was impossible to hit anything with those unruly weapons.

The track up and over Lammer Law is an old drove road, used for centuries to take cattle and sheep to the great southern markets. Whole families would make the long journey – lean husbands, wives, children and dogs, chattering and yapping complaining herds and flocks over the moors.

A magnificent Charolais bull lifts a huge head and stares balefully. Two soft-eyed cows, nuzzled and nudged by new-born calves, chomp contentedly. I call good morning, politely, and hurry by.

My first rest is on a clump of blaze-purple heather by a tiny crystal-clear stream. Westwards, a few lonely sycamores bend against the constant force of the wind. A foolhardy meadow pipit whisks past, followed by an incautious honey-bee. The East Lothian landscape is a patchwork of yellow and green fields, specked white and grey with farmhouses, peeping from dark woods.

Whale-boned Berwick Law broods blackly over fertile fields.

The Bass Rock gauntly guards the Firth of Forth, a grim prison during the seventeenth century. The Romans knew this land and called the inhabitants the Votadini. These ancient Picts peopled the Lothians for a thousand years with hill forts and settlements. I looked towards graceful Tarprain Law, their capital, where, in the early years of this century, a group of workmen discovered an astonishing array of Roman silver and Pictish treasures – a sophisticated, established town enclosing an area of 40 acres.

The wind was even stronger as I struggled on up the hill; it tugged at my coat, whipped tears from my eyes. A brief glimpse of Hopes Reservoir, leaden, sparkling at the foot of Bullhope Law, dotted black by a hopeful fishing boat. At the top of Lammer Law, thankfully, the sun sailed clear from behind thick, dark clouds and the glories of the Lowlands crowded round: Arthur's Seat, a lion crouching over the Auld Grey City of Edinburgh; the blue line of the Pentland Hills; Sir Walter Scott's rounded Eildons and, closer, as though waiting to be stroked, the gentle Moorfoots.

A sudden storm swept in, blanketing the view, and I hurried on towards Tollishill, round Hog Hill and Windy Law to my goal – a single standing stone and the rough outlines of a Pictish fort, ringing the top of a small hill to the west of Tollishill Farm. Vast pylons strode across the hill, like figures from H. G. Wells's *War of the Worlds*. Stark and menacing in the mist. A rabbit scurried over the track, pursued by a bad-eyed stoat. Death in the heather.

Passing under the humming hydro wires I reached Tollishill to be greeted by a laconic collie, securely tied to a barn door. I'm grateful. The outline of the fort is clearly visible: concentric rings, commanding a 360-degree view. These Pictish forts were as much working villages as defensive structures. Gates were barred and spears sharpened only in time of communal danger – generally from the acquisitive aspirations of overbearing neighbours. The single sentinel standing stone is by the side of the road, on the edge of a little wood. Good place for lunch, sheltered and calm.

Wet but refreshed, I retraced my steps back up Crib Law, shadowed by a hungry herring gull and two minister-black crows, wind pushing my back. Before Lammer Law, a deep scar cuts into the hill and I struck right, over the moor, to Bleak Law by Sting Bank Burn. Try falling on your backside to find out why it is so named. On the summit of Bleak Law a tumbled cairn centres a criss-cross of sheep tracks which wind amidst heather and ferns down to a red-rust-roofed shed at the foot of the valley.

Sting Bank Burn bustles into Hopes Reservoir through a wonderland wood of alder, silver birch and hazel. Although Hopes is man-made, it is old enough to have an established, settled look, undiminished by the neo-Gothic water tower and well trimmed lawns surrounding the south end. Beehives nestle in sunny corners and I asked the fishermen how they were getting on. A disgruntled grunt told all.

A dipper, black and white, best-bib-tuckered, kept me company along the outlet burn. The hills around Hopes are scattered with evidence of the Pictish endeavour. Wonder if they had better luck with the fishing? The ghosts of a thousand years keep step with my squelching, sodden boots as I made the last easy miles along tree-lined country lanes back to Longyester.

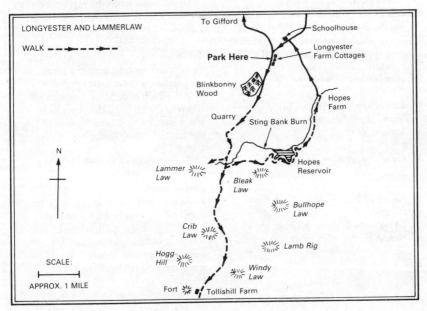

LONGYESTER AND LAMMERLAW

WALK ▪ ▬ ▬ ▶ ▬ ▶

To Gifford

Schoolhouse

Park Here

Longyester Farm Cottages

Blinkbonny Wood

Quarry

Hopes Farm

Sting Bank Burn

N

Lammer Law

Bleak Law

Hopes Reservoir

Bullhope Law

Crib Law

Lamb Rig

SCALE:

Hogg Hill

Windy Law

APPROX. 1 MILE

Fort

Tollishill Farm

WHAT YOU NEED TO KNOW

Time and effort Allow about five hours for this walk, more if it is a fine day so that you can linger on the way. The climbs are gradual, though fairly steep, and most of the route is along a well marked path. The return journey crosses moorland and you might stumble about a bit; try and stick to sheep tracks and you will come to little harm. In dry weather, the descent from Bleak Law could be sudden if you slip. Carry a tea tray and recapture childhood days if you want to get down very rapidly.

Location Ordnance Survey Sheet 66, Edinburgh, second series, scale 1:50,000.

Grid references Longyester Farm Cottages 545651; Blinkbonny Wood 537642; Quarry 535634; Lammer Law 524618; Crib Law 525598; Tollishill Farm 519581; Bleak Law 538616; Hopes Reservoir 547622; Hopes Farm 559638; old schoolhouse 550655.

Route Park the car on the grass verge by Longyester Farm Cottages and walk south along the minor road towards Blinkbonny Wood. Past the wood, a gate leads onto the hill, following a good track. You will see this track winding up the hill ahead of you.

Strike right from the track, at the highest shoulder, to reach the top of Lammer Law. Walk back to the track and continue south to Tollishill Farm, the standing stone and Pictish fort. Return the same way until you reach the deep scar down which runs Sting Bank Burn. Keep to the right of the burn and work your way round the side of the hill, climbing to the top of Bleak Law.

At the north end of Bleak Law, look down to Hopes Reservoir and you will see a red-roofed shed. Follow a convenient sheep track to the shed. Cross the little burn and you will pick up an ill defined track which leads round the side of Hopes Reservoir, eventually bringing you to the dam at the eastern end.

A minor road exits north from the reservoir, following the outlet burn, past the entrance to Hopes House and East Hopes Farm. Cross the bridge over Hopes Burn and walk on to a road junction, by an old schoolhouse and a telephone kiosk. Turn left here and walk past Longyester Farm, back to the cottages.

2
Coldingham Cliff-Tops and St Abb's

COLDINGHAM PRIORY, in Berwickshire, was founded in AD 635. Coldingham Old Church was established on the site of the Priory five hundred years later. Coldingham New Church was built in 1220 and survived intact until the middle of the seventeenth century. Then Oliver Cromwell had a go at it on his way to Edinburgh in 1648.

With the return of Charles II in 1660, and legalised mirth and jollity, the pious people of Coldingham repaired their place of worship, and again in 1854, when a major restoration programme was undertaken. One hundred years later, in 1954, the whole structure was completely renovated and today Coldingham Church is one of the most attractive and best kept churches in Berwickshire.

Understandably, given its turbulent history, the present incumbent, The Revd Daniel G. Lindsay, keeps the little church locked.

When I called recently I had to content myself with wandering round the outside, by trim lawns, through ancient arches, watched by a battalion of suspicious gardeners. Perhaps the same thing happened to Oliver Cromwell and, in order to gain access to his maker, he found it necessary to remove one of the walls permanently.

The village of Coldingham lies amidst fine, fertile, red-soiled Berwickshire farmlands, crowded round a market cross, raised in 1815 by Lord Home to celebrate the defeat of Napoleon – neat red-tiled houses, almost Loire-like in character.

Virginia creeper clings lovingly to the walls of the Anchor Inn but I resisted the temptation for a quick one, striding righteously and soberly past the inviting front door. Never know who might be watching from the shadows of time, bible-breeched and waiting to pounce on poor sinners. Walk first, thirst later.

I walked up the hill, out of the village, and turned right towards Coldingham Loch, two miles distant along a hump-back-bridged country lane, through the old wood that comforts Buskin Burn to Coldingham sands and the North Sea. The sound of running water always reminds me of a senior fishing friend, much given to the love of a dram and always waterless when it came to finding something to dilute his fancy. As the Argo-Cat lurched him lochwards across goat-sided slopes, he would inquire hopefully: 'Is it running water?'

At the top of the first hill, past Bogangreen, a thoughtful bench has been placed in the shelter of the roadside hedge, giving a fine view back to the village, multicoloured roofs across gold fields. Wind whistles through telegraph wires and umbelliferous stalks creak and shake in the breeze.

Hedgerow brambles, missed by birds, prick my fingers and stain my hands. Van-Gogh-black crows hover above stubble and balers work busily up and down the long rows of straw bundles. A fringe of pines guards the road up to Pilmuir Farm and, in the distance, Westloch House and the wood round Coldingham Loch, one of Scotland's oldest and most famous trout fisheries.

Coldingham Estate used to belong to the Scottish brewing family of Usher. It is now owned by Dr and Mrs Wise, who offer a range of well-sited, comfortably furnished self-catering cottages to anglers and other holidaymakers in search of peace and quiet. The loch is regularly stocked with brown trout and has the distinction of being the first loch in Scotland to stock rainbow trout. Both thrive mightily in the lime-rich waters.

The most attractive cottage on the estate is Lochside Cottage, built over a boathouse and the perfect place for an away-from-it-all winter break. Access is either by suspect grass track or by rowing across the loch. The sound of the sea breaking endlessly on mighty cliffs hurried me round the west shore of the loch, past curious head-bobbing white-crested coots and nervous wildfowl.

First sight of the sea, sparkling with a million colours. From the north, a narrow track picks its way along the cliff and I join it close to where a tiny stream blossoms into a silver waterfall, plunging down Heathery Carr, dashing against ebony-black seagull-screaming rocks. On the horizon, the ominous, unmistakable shape of a warship trails a long white furrow northwards, heading for Bass Rock and the Firth of Forth.

The 500-foot hilltop is spread with a continuous array of grass-covered mounds, sudden hollows and heaps of boulders: remains of ancient hill forts and settlements. People lived and worked here for thousands of years and there are outlines of defensive ramparts, ditches and an enclosed fort which measured almost 200 feet across. There are foundations of circular stone-built houses and evidence of a community occupying the site down to post-Roman times. In 1931, relics dated between AD 150 and 400 were discovered during excavation works.

I stopped in the old circles and shared lunch and memories with my ancestors. Must have been a hardy lot to survive here. No danger of a surprise attack from the east, the cliffs would have seen to that, but no way out either. I wondered how many of the villagers had met their pagan gods half-way down the sheer face of the cliff?

After lunch, eastwards along the track to Pettico Wick and my first glimpse of a marine nature reserve. Don't see much of the reserve, not from the shore anyway; but a convenient notice, by the little slipway, tells me that Pettico is jointly sponsored by Britoil and the Nature Conservancy Council. I was reminded that, under-water, spear guns, spears and gaffs were not allowed. Nor was I to disturb marine life or remove any plants. Got to be rules, I suppose, even on the bed of the North Sea.

St Abb's Head, crowned by the white-painted lighthouse with its red-lead fog-horn perched precariously over the cliff, seemed civilization after the wilds of the hill forts. An all-weather road leads to the top and this is much used by visitors to the St Abb's Head Nature Reserve: 200 acres of coastal grasslands and cliffs. More notice-boards. Why does officialdom seem incapable of existing without littering the countryside with notice-boards?

When I first visited St Abb's Head, more years ago than I care to remember, there wasn't a single, solitary notice-board to be seen. Only wild-flower-carpeted cliffs, kittiwakes and puffins and snow-white gannets dashing into blue waves. Now we have high-heeled hair-dressed matrons trailing overweight, grumbling husbands: 'Look at the lovely view, dear, isn't it nice?' So I'm prejudiced? Can't I be fifty and prejudiced?

The path round St Abb's Head is wonderful, and you soon leave most of the single-step-trippers behind. I walked into the tiny fishing village of St Abb's, and back decades in time to a family holiday we spent there in 1947.

The row of brightly painted cottages still crested the hill over-looking the harbour. The bedroom window, where my brother, Ian, and I waited breathless with impatience for the sound of stones rattling on our window – Jake, come to take us to sea.

Jake Nisbet was our hero, full of grand tales of whaling days in the South Atlantic and endless patience with the excited chattering of two small boys. A clinker-built fishing boat edged cautiously out between narrow harbour walls, and I remembered the windy night, sailing home, cold and shaken with rough seas, when mother comforted me with a 'Scotch muffler', a breath-stopping warm hug.

At the white sands of Coldingham Bay I turned my back on the sea and walked slowly back to the present, up the hill to the church. Happily, no one had knocked it down during my thousand-year absence, and the door of the Anchor Inn was still open and just as inviting.

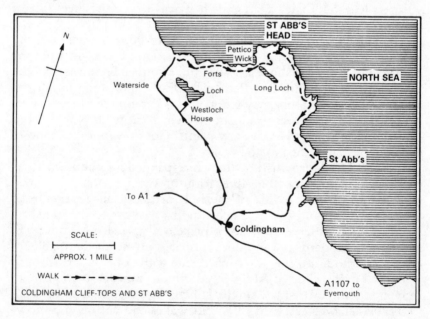

WHAT YOU NEED TO KNOW

Time and effort This is an easy, comfortable walk, with little to make the pulse race; part road, mostly along a cliff track. If you do not have a head for heights, keep well back from the edge. Even if you have, stay clear; the grass can be very slippery and it is a long one-way ticket down. Take extra care to keep well back if it is windy. A sudden gust could catch you unawares. Including a visit to the Priory, allow about four hours for the walk. Longer, if it is a fine day and you fancy a doze on cliffs or beach after lunch.

Location Ordnance Survey Sheet 67, Duns and Dunbar, second series, scale 1:50,000.

Grid references Coldingham 903659; Coldingham Loch 897685; hill forts and settlements 895691; Pettico Wick 908691; St Abb's Head 914693; St Abb's Village 920670; Coldingham Bay 917664.

Route Free parking, last time I was there, opposite Coldingham Priory. Walk past Anchor Inn and up the hill. Turn first right and follow this road out to Coldingham Loch. This is private property and if you wish to view the loch, or walk round the west shore, you must call at Westloch House and seek permission before doing so. Otherwise, continue to the end of the road and at Waterside walk north-east to the cliff path.

Turn right along the cliff path and follow it down to Pettico Wick and the marine nature reserve. A road leads up the hill, through the NCC reserve, past the Long Loch, to St Abb's Head and lighthouse. Climb past the pristine notice-board, round the back of the lighthouse; continue along the cliff, eventually reaching the village of St Abb's.

Walk past the front of the row of multicoloured two-storey cottages on the edge of the hill above the harbour. At the end, you pick up a tarmac path which leads to Coldingham Bay. From Coldingham Bay, walk back to the church. No need to walk on the main road: a good pavement will be found, on the right of the road, behind the hedge. This will almost see you home, safe from oncoming traffic.

3

Eildon, Tweed and Melrose

HEATHER-LAZED on Eildon, gazing skyward, lulled by prima donna larks. A soft west wind fingers my hair. White cloud-whisps sail silently by. In the valley, microdot figures inch over golf-green swards. Faint murmers of Melrose, a million miles away, drift up on summer airs. 'God's in his heaven, all's right with the world.'

Abbey pinnacles pierce the trees and, barely discernible amidst the grey cluster of the old Border town, I see the railway station where, centuries past, I parked. Tweed, a silver thread, winds and wends through rich farming lands – squared fields of gold, green and blue – hurrying seawards by deep pools where salmon lie, past the Wallace Monument and ox-bowed Dryburgh Abbey.

The spread of Galashiels edges eastwards and the stark concrete of the County Administrative Buildings in St Boswells intrude harshly onto the gentle landscape. Westwards lies Abbotsford, mighty home of mighty Sir Walter Scott, who made the Eildon Hills his own, his favourite walk, ringed by the magic of Moorfoot,

Lammermuir, Cheviot and Lowther.

The triple hills of Eildon dominate these Border lands. Because the surrounding countryside is flat, they stand proud, like ancient watch-dogs keeping guard over the four abbeys: Melrose, Dryburgh, Jedburgh and Kelso. Melrose Abbey was founded in 1136 by monks from Rievaulx in Yorkshire and for hundreds of years it played an important part in the making of Scotland. King David I granted the abbey the three granges of 'Eildon, Melrose and Darnick together with the royal lands and forest of Selkirk and Traquair with pasturage for sheep and cattle, wood for building and burning and rights of fishing in the Tweed. In addition the monks received Gattonschauch and the lands and woods of Gattonside.'

Like so much of the Borders, Melrose and the other great Scottish abbeys suffered dreadfully during the Scottish Wars of Independence and Edward II sacked the abbey in 1322. Richard II did likewise in 1385 but, in spite of such rough treatment, Melrose Abbey always managed to recover and became the most prosperous religious house in the kingdom.

However, the troubled times of the sixteenth century and constant feuding between Border families brought eventual ruin to the four abbeys. After two successive raids and burnings in 1544–5 the majesty of Melrose Abbey declined. In 1590, 'Jo Watsonn, pensionarius de Melrose, the last member of the convent, passed away' and the great days were over.

The track round Eildon is well marked and earlier that morning I had left the car by the railway station, now a thriving arts and crafts centre, and walked up Dingleton Road, under the bridge, left down the steps and onto the hill. Soon wiping a sweat-wet brow, I rested and looked back, the town turning doll-like below me. Eager midges swarmed in the long grass, anxious for lunch, so I lurched upwards to gain the open heights and welcome breeze.

The track shows well-trodden signs of horses hoofs' in thick red soil and the ground is soft and muddy after overnight rain. An unexpected flag-post marks the way and I begin to think of photographs. Stupid, for, as though reading my thoughts, skies darken and clouds gather. Sat on my lunch-time banana. On the crest, where grass and heather meet, house martins swoop and tumble. Must be on a training exercise, preparing youngsters for their long journey south, fattening them up on Eildon flies.

Before the Romans came, Picts castled the crest of North Eildon with a circular fort. Within the immediate area of the hill, more than three hundred settlements of the Selgovae tribe have been identified. These wild, fearless men must have looked out from their hilltop fastness, over ancient forests, and wondered at the coming of Cnaeus Julius Agricola's legions; the sharp rattle of civilization knocking at old time's door.

The Romans quickly subjugated the Selgovae and routed them from their Eildon fortress. A signal tower was built and a major camp constructed on the Roman road of Dere Street, near Newstead, a mile east of Melrose. The camp was an important staging post for Roman expansion northwards and, at its height, accommodated two legions and a detachment of 500 cavalry.

If you examine Eildon carefully, the outlines of these Pictish settlements are still visible – regular heather-covered ridges, where no ridges should be; strange mounds and hollows on the hillside. The Commendator's House, in the grounds of Melrose Abbey, is a superb museum which includes details and artefacts from the days of Roman occupation.

Another ancient hero, King Arthur, is reputed to have known and loved the Eildon Hills. Romantic legend has Arthur and his knights buried here, awaiting the call for help from a threatened nation; then they will rise from sleep, swords brightly burnished, to vanquish our foes. King Arthur must have been a man of many parts – the same story is told of a dozen other British hills – but I like to imagine the whole Round Table sleeping under tranquil Border skies.

I paid for lunch, a magnificent, well-filled roll, followed by wild bilberries, scattering crumbs amongst the scree for my songstress lark, then stumbled downhill towards the village of Newstead. The track leads to a narrow little wood, famous for the Eildon Tree of Thomas the Rhymer. A stream keeps the track company through the woods and my boots splash droplets over wet socks.

Squirrels dart across the path; stop, bright-eyed and motionless, whisker-twitching, testing the air; then spring, rocket-like, into overhanging branches. A fat pheasant coughs nervously, the sound of its pattering feet quickening as it launches itself into clumsy, frightened flight. Now the main road. The sudden shock of cars.

Newstead is a dream of a village, almost unreal in Scotland – pink-washed cottages, wallpapered with honeysuckle, clematis and roses; trimmed lawns fronting well maintained houses, flanked by two-car garages. Down Clymires Lane, right over the road, then left by the telephone box. The path leads to the River Tweed and my excitement mounts with every step.

For me, the Tweed is the Borders. I grew to love it as a boy, when I first committed the sin of angling amidst its tumbling streams and gentle glides. The Tweed has an unforgettable smell, like no other river I know: warm, friendly, inviting, promising perfect peace, absolute contentment.

By the river, three herons are busy fishing. They flap awkwardly airborne as I arrive. Upstream, a couple of salmon fishers flay the water. Wager the herons have had more sport. A grey wagtail bobs greeting and, in the slow eddies, trout feed hungrily. Mr Dipper watches with tiny-eyed caution.

The riverside track wanders upstream towards the suspension bridge at Melrose. Beech and sycamore shade the water and a salmon turns lazily, silver flanks shining in afternoon sunlight. The urgent buzz of a sawmill startles a flight of mallard from the cover of a reed-covered island. Crows harry a marauding kestrel from their nests and, as I lingeringly watch the river, a stream of ants carry seeds home to their night's rest.

Sitting in the ruined transepts of the great abbey, I wonder where King Robert the Bruce's heart lies. Carried in a silver casket to the Crusades, it was flung by ever-faithful Douglas into the thickest of the fight. After the battle, Douglas was found dead, his body lying over his king's heart. The casket was brought back to Scotland and buried at Melrose Abbey.

Light fades, sending long shadows filtering through the broken windows, washing mellow stones in soft reds and grey. Time stands still, hovering mystically as the sun slowly fades below the gentle peaks of Eildon.

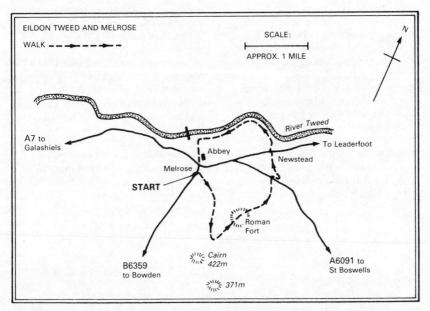

WHAT YOU NEED TO KNOW

Time and effort   This is an easy walk which will take about four hours, depending upon how long you spend visiting Melrose Abbey. The climb up to North Eildon may make you puff a bit – it did me – but there is no hurry, so take it at your own pace. The total distance is in the order of seven miles. Wear stout walking shoes – the track gets very muddy.

Location   Ordnance Survey Sheet 73, Galashiels and Ettrick Forest, second series, scale 1:50,000.

Grid references   Melrose 545343; North Eildon Hill 555328; Newstead 563342; Tweed 563343; Melrose Abbey 549341.

Route   In the centre of Melrose, by the Market Cross, follow the B6359. Within fifty yards, before you go under the railway bridge, turn right and within one hundred yards park in front of the old railway station.

Walk back to the road and turn right under the railway bridge. On the left, you will see a notice indicating the start of the Eildon Walk. Go down the steps and follow the track up through the wood onto the hill. After leaving the fields behind the track bears right. Walk round the side of the hill, making for the white-painted flag-pole in the distance.

From the flag-pole, walk directly up to the shoulder between the two hills; thence, an easy walk to the top of North Eildon. From the top, go down the north side, making towards the wood which lies directly below. A track leads through this wood to the main A6091 Melrose–Jedburgh road.

Turn right along the main road and, after about a hundred and fifty yards, left down a muddy track – once again signposted 'Eildon Walk'. Follow this track until you pass under a bridge. Eildon Walk is posted left; you turn right and walk into the village of Newstead.

To the left of the telephone box a track leads past a few houses down to the banks of the River Tweed. At the river, turn left and follow the bankside path back to Melrose. On the way, walk along the top of the well made wall rather than in the field; this leads back to the path.

Just after the sawmill, and before the suspension bridge, turn left, away from the river, and walk into Melrose. There is a motor car museum on your right and the Abbey is signposted on your left.

After visiting the Abbey, walk back past the market cross to the car. There is a café within the old railway station and this will provide you with welcome refreshment – tea or otherwise!

4

The Silver Tyne and Crichton

The admirable village of Crichton is a neat collection of houses thirty minutes' drive south from Edinburgh, but my first journey there took an hour and a half – by bicycle. Couldn't drive at the age of fifteen, although considerate father had given me one or two sneaky shots on quiet country lanes. I had decided to become a world-famous artist and intended to sketch the gaunt ruins by way of a preliminary to fame and fortune.

The Wizard of the North, Sir Walter Scott, had aroused my interest by his description of Crichton in *Marmion*:

> That Castle rises on the steep
> Of the green vale of Tyne;
> And far below, where slow they creep
> From pool to eddy, dark and deep,
> Where alders moist, and willows weep,
> You hear her streams repine.

Or perhaps my imagination had been fired by stories of Mary, Queen of Scots, and her ruthless lover, James, Earl of Bothwell, whose home Crichton was in the seventeenth century. Anyway, I stumbled up and down the jagged stairways and round the well kept courts, sketching busily for most of an afternoon, and the results pleased me mightily: which was all that mattered.

These childish drawings have long since disappeared, which is just as well; but the mystery of the castle, glooming over the silver river from its bracken-covered ledge, remains undiminished, as clear and awesome as ever it was on that first, bright day.

Thirty-four years later, in the warm sunlight of an early-autumn morning, I parked my car by the old parish church at the start of the short track to the castle. Gathering together cameras, notebook, lunch and map, I made for the church, intent upon a few words with my maker prior to setting off for the grim ruins. Best to be prepared.

All the doors of the church were securely locked and bolted. Sad times. I remember, as a boy, when you could walk freely into any Scottish church, Highland or Lowland, without let or hindrance. The Good Lord was always at home in those days.

The parish church was established in 1454 by William Crichton, Lord Chancellor of Scotland, 'as destitute of faith, mercy and conscience as of fear and of folly'. William was one of the most powerful and feared men in Scotland, jealously guarding his privilege of caring for the infant king, James II.

His arch-rivals, and arch-enemies, were the Douglases, and William constantly plotted their downfall. The Lord Chancellor feigned friendship and forgiveness and persuaded the young king to invite the Douglas youths to Edinburgh Castle. The boys stopped at Crichton on the way and, no doubt, were well entertained by William Crichton.

He entertained them better the following evening during the 'dinner of the black bull's head'. At the entry of the platter bearing this ominous sign, Earl Douglas and his brother were dragged from the table and brutally stabbed to death.

As I left the churchyard and walked along the track to Crichton it was as though three decades had vanished. The same clouds seemed to chase the same shadows over the still-golden ferns. Shafts of sunlight danced on red walls and the air was full of the sound of the busy river and sky-high singing larks.

Crichton Castle reached its peak in the ownership of Francis Stewart, Earl Bothwell, when King James VI was entertained there in March 1586. Francis had an unmatched reputation for evildoing and violence, even for those harsh times – 'a terror to the most desperate duellists in Europe and a subduer of the proudest champions'.

Sitting in the courtyard of the castle, gazing up at the superb Italianate Renaissance façade, erected by Francis Stewart, I pondered moodily on my fellow Scots, wondering what manner of men could build such delicate works of art one day and happily murder, rob, pillage and rape the next.

Leaving the castle, I walked past the sandstone ruins of the stable. At first sight, because of the vaulted roof, it could be taken for a chapel but the window above the main door gives the clue: it is shaped like a horseshoe. The stable was a two-storey building – animals below, grooms and retainers above.

To the right of the stables a track leads downhill to the Tyne, crossing a gurgling little tributary on the way. A small meadow, spread with sweet-smelling grasses, carpets the valley and the track then meanders up a muddy slope, through waist-high bracken. Silver-specked spider webs danced between leaves, crystal droplets shaken by my passing, and my trousers clung damply to cold legs when I reached the top.

Here a drunken notice nods the way south to the village of Borthwick. Farmers were busy with harvest as I damply passed. Ahead, the line of the old railway cuts over the hill. Behind, the triple peaks of the Eildon Hills proudly dominate the horizon. On my right, a long line of Pentlands point the way to Scotland's capital city.

From the top of the hill, below me, the tower of Borthwick Castle peeks from surrounding woodlands. The trees are magnificent: oak, ash, beech, sycamore, elm, willow, birch and ancient Scots pine – a proper wood, with space to breathe beneath the leaves.

Woodland birds – blue tit, wren, treecreeper and goldfinch – join me for lunch, as does another sudden rainstorm. I shelter under the umbrella of an old oak. Glossy, aristocratic horses eat also, chestnut and black backs turned carefully against the rain, tails switching as they chomp.

An enigmatic sign offers two ways into Borthwick and I choose to walk left, round the walls of the castle, which is now an exclusive hotel. The road leads down to little Gore Burn, a tributary of the Tyne, made big and proud by heavy rain. Maple trees blush, burnt crimson with the first flush of autumn.

At the end of the road, a wet track invites me down through the woods, leading to a gated wooden bridge and up to Borthwick churchyard. The roof of the church is an intricate pattern of rectangular and diamond-shaped stone tiles, bright and glistening from recent showers. Ranked tombstones tell sad stories of young hopes brought early to earth.

The last time I had walked this way was as a Scout, on a night adventure exercise; two, small, semi-fearful boys, peering at a map by weak torchlight at 3 a.m., hopelessly lost. Then my mind was filled with thoughts of wicked earls and murderous lords lurking behind every bush, razor-sharp blades poised, ready to slit my unsuspecting throat.

Leaving the church, I followed the road through the small village, back over rushing Gore Burn, up to the high bank of the railway, then over the fields to Loquhariot Farm. The view across the valley was dominated by Crichton Castle, softly lit by evening sunlight, with the road leading down to tree-banked Tyne. At the top of the hill, to the left of the village, are the remains of an even earlier fort, dating from the Iron Age, enclosing an area 300 by 190 feet.

I wondered if the inhabitants of these grassy mounds plotted and planned to rule their world as hard and ruthlessly as their latterday neighbours along the road at the castle: Couldn't ask our dour Scots Lord for the answer; when I called at the church again, he was still out.

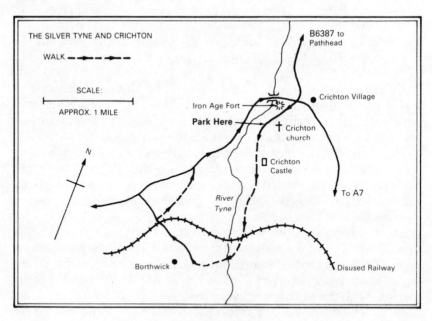

WHAT YOU NEED TO KNOW

Time and effort   This is a pleasant afternoon outing which takes about three or four hours, depending upon how much time you spend exploring Crichton Castle. In wet weather, the track from Crichton to Borthwick can be very muddy, so be prepared. From Borthwick, the route follows a quiet minor road back to Crichton, through farmland and the valley of the River Tyne. There are no harsh hills or heart-bursting climbs and this route offers an easy, gentle, country walk.

Location   Ordnance Survey Sheet 66, Edinburgh, second series, scale 1:50,000.

Grid references   Crichton parish church 381616; Crichton Castle 380612; Borthwick Castle and church 369596; Loquhariot Farm 370608; Crichton Fort 385619.

Route   Park the car at Crichton parish church. Directly ahead lies Crichton Castle, a short walk across the hill. The castle is in the care of the Historic Buildings and Monuments Commission and is open April to September: weekdays 9.30 a.m. to 7 p.m., Sundays 2 to 7 p.m.; October to March: weekdays 9.30 a.m. to 4 p.m., Sundays 2 to 4 p.m. Entrance charge is about £1 per adult.

From the castle walk to the right of the stable building and you will find a narrow track leading down the hill, through a small wood. This track crosses a small tributary of the River Tyne, then over a meadow and up a muddy slope to a stile. Borthwick is signposted here. Follow the sign to the line of the old railway, where there is a farm bridge over the disused track. Take care here and make sure that you cross the track and walk round the side of the hill, to the right, in front of you.

From this hill you will see Borthwick Castle, and the track down through the wood is clearly marked. Once down, cross the stile by the field with horse jumps and walk the few hundred yards to the road. Here turn left, round the side of the walled garden. The road passes over the Gore Burn and wends uphill to a private house. When you see the house, look right and you should find a track down through the woods to a gated bridge over Gore Burn. This path leads up to Borthwick church, through a white-painted gate at the top.

After visiting Borthwick church, follow the little road down through the village to the bridge over Gore Burn. From here, go up the hill and, when you see the railway embankment, turn right and follow the track through the fields to Loquhariot and onto the minor road.

At the next road junction bear right, down into the Tyne valley. On the way up the hill you may if you wish follow the inviting little track on your right, up the hill, through the woods; it leads back to the road. At the top of the hill, at the road junction, turn right. Immediately on your right is the entrance to the site of the Iron Age fort – and a well disguised water storage tank (I think). Walk back to the road, turn right again, and this brings you back to the church and car park.

5

Broad Law, Talla and Tweed

THE BORDER hills of Scotland were born out of millions of years of geological turmoil. Ancient sands and shales, compressed into rock by mighty forces, split by molten lava, crushed beneath ice-sheets and glaciers half a mile thick. The retreating ice left fertile soils which have given comfort and sustenance to man down the ages.

Nearly three thousand years ago our Pictish ancestors tilled these soils and grazed their cattle, protected from attack in fortified villages and hill forts. Double stone walls were laboriously constructed, in-filled with rubble, often up to 15 feet high, surrounded by deep ditches. Huge wooden gates between twin watch-towers guarded the entrance to the village and life was secured only by constant vigilance.

Deep in these green hills, close to the well-springs of Mistress Tweed, I stood by the banks of the gentle river at Hearthstane and looked eastwards, towards the rounded heights of Broad Law, rising 2,723 feet above the stream. I parked the car near to where Hearthstane Burn hurries into Tweed and followed the track, past the farm, along a forest road, up the hill.

This is John Buchan country: writer, soldier, statesman, created Baron Tweedsmuir in 1935 and Governor-General of Canada until his death in 1940. G. M . Trevelyan, the historian, wrote: 'I don't think I remember anyone whose death evoked a more enviable outburst of sorrow, love and admiration.'

Like many boys before me, I had thrilled to the exploits of Richard Hannay in *The Thirty-Nine Steps*; but, to me, the most entrancing piece John Buchan ever wrote was a little memorial poem to a fishing friend, killed during the First World War, called 'Fisher Jamie'. As I climbed the hill, I recited the lines, smiling with pleasure at their simple beauty:

> Puir Jamie's killed. A better lad
> Ye wadna find to busk a flee
> Or burn a pule or wield a gad
> Frae Berwick to the Clints o' Dee
>
> And noo he's in a happier land. –
> It's Gospel truth and Gospel law
> That Heaven's yett maun open stand
> To folk that for their country fa'.
>
> But Jamie will be ill to mate;
> He lo'ed nae music, kenned nae tunes
> Except the sang o' Tweed in spate,
> Or Talla loupin' ower its linns.
>
> I sair misdoot that Jamie's heid
> A croun o' gowd will never please;
> He liked a kep o' dacent tweed
> Whaur he could stick his cast o' flees.
>
> If Heaven is a' that man can dream
> And a' that honest herts can wish,
> It maun provide some muirland stream,
> For Jamie dreamed o' nocht but fish.
>
> And weel I wot he'll up and spier
> In his bit blate and canty way,
> Wi' kind Apostles standin' near
> Whae in their time were fishers tae.
>
> He'll offer back his gowden croun
> And in its place a rod he'll seek,
> And bashfu'-like his herp lay doun
> And spier a leister and a cleek.

31

For Jim's had aye a poachin' whim;
He'll sune grow tired, wi' lawfu' flee
Made fra the wings o' cherubim,
O' casting ower the Crystal Sea . . .

I picter him at gloamin' tide
Steekin' the backdoor o' his hame
And hastin' to the waterside
To play again the auld auld game;

And syne wi' saumon on his back,
Catch't clean against the Heavenly law,
And Heavenly byliffs on his track,
Gaun linkin' doun some Heavenly shaw.

A sudden flurry of rain sent me chasing for the shelter of a beautifully built circular sheepfold – well-knit grey stones topped with old turf. Crouched inside, sheep-like, it was as though I was on another planet, but the storm soon passed and I trudged on, past numbered posts which zigzag up the slope, each 22 yards apart. Suspicious.

I won't tell you how many posts there are – might be depressing – but when I finally cleared the forest, over a stiled gate, they still marched ahead, incongruous sentinels marking the way. Cattle grazed happily in the wind, cropping fine grass-covered slopes at 1600 feet. A high-altitude pheasant shot past, with startled look and worried shriek. The Lowther Hills crowded the horizon, amazingly folded as though someone had softly smoothed them. God, I suppose.

One of the black cattle had its head up a huge culvert, drinking heavily from the rushing stream which charged down the hill towards Geddes's Well. No sign of Mr Geddes but he must have walked here some time to be so famously remembered on the map. The road is well maintained and, apart from the unremitting marker posts and three-mile slog, going is easy.

As I rounded the final twists and curves, panting, the reason for the well ordered access became clear: a space-age-like structure of dishes and domes, surrounded by a high wire fence, loomed before me. 'Warning, High voltage. Property of the Civil Aviation Authority.' An anxious greenshank flitted by. Hope it has read the warning.

Although the aviation station comes as a bit of a shock, once on top of Broad Law there is a superb panoramic view over half of southern Scotland and the tiresome uphill walk is well rewarded. Unending hills surround me, gentle green-topped slopes full of light and shadow. Hidden corries beckon. White clouds scud over dark ridges. Small patches of bright-yellow fields carpet deep valleys. An empty windswept wonderland. A sweet upland dream.

Leaving the top of Broad Law, I walked in a happy daze along the flat grassy summit to Cairn Law. Talla Reservoir sparkled 2,000 feet below, with the buildings of Talla Linnfoots crouched, tiny black specks, by the edge. Waterfalls on Megget Burn flashed silver as sunlight chased shadows up the sheer sides of Garelet Hill, towering starkly over the west shore of the loch.

I followed a spur to Muckle Side and, after a magnificent two-mile walk, all above 2,000 feet, I rested for lunch. Nestling in a sheltered corner, close to the source of Glenrusco Burn, I attacked a sandwich greedily. By the jagged rocks of the burn, in a warm corner, pale, white flowers nodded sleepily – a sudden, magical garden of grass of Parnassus. A harsh, angry, cackle turned my gaze skywards, and I caught a quick glimpse of a raven slipping away on silent, bible-black wings.

The west shoulder of Muckle Side gives a gradual, safe descent to Talla. Any other way down would be difficult; it is as easy to slip on a grass slope as it is on rock, and from 2,000 feet the result is just the same – not at all nice. Funny how sheep seem to manage. Probably glued to the side of the hill.

The walk north by the side of Talla Reservoir is along a minor road which joins St Mary's Loch with Tweedsmuir, twisting through the Lowther Hills past Megget Stone and Fans Law. During summer months it can be busy, and even in October, when I last walked it, cars passed frequently.

Victoria Lodge, at the end of the loch, sits smothered in conifers like an extravagant lost Highland shooting lodge looking for sport. I walked along the dam wall and down to the keeper's cottage, where fishing permits are issued for those wishing to do battle with Talla trout. Fisher Jamie would have been a regular.

Crossing Talla Water, I found the line of a dismantled railway and followed it round pine-clad Cockiland Hill to Glenrusco, where the old railway bridge still crosses Tweed. There is something special about the scent of Tweed. It has lived with me for nearly forty years, yet it still produces a sense of excitement, of mounting anticipation, and I believe that I could recognize Tweed blindfold from a thousand miles by the magical smell of its tumbling streams.

I paid my respects to Pictish ancestors as I passed their old fort by the stream on the hill across the river. Then, footsore but content, I let lovely Lady Tweed murmur me home.

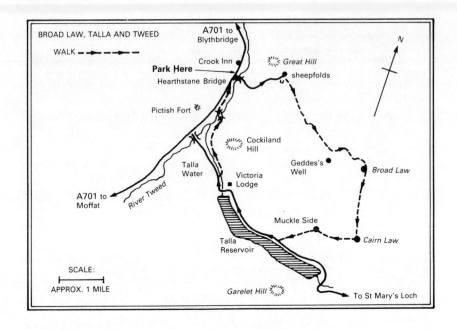

BROAD LAW, TALLA AND TWEED

WALK ‑ ‑ ‑►‑ ‑ ‑►

A701 to Blythbridge

Crook Inn

Park Here

Hearthstane Bridge

Pictish Fort

Great Hill

sheepfolds

Cockiland Hill

Geddes's Well

Broad Law

Talla Water

Victoria Lodge

A701 to Moffat

River Tweed

Muckle Side

Cairn Law

Talla Reservoir

SCALE:
APPROX. 1 MILE

Garelet Hill

To St Mary's Loch

N

WHAT YOU NEED TO KNOW

Time and effort Quite a lot. Allow about five and a half hours for the round trip – more if it is a fine day, because once up you will not want to come down. The only real slog comes at the beginning, hiking up the rough road to the top of Broad Law. Be like me and stop for plenty of rests. Once up, it is easy all the way. Take great care descending from Muckle Side. Follow the spur and do not attempt a glissade, planned or otherwise, down the steep sides: Talla Reservoir, at the foot, is deep, dark and very cold. The Crook Inn is nearby for welcome after-walk refreshment.

Location Ordnance Survey Sheet 72, Upper Clyde Valley, second series, scale 1:50,000.

Grid references Crook Inn 111265; Hearthstane Bridge 110260; sheepfold 123261; Geddes's Well 137238; Broad Law 147235; Muckle Side 134217: Victoria Lodge 107231; Glenrusco Railway Bridge 105251.

Route Park near the bridge over Tweed at Hearthstane, half a mile south of Crook Inn on the A701 from Blyth Bridge to Moffat. Cross the bridge and at the cottage on your right cut up the hill towards the track you see in front of you. Turn left along this track, round the hill and down to cross Hearthstane Burn.

Then right, and follow the well maintained path, past the sheepfolds, up through the wood. On the top of Broad Law, where you should now be, go past the right-hand side of the civil aviation station and make for the trig. point at the junction of a fence line. The fence pointing quarter-right is your route. Walk due south, over good, springy turf, down and up again to Cairn Law.

Bear right here and go along the shoulder of the hill to the top of Muckle Side. At the west of Muckle Side a spur drops reasonably gently to the road. Walk down this spur, turn right at the road and go on to the head of the loch and dam wall.

Turn left along the dam wall and follow the road down until you reach the cottage where fishing permits are obtained; a notice outside says so. Just past the house, a track on your right leads down to Talla Water. Follow this path, cross the bridge.

Now, angle quarter-left through the woods. Cross a field and you see the line of the dismantled railway. Turn left and follow this back to Glenrusco. Where the old bridges have been removed, you have to leave the track and then climb back up. Don't be tempted to go too fast or you might end up shooting into space where there is no bridge.

Cross the Tweed at Glenrusco, alongside massive water pipes from Talla Reservoir, then a last couple of hundred yards and you are deposited back on the road, where the old railway line used to cross. You should now be able to see your car. If not, head directly for the Crook Inn and drown your sorrows!

6

Culzean Cliffs and Woodlands

M Y SECOND son, Charles, recently stayed at the Gas House of Culzean Castle. It was built towards the end of the last century so that Culzean could receive the benefice of carbide lighting. When he told me, I was tempted to remark that he and his colleagues from art school must have felt delightfully at home amidst so much hot air; but common sense and a high regard for personal safety prevailed. Charles Sandison is nineteen years of age, a near-six-footer, fourteen stone square, and notoriously short-fused.

The Gas House, redundant after mains electricity was installed, has been converted into student accommodation used by Glasgow College of Art, and aspiring bands of embryonic Leonardos and Michelangelos rest there between artistic endeavours. Nearby is Culzean Park Centre, where most of Culzean's other 300,000-a-year visitors rest.

Robert Adam designed the beautiful soft-stoned buildings as a home farm in 1777 and the Park Centre, with its dramatic arches and central court, has been carefully developed into a focal point for Culzean Country Park – exhibitions, snack bar, shops and administrative offices.

Which all sounds highly organized, thick with tourists and not really the place for a peaceful afternoon amble. Well, it is and it isn't. Yes, organized and, yes, often busy; but nevertheless a splendid place for stroll and a surprisingly quiet corner of otherwise busy Ayrshire.

The National Trust for Scotland was given Culzean and its 560 acres in 1945, by Charles Kennedy, 5th Marquess of Ailsa, and in 1969 the Trust declared the grounds Scotland's first country park. Herculean effort has restored castle, gardens, woodlands, ponds and pathways to former glory. The result is a wonderful re-creation of a magnificent Scottish estate, complete with swan pond, walled garden, ice house, camellia house, ornamental arches, fountains and delightful tree-shaded walks.

The Castle stands on the edge of 400-million-year-old volcanic cliffs and was originally a square Scottish tower, glowering balefully seawards, defying Atlantic slings and arrows since the Middle Ages. Kennedys have been associated with Ayrshire since the twelfth century; James Kennedy married a daughter of King Robert III in 1407 and he and his five brothers owned half the county between them.

A Kennedy was with Joan of Arc at the relief of Orleans; another fell on Flodden Field with King James IV in 1513. The 2nd Earl was murdered, the 3rd poisoned. The 4th Earl, following the fine traditions of medieval Scottish diplomacy, persuaded the Commendator of Crossraguel Abbey to consign valuable lands to Clan Kennedy – by roasting him alive in the grim dungeons of Dunure Castle.

The present castle is the work of David Kennedy, who succeeded his brother in 1775 and invited architect the Robert Adam to prepare plans for a major restoration and building programme. Of all the splendid rooms Adam designed, in my opinion, there is none finer than the Saloon, a circular, simply-styled, dreamlike room overlooking the Firth of Clyde.

Recitals of Beethoven piano and cello sonatas have been broadcast from the Saloon and a more perfect setting for these glorious masterpieces is hard to imagine. Recently I found myself alone in this sweet room. Soft sunlight streamed through tall windows and I watched, spellbound and silent, as evening stretched out all the Arran hills, and the sun dipped gently into western skies.

Earlier, I walked round the estate on a well marked path, nose-deep in the excellent National Trust booklet which guides you on your way. I started the walk from the main car park, pulling on stiff, cold boots, watched by a herd of haughty red deer, studiously ruminating behind a leap-proof fence, carefully gauging the height to greener grass.

The Gas House was still standing. Given my knowledge of what Charlie does to his room at home, this surprised me. I followed the path down the cliff, onto the foreshore. There are two caves at the foot of the cliffs, reputed home for hibernating moths, and, no doubt, smuggled booty in days gone by.

The shore is an archaeological delight, strewn with pebbles of agate, lava, quartz, flint and calcite. Culzean Park rangers lead parties of visitors on conducted tours and one of the most successful aspects of their work has been the establishment of a young naturalists' club; hundreds of children are introduced to the mysterious world of nature by a team of excellent instructors, adept at capturing youthful imaginations.

Gannets, from their breeding ground on Ailsa Craig, dive spectacularly – spears of white, yellow and black, plunging into the sea from heights of 100 feet. In times past the 'solan goose' was greatly prized for its feathers and soft down. It was also eaten 'by those who can get no better food' and sometimes even domesticated. Sea-swallows, globe-circumnavigating terns, hover and swoop over the waves. Straight-winged fulmars glide by, fingering cliff-side thermals. Red-beaked oystercatchers busily poke.

A total of 155 species of birds have been recorded at Culzean, attracted since the late eighteenth century by the planting of more than five million trees. The Trust has produced an ornithological check-list giving details of residents and visitors, vagrants and rarities. Recent records list goshawk, peregrine, jay, corncrake, grasshopper warbler and barn owl. There have also been single sightings of osprey and little bittern.

There are several buildings along the shore: Dolphin House, a laundry, used until 1900; the Round House, where hardy bathers changed and shivered from the Firth; and the remains of a private oyster pool, to ensure fresh supplies for the great folk at the Castle. Just before the path hikes you back up the cliff, a track goes on to Port Carrick, grander in name than in reality, but a perfect place to stop for a picnic, complete with small sandy beach.

Up Barwhin Hill now, on to the ornate pagoda, fronted by an aviary, built in 1860. I wandered over to Swan Pond, to see what I could see, closely followed by my golden retriever, Breac, the Gaelic word for trout. Still understands English, though, and walked perfectly to heel, eyeing mute swans and wildfowl with feigned indifference.

Morriston Bridge takes the path under a disused railway and the track turns north along the old line. It was opened in 1906 and carried passengers and freight between the village of Maidens, south of Culzean, to Dunure, close to where the old Kennedy stronghold still clings precariously to the cliffs. Left then, leaving the railway at Kennel Mount, and down through the woods, back to the car.

Everything about Culzean charms the senses and delights the eye

– the dramatic arch at the entrance to the castle, creeper-clad, looking like a centuries-old ruin, cleverly designed to do so; Adam and Eve, two Sitka spruce, nodding sleepily in Happy Valley Wood, planted in 1851 and now 140 feet high; and the famous walled garden, with its compass-point corners, ablaze with colour.

I stood in the armoury, surrounded by an astonishing display of weapons ancient and modern, and wondered about the magnificence of Clan Kennedy: great, powerful people; people to be reckoned with, envied and, no doubt, feared. Not so very far distant from the splendour of Culzean, at Alloway, a great man was born – not in palace or mighty castle, but in a simple cottage, shared with his father's cattle.

Whilst David Kennedy and Robert Adam were changing the face of the material world at Culzean, Robert Burns was changing the hearts and minds of people with wild, romantic verses. For all Culzean's grace and glory, perhaps Burns's poetry is the more enduring monument. Souter Johnnie, Tam o' Shanter's drinking partner, lived a mile from Culzean Castle at Kirkoswald. Call at his cottage after your visit, and ponder these matters.

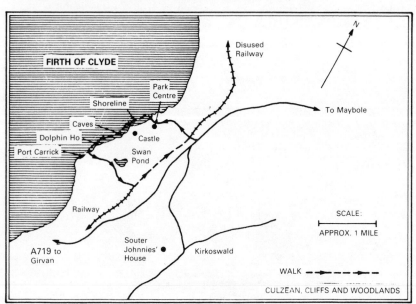

CULZEAN, CLIFFS AND WOODLANDS

WHAT YOU NEED TO KNOW

Time and effort   More of the mind than of the feet. There is so much to see and do at Culzean that you could spend a week there and still not properly explore all that the castle and estate have to offer. Allow at least a whole day. The walk round the boundary takes three hours; more if you are ornithologist, geologist, botanist, or even just plain amateur naturalist. Some of the going is wet and rough so you will probably feel more comfortable in strong walking boots. You can always remove them before you visit the castle. I combined my visit to Culzean with a stop-over at Burns's Cottage in Alloway, near Ayr. You may care to consider doing likewise; the contrast is fascinating.

Location   Ordnance Survey Sheet 70, Ayr and Kilmarnock, second series, scale 1:50,000.

Grid references   Culzean Castle and Country Park 233101; Burns's Cottage 335187; Souter Johnnie's House 241076; Dunure Castle 254158.

Route   You are in good hands. The Park Centre at Culzean will furnish you with an excellent series of descriptive literature, giving details of a number of short and long walks through the estate. The brochure is entitled 'Culzean Country Park Walks'. There are also companion leaflets on other subjects which are invaluable if you wish to get the greatest benefit from your visit. Otherwise, from the Park Centre, follow your nose, and the path, down to the shore and south along the foot of the cliffs.

7

Mary, Merrick and Bruce

*E*LEVEN HECTIC days after her dramatic escape from Loch Leven Castle, Mary Queen of Scots faced her enemies at the Battle of Langside on 13 May 1568; but the bleak moorlands between Dunblane and Comrie saw her father's prophecy fulfilled: 'It cam with ane lass and it will pass with ane lass.' Mary's forces were routed and she fled southwards, arriving at Dundrennan on Solway two days later.

When you come to think about it, Mary never stood a chance anyway. Her Catholic brother, King Henri of France, and all the Scots Catholics expected her to re-establish the 'one true church', preferably by force. Mary resolutely refused. Scottish Protestants, led by ranting Knox, demanded that she abjure her faith and root out the evil of Catholicism. This she would never do. With hindsight, her defeat and downfall were foregone conclusions.

Mary crossed into England, where cousin Elizabeth solved the problem – by removing Mary's head at Fotheringay on 1 February 1587. She remained steadfast to the end. Dr Fletcher, Dean of Peterborough, on the scaffold, attempted to persuade Mary to 'repent you of your former wickedness' but Mary replied: 'Mr Dean, trouble not yourself any more, for I am settled and resolved in this my religion, and am proposed therein to die.'

Which, a few moments later, she did; and the Earl of Kent stood over her poor body saying: 'Such end of all the Queen's and the Gospel enemies.' Meanwhile, safely on the throne in Edinburgh, her son, King James VI, turned a blind eye, whilst his nobles and clerics no doubt tucked heartily into their sanctimonious Scottish breakfasts. For them, Mary's death in England was a startling break with tradition: normally, they managed to murder their own monarchs.

During her flight from Langside, Mary passed through the wild highlands of Dumfries and Galloway – a desolate wilderness of dangerous cotton-grass-covered silver flows, jagged peaks and windswept moorlands, crowned by mighty Merrick, towering 2,770 feet over tiny lochans with magical names, Neldricken, Valley, Glenhead, Dungeon, Enoch and Aldinna.

There are a dozen hills here, by the ragged Rig of Jarkness and Rhinns of Kells, all over 2,000 feet, including Meikle Millyea, Corserine, Cairngarroch, Cairnsmore, Kirriereoch, Shalloch on Minnoch and Benyellary – ancient granite rocks, laid bare by millions of years of weathering, covered by Caledonian forests, warmed by mild Atlantic winds.

But the forests where Robert the Bruce and Douglas plotted the overthrow of usurping English neighbours were cleared, and now, in their place, we have the new plantations of the Forestry Commission: dense, closely packed, impenetrable conifers, blanketing more than 35 per cent of the south-west. Called 'National Parks', they presuppose some scenic value; in fact, they have created a sterile desert beneath their light-excluding canopy. Colonel Gadaffi of Libya could well declare the Sahara Desert a 'National Garden Centre' and claim for it more beauty and diversity of wildlife than there is in the monotonous, monstrous forests of Dumfriesshire and Galloway.

On a fresh August morning I stopped at the head of Glen Trool and prepared myself for something I had long planned: the ascent of southern Scotland's highest peak, Merrick. Loch Trool – owned by the Liverpool football-pools family, the Moores – winds like a silver ribbon through the glen and I set off, up the side of Buchan Burn, weighted down with cameras, lunch, notebook and pencil.

Heavy rain the previous night had turned Buchan Burn into a spectacular display of waterfalls and deep pools, urging the crystal-clear stream over massive boulders, by banks alive with birdsong and heather so purple it dazzled the eye and dazed the mind. Slender mountain ash arched the torrent, bright red clusters of berries above dancing rainbow spray.

The bad news is that it was also very wet. Can't have it both ways, I suppose – foaming river and dry banks. I climbed hotly over the rocks to the soggy plain above, wading through spongy grass to reach the cottage at Cul Sharg. This is well maintained and provided welcome shelter from a sudden shower. I sprinted the last hundred yards, size eleven boots splashing mud round legs. Took three minutes. Record-breaking for the likes of me.

James Cameron, Toronto, Canada, had beaten me to it – by about a week, according to a name inscribed on the wall of the cottage. Rest and dry, then on again, through the woods, out onto the hill proper. Loch Trool has vanished, hidden in its deep, cleft-like valley. Benyellary looms above, with Merrick lurking north. The sun was very hot so I quickly removed several layers of clothing to ease the steep, relentless climb.

A drystane dyke greeted me on the ridge and I stopped a moment, looking back down the hill, across to Rig of Jarkness – a magnificent crest of jagged peaks enclosing upland valleys, streaked with tumbling streams, caressed by soft shadows of passing clouds.

Some of them weren't passing and, from the west, ominous nimbus gathered. Within minutes a violent storm swept in and I broke more records, struggling back into mountains of pullovers. With wind-driven rain battering my face I battled to the tall cairn of Benyellary and searched through the downpour for Merrick. The top was shrouded in mist, a thick grey bank rolling rapidly to meet me.

Given the broad summit track and small cairns marking the way, I decided to walk on, hoping for a break in the clouds when I reached the top. Hills have a strange, mystical quality in mist. Danger ever-present. Senses sharpened. Caution walking alongside. And something else: an awareness that anything might come charging from the gloom, hobgoblin or foul fiend, and that you are alone in the hands of fate.

The climb had tired me. Mist, rain, wind and cloud depressed my spirits, but I trekked wearily on, determined to reach the top. Nearing the summit, with sudden shock I saw a huge, dark shape ahead, moving towards me through the mist. Was this the black creature of my dreams? I tensed, expectant.

Then clouds cleared, sun broke through and I saw, walking strongly downhill, a hand-in-hand couple, who waved me a cheery good afternoon as they passed. I judged from their appearance that they were at least twenty years my senior, and I won't see fifty again; yet they strode happily across the mountain like a couple of youngsters on a Sunday-school picnic.

The trig. point on top of Merrick is white-painted and surrounded by a circle of heaped rocks. I lunched in solitary splendour in the finest dining room in southern Scotland.

Proud, isolated Ailsa Craig and Arran's 'sleeping warrior' hills shimmered on the white and blue wave-ridged Firth of Clyde. A distant outline of Northern Ireland peaks. Green Lowther Hills and Cheviot, eastwards. South, the flat, blood-stained plain of the 'Debatable Lands' of Border feuds and battles. Beyond, Cumbria's purple-painted lakelands.

The crags north of Merrick, Black Gairy, are daunting and steep, but I followed the eastern ridge and carefully descended, overlooking island-clad Loch Enoch. I made for the little saddle on Craig Neldricken and Helen's Stone; no clear sign of stone, or, for that matter, of Helen either. The ground is rough, wet, tussocked, hollowed and hummocked and I edged my way slowly past Crocket's famous Murder Hole to the side of bleak Buchan Hill at the west end of Loch Valley.

The Gairland Burn, main feeder stream of Loch Trool, chummed me home, singing all the way, a torrent of sound-hurrying water. As the path rose round the hill, glimpses of Loch Trool, cradled between steeply wooded banks, filled the view and I walked past Buchan, uphill to the monolith of Bruce's Stone.

On one side is a description of a battle fought by Robert the Bruce in Glen Trool, when he defeated an English army by rolling mighty stones down onto their unsuspecting heads, thereby causing them great distress and probably quite a few headaches.

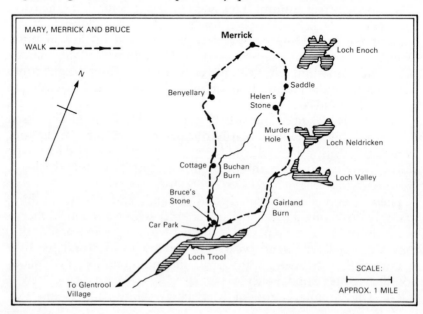

On the other side of the stone is the date when the monument was raised – 1926, if I remember right, but by this time my notebook was a soggy unusable heap and my pencil long lost on top of Merrick. Why, I thought, did it take my fellow Scots more than six hundred years to commemorate our hero king's victory? Luckless Queen Mary would understand.

WHAT YOU NEED TO KNOW

Time and effort Getting to the start, at the head of Loch Trool, is an expedition in itself. The roads through the forest are narrow, twisting and dangerous, with conifers blocking most of the view. The walk I describe takes about six hours so make sure you leave early and plan the day with great care.

Weather conditions change rapidly in this part of the world, so go prepared for the worst, regardless of time of year. I found it a most rewarding, exciting walk – but tiring, probably due to the fact that it was very wet and muddy .

This is particularly so from the bottom of the east slope of Merrick onwards, when you have to plot your own route across the flows. Certainly map and compass country. However, if you want to see one of the finest views in Scotland, then this is a walk you must make; and, once made, it will never be forgotten.

Location Ordnance Survey Sheet 77, New Galloway and Glen Trool, second series, scale 1:50,000.

Grid references Glen Trool car park 417803; Bruce's Stone 419804; Cul Sharg Cottage 416819; Benyellary 415839;Merrick 428854; Descent from Merrick at 420853 towards 437851; Loch Enoch 445850; Helen's Stone 436837; Murder Hole 439830; Loch Valley

445817; Buchan Hill track from 438820 by 428807 to car park.

Route The Merrick Walk is well signposted from the car park at the head of Loch Trool. Follow the signs to Buchan Burn and climb the left-hand side, up a rough, muddy track to the moss above. At the top you will see the little cottage of Cul Sharg ahead, in front of the forest.

Leave the cottage – I did so by the back window – and the track bears slightly right, still signposted, up the hill, through the new plantation. Cross a forest road and continue up, and up and up. As you clear the trees, the summit of Benyellary appears and at the top, a drystane dyke runs northwards. Follow this dyke; it leads to the top of Benyellary and on to Merrick.

The track dips from Benyellary, before the long, gentle ascent to the top of Merrick. From the end of the east spur of Merrick, map in hand, plot your route over the floor of the flow below, marking in your mind the saddle on Craig Neldricken, before you descend. Keep well to the south of Loch Enoch and make for the end of Loch Neldricken.

Skirt the loch – unless it is very hot and you want a cold spash – and trek over the hill towards Loch Valley. From Valley, a wet, broken track leads round Buchan Hill, back to the car park. You empty out at Bruce's Stone, above the track, and a last challenge to tired legs.

8

Riccarton, Hermitage and Roughley Sike

M Y WIFE, Ann, doesn't use maps to find out how to get there; she uses maps to find out where she is once she is there, wherever 'there' might be. The woman seems to have an almost supernatural sense of direction. Whilst I ponder at the bottom of a hill, trying to interpret contours, she is half-way up, calling for me to get a move on.

A walk with Ann is an adventure. Others, less considerate, describe her hikes in less kindly terms – such as 'nightmare'. These special days are action-packed, full of incident, never-to-be-forgotten experiences; and when mist rolls down the mountain there is never argument about who should be pathfinder. Breac, my golden retriever, and I fall meekly into step behind Heathcliff, Ann's Yorkshire terrier, and humbly dog them home.

So, when Ann offered to contribute one of her walks to my book, I accepted, courteously but with mixed feelings – anticipation tempered by a strong foreboding of disaster. I had been there before, often. Still, I reasoned, what possible harm could we come to, walking round her childhood, Border hills? During the last war, having been blitzed out of the fair City of York, Ann's mother found employment as schoolteacher at Riccarton Junction, a road-less railway halt deep in the Cheviots fifteen miles south from Hawick.

The construction of a railway line between Hawick and Carlisle was the dream of Richard Hodgson, Chairman of the North British Railway Company in 1858; and, when the decision to start work was announced, Hawick declared a public holiday. But building the line was a Herculean task. The proposed track crossed some of the wildest country in Britain and a tunnel had to be driven 1,260 yards through Limekilnridge. The line between Copshaw and Whitrope Summit was an almost unbroken run of eight miles at 1:75, and the route had sharper curves and steeper gradients than any other track in Britain.

Time and fate eventually caught up with the Waverley Line one hundred and eleven years later. David Steel, Liberal Member of Parliament, rode the last train through Riccarton on the night of 6 January 1969. The following morning a section of track was lifted.

Ann's plan was to retrace one of her favourite walks: round the north side of Arnton Fell and Blackwood Hill, down Roughley Sike, and across the moor to gaunt Hermitage Castle, by Lady's Knowe and Flowsware Rig. In this part of the world, little streams are called 'sikes' and Ann recalled, as a child of seven, swimming in Roughley Sike, summer-warm pools at the foot of a waterfall rushing down the glen.

We knew Riccarton was in ruins, only Ann's schoolhouse being occupied, and that the tree-planters had moved in. However, nothing could have prepared us for the shock of devastation that greeted our arrival: as far as the eye could see, row after row of conifers. Regimented lines of lodgepole pine and Sitka spruce blanketing the horizon, obliterating once open moorlands. Worse, the last traces of the railway village, platforms and signal boxes were being torn up to extract hard core for more forest roads. The route round Arnton Fell had gone for ever.

Sadly Ann abandoned her plan, and we drove back through endless close-packed conifers to the road. But I saw the light of battle glint. 'Just because they have ruined Riccarton doesn't mean that we can't have a walk. Let's go over to Hermitage anyway, and try another route.' Long experience had taught me it was useless to protest. So I turned left on the B6399 and we drove a few miles south, by Whitrope Burn, then up to Hermitage.

My second daughter, Jean, had decided to accompany us. Heaven knows why, given her previous experiences of 'mother's walks'. To get matters off to a proper start, Jean opened the car door and, tangled in the seat belt, tripped into the mud, tearing new trousers and badly grazing her knee. Amidst the ensuing uproar, Heathcliff, having spotted a few sheep and the chance of escape, disappeared over the dyke, a happy brown flash, teeth bared, his face in a hideous grin.

Ann deserted her howling daughter and dashed off in hot pursuit, yelling, uselessly: 'Heathcliff! Come back here at once.' By this time, Breac had found Hermitage Burn and was snorting and snuffling his way quickly downstream. Jean was still hopping around, complaining that she wanted to go home immediately. Good Lord, I thought, and we haven't even started.

An exhausting half-hour later, Clan Sandison reformed. Hot sweet tea was administered and Heathcliff securely tethered to a nearby tree. I managed to get in a surreptitious swipe at the brute whilst 'she' wasn't looking and felt better – not a lot, but better. Breac jumped in to join us, a golden mound of dripping dog. Then Ann announced the fatal words 'I'll just have a quick look at the map.' My heart sank. 'Is there a dungeon in the castle?' I inquired, hopefully.

Hermitage, 'The Strength of Liddesdale', is an overpowering, massive, dark slab of history. Since 1242 it has guarded the south-west gateway to Scotland and throughout turbulent Border feuds and battles Hermitage has occupied a strategically unique position in Scottish history. The castle belonged to the Douglas family and Sir James, 'The Black Douglas', was one of Robert the Bruce's staunchest supporters during the Scottish Wars of Independence.

We explored the castle, marvellously preserved outside but little more than an empty shell inside. The bedroom where Earl Bothwell lay wounded when Queen Mary visited him on 15 October 1566. Mary rode there and back in a day from Jedburgh, over fifty miles of bleak windswept moorlands, to comfort her lover. The great hall, where dubious Francis Stewart of Crichton, 5th Earl Bothwell, entertained – a monstrous, fearful, pitiless prince.

In sombre mood, we left the grim castle and walked down to the road junction. Even Heathcliff was quiet. The cottage on the corner has been converted into a craft centre and shop. Long pause whilst the owner was routed out and forced to sell Jean comforting lemonade and crisps. Turning north, we walked up the road, past Hermitage Cottages.

Ann doesn't like roads. 'Come on now, over the fields and on to Roughley Burn,' she said encouragingly. The roadside dyke scaled, we all landed in a thick, glutinous mire lurking unseen on the other side. Loud howls of protest and outrage from Jean. Heathcliff was instantly transformed into a small, ragged, filthy black ball.

Half-way over the field I spotted the bull. At about the same time it spotted us and lumbered into first gear. Trying to keep calm, I urged the tribe to greater speed and we scrambled over a convenient gate, just ahead of about a ton and a half of steaming, angry Border beef. Roughley Burn lay before us, closely tree-clad, at the foot of a steep slope.

I suggested following the near bank, upstream, until we could find a suitable crossing place; but Ann doesn't like detours. Roman-like, she steers a straight course. Anything in the way has to be surmounted, not rounded or avoided. Just another challenge. Struggling down through the trees, we arrived at the burn, which was full, deep and fast-flowing.

I waded over with Jean first, stumbling amongst slippery stones. Then with Heathcliff: he is afraid of water. Then Ann, although I must admit that she did offer to wade the stream herself. Neat, I thought, standing there, wet to the waist, waiting until then to make her offer. Breac just stayed in the middle of the burn and paralleled our passage up the other side.

Which was not as easy as it sounds. Scrub, bramble, birch and willow crowded the muddy track, bounded by a malignant electrified fence. We crawled, Indian-like, through the tangle. At the first clearing we rested. Within seconds, Ann and Jean had been stung by a resident wasp, sending Jean off into further screams of terror. Me, I thought it was poetic justice.

Roughley Sike reached, we assaulted the hill, searching for the waterfall and pools of Ann's childhood. Sure enough, they were still there, but completely enclosed by mature trees which shaded out all light and gave the glen a forbidding feel. Jean, tired, cold, dismal and disillusioned, grabbed the fence to help her up hill. She shrieked with fright and leapt back. Even here the fence was electrified.

Lunch in the rain at the bottom of the hill. Another ferry session over the river, then the long, wet hike back across the moor to the car. Ahead, the black outline of Hermitage Castle beckoned and Jean and I instictively quickened pace. With any luck, we could get there first and barricade ourselves in. It had held out against invading armies in the past. Perhaps it would protect us today?

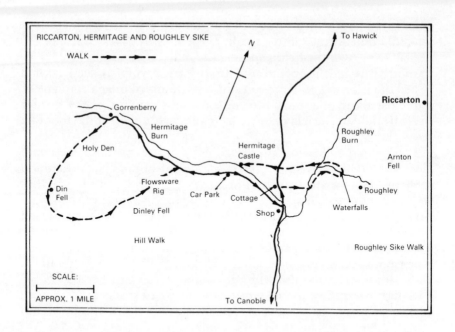

RICCARTON, HERMITAGE AND ROUGHLEY SIKE

WALK ▶ ▬ ▶ ▬ ▶

N

To Hawick

Gorrenberry

Hermitage
Burn

Holy Den

Hermitage
Castle

Roughley
Burn

Riccarton

Arnton
Fell

Din
Fell

Flowsware
Rig

Car Park

Cottage

Roughley

Dinley Fell

Shop

Waterfalls

Hill Walk

Roughley Sike Walk

SCALE:

APPROX. 1 MILE

To Canobie

WHAT YOU NEED TO KNOW

Time and effort A visit to Riccarton Junction will only be of interest to railway buffs or, like us, to people with ancient memories. Forestry has completely destroyed everything else. The walk to Roughley Sike is difficult and tiresome; much of the way is travelled bent double, climbing over and under trees, through tangled undergrowth, across streams. Not long in distance, but long in the mind. If you are foolish enough to attempt it, wear thigh waders and allow about three hours.

I have noted an alternative walk on the map, also starting from Hermitage Castle, but to the south and west: from Gorrenberry to Din Fell, Dinley Fell and Flowsware Rig – a fine moorland and hill walk with excellent views from the top of Din Fell, with summit amble. Be well shod and clad and allow about four hours, plus time to visit Hermitage.

Location Ordnance Survey Sheet 79, Hawick and Eskdale, second series, scale 1:50,000.

Grid references Hermitage Castle 497961; craft centre and shop 507952; Roughley Burn 515955; Roughley Sike Waterfalls 522958; Gorrenberry 470970; Din Fell 460960; Dinley Fell 473951; Flowsware Rig 478958.

Route Leave your car in the car park at Hermitage. For Roughley Sike, walk back down the road to the cottage at the junction with the B6399. Turn left, northwards, and walk up to Hermitage Cottage, on the left of the road. Cross the dyke, into the bog. Stumble over the soggy fields to meet Roughley Burn, a distance of about three-quarters of a mile. Wade the stream and crawl up to where Roughley Sike enters. Climb the hill up Roughley Sike Glen. At the top, by Roughley Cottage, cross the sike and go back downhill. From there rewade the burn and take the most direct route over the moor to the road and Hermitage.

For the hill walk, turn right out of the car park at Hermitage and follow the road west to Gorrenberry. By the telephone kiosk, turn south and climb the shoulder of Din Fell, past Holy Den. This is a steep climb but the ground is relatively dry and going is easy, sort of. From the top, walk south-east, angling down the hill to the promontory of Dinley Fell. From here, an easy walk downhill brings you over Flowsware Rig and back to the minor road. Turn right, alongside Hermitage Burn, back to the car park.

9

Eagle Rock, Romans and Queensferry

ONE OF my best-loved walks near Edinburgh is from the village of Cramond to South Queensferry and back – a distance of ten miles along the shores of the Firth of Forth. As a boy I had often made the walk with my parents so it was with a feeling of returning to an old friend that I once again walked down the winding road to the Firth.

Cramond – Caer Almond, the fort on the River Almond – was an important Roman garrison town, and excavations have revealed much of the signs of early occupation by these methodical early invaders of Scotland. The white-walled Cramond Inn provides a focal point for the village and is well known for the excellence of its food – and drink. Time your walk in accordance with opening hours and work up a thirst for the end of the day.

Robert Louis Stevenson, author of *Treasure Island* and *Kidnapped*, was a frequent visitor to the old inn and, at the other end of the walk at South Queensferry, there is an equally famous watering-hole, the Hawes Inn, built in 1683. Stevenson dreamed up the plot for *Kidnapped* whilst staying at Hawes, in bedroom number 13, 'a small room, with a bed in it, and heated like an oven by a great coal fire'.

It was low tide when I arrived and the Almond lay exposed, mudflatted between tree-lined banks, dotted with small sailing boats. A group of youngsters in kayaks ploughed up and down, yelling with delight when one of their companions capsized. Visitors wandered ice-creamed in warm sun.

A mile off shore, connected to the mainland by a causeway, lies Cramond Island. It is possible to walk over at low tide, but get it wrong and you have a long wait before being able to return. From time to time foolhardy drivers attempt the journey in four-wheel-drive vehicles and, recently, a Range Rover stuck and was soon covered by the incoming tide.

For centuries, passage over the Almond has been provided by a small boat, sculled back and forth on demand by a ferryman who lives in a cottage on the west bank. I stood by the steps leading down to the river, looking hopeful, and in a few minutes the ferryman appeared.

The boat is propelled from the stern, by one oar, manoeuvred in a figure-of-eight rhythm. Not as easy as it sounds. Whilst I was employed by Her Majesty the Queen as a seaman in the Water Transport Regiment, Royal Army Service Corps, I mastered the art of sculling on the River Yar, Isle of Wight. It's like riding a bicycle – once learnt, never forgotten – and it was hard to resist the temptation to ask the ferryman for a go.

I paid my dues of 20 pence and set off westwards along the well remembered path through magnificent woodlands peopled with ancient trees: oak, ash, beech, sycamore, plane, birch, tall Scots pine, larch and nodding old elms, survivors of the dreadful disease that has decimated so many of our native trees in recent years.

A few hundred yards on I turned right, down to the shingle shore to revisit Eagle Rock. As a boy my mind blazed with images every time I surveyed the carving on the face of the huge volcanic boulder. The shape of an eagle has been chiselled in the stone – a Roman eagle, reputed to have been the work of the garrison stationed at Cramond.

Whilst there is no proof that the legionaries actually carved the eagle, I firmly believe they did. Otherwise, all my childhood dreams, wild adventures and fights round the rock would have been pointless. I was always a Pict – and the Romans never won, in spite of what history might say.

On the edge of the tide statuesque herons solemnly stalked lunch;

oystercatchers screamed and squeaked in noisy, black-and-white flights. Long-beaked redshank and curlew poked busily in the sand. Hunch-shouldered mallard stared gloomily at nothing in particular. A pair of mute swans gracefully adorned the flats, haughtily marking my passing.

Walking along the Firth is like a journey in and out of history. The sea is scattered with passing ships: ponderous tankers; a Rosyth-bound Royal Navy frigate, inching menacingly towards port; drilling platforms; and pleasure craft. The Romans would have passed this way, dreaming of distant loved ones and sun-drenched Italian lands.

An RAF fighter plane screams low over Inchcolm, shaking the ruins of the island's ancient abbey, founded in AD 1123, ripping past gaunt pillboxes, relics of Second World War defences. Barnbougle Castle looms near, built in the thirteenth century by the Mowbray family, on the edge of the sea, ideally placed for smuggling; and Hound Point, haunted by the ghost of Sir Roger Mowbray's dog, Baskerville-howling for his dead master, killed during the Crusades.

Glimpses eastwards, of grey-painted Granton Gasworks and Edinburgh and the crouching lion of Arthur's Seat. North over the Forth to the Kingdom of Fife, busy with Burntisland, Methil, Kirkcaldy and Dysart. The view spans the centuries, stretching mind and imagination over Scotland's turbulent past and hopeful future.

Dalmeny golf course interrupts the cool woods, precisely mani-cured in well ordered calm. A notice warns me to take care. Presumably from flying golf balls, but the greens and fairways are empty this morning. Time to visit Dalmeny House, home of the Primrose family, Earls of Rosebery, who have lived there for more than three hundred years.

I never think of Rosebery without reciting to myself the brief lines Robert Burns once gave a previous Lord and Lady Rosebery to say:

> Rosebery to his Lady says,
> My hinnie and my socour,
> Oh, shall we do the thing ye ken,
> Or shall we tak our supper?
> Wi modest face, sae fu of grace,
> Replied the bonnie lady,
> My Noble Lord, do as you please,
> But supper isna ready.

The parents of the present Lord Rosebery divided their time between Mentmore and Dalmeny, 'driving north with two dogs, a cat, a parrot, about twelve staff, three cars and a horse box full of luggage every August in time for the grouse shooting and the Edinburgh Festival'.

Dalmeny House is the work of the 4th Earl, who, one year before the Battle of Waterloo, commissioned the architect William Wilkins to prepare plans for a new house. Barnbougle, the old house, was 'much neglected'. A story is recounted by Lady Rosebery, in her excellent guidebook to Dalmeny, of how the 3rd Earl was once drenched by a wave breaking through the dining-room window of Barnbougle, but the Earl maintained that what had been good enough for his grandfather was good enough for his grandchildren.

Wilkins's building was the first Tudor Gothic Revival house to be built in Scotland and Dalmeny is open to the public. The house contains a wealth of treasures from all over the world: Scottish portraits by Reynolds, Gainsborough, Raeburn and Lawrence; Goya tapestries and the famous Rothschild Collection of eighteenth century furniture, porcelain and other works of art.

From Dalmeny, I walked on to the Forth bridges and Queensferry. The railway bridge was designed by Sir John Fowler in 1890 and in its day was one of the wonders of the modern world. Even now, the imposing structure dominates the feather-like span of the new road bridge.

Before the road bridge was built, passage across the Forth was by ferry, established in the twelfth century by Queen Margaret; and the seaside town named for her is now a quiet, traffic-less, peaceful haven. In my young days, the narrow streets were always jam-packed with cars and crossing the Forth could take anything up to three hours, shuttled below the bridge by side-paddle steamers. the *Queen Margaret, Robert the Bruce* and *Sir William Wallace*.

Time for a closer look at the Hawes Inn and stirring of old memories before the return to Cramond. Must be back at the Almond before 7 p.m. from April to September or before 4 p.m. during winter months. Otherwise you might end up having to swim for your supper – and who needs that?

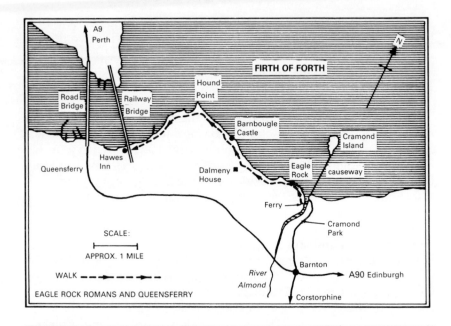

In the map:

A9 Perth

FIRTH OF FORTH

Hound Point

Road Bridge · Railway Bridge

Barnbougle Castle

Cramond Island

Queensferry · Hawes Inn

Dalmeny House

Eagle Rock · causeway

Ferry

Cramond Park

SCALE:

APPROX. 1 MILE

WALK - - ➤ - - ➤ - -

Barnton

River Almond

A90 Edinburgh

Corstorphine

EAGLE ROCK ROMANS AND QUEENSFERRY

WHAT YOU NEED TO KNOW

Time and effort This is an easy walk, along a good track, through woodlands and by shoreline. There and back the walk takes up to four hours, depending upon how long you linger at Dalmeny House. Worth carrying binoculars to get a closer look at wildlife on the shore. The total distance is 10 miles.

Location Ordnance Survey Sheet 65, Falkirk and West Lothian, second series, scale 1:50,000.

Grid references Cramond 190770; Eagle Rock 185775; Dalmeny House 169781; Barnbougle Castle 169785; Hound Point 158796; Hawes Inn 139784.

Route Parking is restricted on the sea-front, so park up the hill in Cramond Village and walk down to the shore. Steps lead down to the ferry. Stand at the top until the ferryman comes over – don't worry, he will see you.

Pass through the turnstile on the other side, by the ferryman's cottage, and the track leads you easily westwards. Within a few hundred yards watch for the little junction on your right, down to Eagle Rock.

Once you reach the golf course, walk inshore of the trees and you will see Dalmeny House set on a promontory to your left. From the house a road continues west, once more through the trees. This soon becomes a track again and leads directly to South Queensferry. Return the same way. Make sure that you check ferry times.

10

Gladhouse, Dundreich Hill and Portmore

Tom wood heated milk and poured it over sugar-covered Weetabix. We sat outside our tent by the shores of Gladhouse Reservoir luxuriating in early morning sunlight, the wild, rain-soaked night forgotten. What ever happened to Tom? Thirty-five years have passed since that breakfast, but I still feel its warmth as keenly as though it were yesterday.

We had spent the previous night, on a Boy Scout exercise, walking in the Moorfoot Hills. After gathering up our damp gear, we limped soggily back to Edinburgh and headquarters at Hermitage of Braid. Although I can't remember the purpose of the hike, I shall never forget that special breakfast. Wherever you are, Tom, thanks again: it was a life-saver.

The little wood we camped in was still there as I lumbered by last summer, heavily booted for the hills. Gladhouse lay calm and peaceful, bedecked with black specks of fishing boats inching eagerly round tree-clad islands, searching shallows for shy brown trout.

Fishing on Gladhouse used to be organized by ballot. In the dark depths of the Water Department of Edinburgh City Council in

Cockburn Street, a mysterious hat was produced and the names of anglers seeking permission to fish on a particular day were chucked in and, presumably, stirred about a bit. First out got the boats. Took me years to realize that in order to be first out you really had to be 'first in' with one of the officials. Father always used to say I was naive.

The road along the south side of the reservoir leads to Moorfoot Farm, a cluster of neat buildings surrounded by well kept, busy fields. Contented cattle and black-faced sheep gazed curiously as I passed, probably wondering if I was for eating. Turning south along a good track, I noted tumbled ruins marking the site of Moorfoot Chapel and Grange.

King David I gave the lands of Moorfoot to the wealthy Abbey of Newbattle in AD 1120. Then, Moorfoot was a considerable community – robe-clad, hooded monks tilling thin soils and tending sheep in upland valleys. Now only bare stones remain by the clear waters of the infant South Esk, as it wends towards captivity in Gladhouse.

The South Esk rises from secret valleys, deep in Moorfoot on Blackhope Scar. It rushes 1,200 feet down Long Cleave to a stem at Gladhouse Cottage, where it is bunched into order for the journey north. The ruins of Hirendean Castle stand on a small knowe overlooking the river – a stark shell guarded by an ancient ash and four windswept sycamores.

I climbed past the sheepfold on the lower slope and sheltered from rising wind in the lee of the single jagged wall. Hirendean was built in the sixteenth century by the Kerr family and little is known of their pastimes and pleasures. Behind me were outlines of a great fireplace, so I was probably crouched in what was once the main hall. Wonder what they got up to, in their balmy days of power and glory? Poor old house; no one seems to care for you now.

'Esk' is the Pictish name for water and the little river glistens and sparkles by an easy track which climbs slowly southwards. Every step of the way is sheer delight. The stream turns and twists, now cascading over tiny waterfalls, now swirling into deep, foam-churned pools. Heather-purple banks and bracken-sided hills colour the scene. Dippers and pied wagtails dart and splash amongst grey and yellow stones. Red-capped grouse wing wildly across the moor and the sound of the stream is never-ending Mozart.

A ford crosses the river at head of Glen Esk, but I balanced, dry-shod, over a twin-poled bridge. As I left the river, I thought how sad it was that the Esk should be so filthy and ill kept downstream by the pits and papermills of Midlothian when it had gone to so much trouble making itself beautiful in childhood hills.

The track reared ahead, climbing round the slope, following a narrow burn bursting with eagerness to reach Lady Esk. A hobgoblin bridge led to a small hut, already winter-fodder-packed for hardy Moorfoot sheep. I turned left, still by the stream, which fell through an ever-darkening, deeply scarred gorge, the sides stripped naked by dashing rivulets. Rowan cling precariously, hopefully berried for autumn birds.

Dundreich Hill, my goal, disappears behind a false summit. Hard going, for me, with plenty of pauses for rest. As I crested the ridge, Dundreich appeared again, a mile distant over an undulating wet moorland plateau. I trudged on, rain now keeping me company. A criss-cross of drainage ditches covers the moor. Deep black and brown peat hags hung dripping with raindrops as I turned and twisted towards the summit.

Dundreich, at 2,040 feet, is second highest of the Moorfoot Hills. A trig. point and cairn of basalt boulders mark the top. Lunch and welcome. The dark ridge of Salisbury and outline of Edinburgh Castle lie enfolded northwards, between Pentland and Lammermuir Hills. Across the Firth of Forth, Ochils and Campsie Fells preamble Highland peaks. Blackhope Scar, Black Knowe and Black Law, a ruffled green carpet, stretch southwards to Tweed.

Below, the dormitory sprawl of Penicuik, 'hill of the cuckoo', edges Edinburgh-wards and the soft Lothian landscape is stabbed with the blades of coal mines, mills, power stations and factories. Godlike on the hill, I ponder man's unending greed and desire to despoil everything around him in the name of commerce and progress. Only the very top of Totto Hill is treeless; Lamb Law, Sherra Law, Dunslair Heights, Cardon Law and Caresman Hill are now smothered by impenetrable conifers.

I walked south from the cairn, along a springy grass summit, to the spur above Portmore Loch. Once spent New Year's Day there, nursing a badly sprained ankle. My fault. Should never have tried to dance a foursome reel, on my own, half-sheets to the wind on Auld Year's Eve. Portmore was always a special place for my wife Ann and me. We used to buy provisions at the Aladdin's cave of Messrs Valvona & Crolla, Elm Row, Edinburgh, and repair to the lochside to eat. Salad summer days, filled with French loaves and cool white wine.

On a small hill south-west of the loch lie Northshield rings – and no finer place to view this Pictish fort than from 2,000 feet above. Three concentric circles of ramparts and ditches enclose an area 240 by 210 feet. The hill is clad with heather and bracken and, from nearby, the outline of the fort is easily missed. Now, from Dundreich, with sun slanting over the shoulder of the hill, I could almost see skin-clad spear-carrying figures, dog-heeled, scurrying homewards.

The reed-fringed south shore of Portmore was clustered with quacking, squabbling mallard. Bad-tempered birds. An expectant angler whisked his fly out over the dimpled rise of a feeding trout. To no avail. I stopped to commiserate and offer advice, conveniently forgetting to mention the fact that during three years of regular piscatory visits I had caught far fewer fish than my wife – who caught only one.

A pleasant lochside track meanders along the east shore to the dam wall and I relaxed for a few moments in a chair outside the fishing hut for coffee. With midges beginning to think I was supper, I started the three-mile walk back to Gladhouse, following the line of an old underground water-pipe. Meant to find out if it was still in use but never did. Ornate iron uprights mark the way, regularly spaced 200 yards apart. They are dated, alternately, 1880 then 1889, and marked as being the property of E & D W T: Edinburgh and District Water something or other?

The wet whirr of snipe, and pheasants, chortling safely from turnips, accompanied me over the fields. By the car I stopped for one last look back up the Esk Valley to Dundreich. Clouds were gathering where I had been. A lone curlew whistled down the hill. I said 'thank you'.

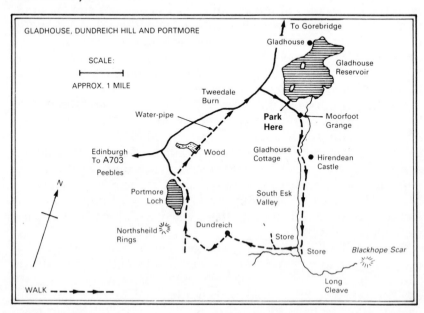

WHAT YOU NEED TO KNOW

Time and effort About twelve miles and five hours. The only section likely to make you puff – it did me – is the climb up from the head of the Esk Valley to Dundreich Hill. You will require waterproof boots: the plateau before Dundreich is damp and soggy. Nor should you underestimate the rapidity of weather changes in the Moorfoot Hills; modest they may be, but it can be very cold and inhospitable on the tops. Carry spare warm clothing, just in case.

Location Ordnance Survey Sheet 73, Galashiels and Ettrick Forest, second series, scale 1:50,000.

Grid references Gladhouse Reservoir 295535; park at 292527; Moorfoot Grange and Chapel 297524; Hirendean Castle 297513; head of Esk valley 297486; Dundreich Hill 275491; Northshield Rings 257494; Portmore Loch 260500; water line from Portmore at 260508 to Tweeddale Burn at 276526.

Route Park on the minor road leading to Moorfoot Farm, at the south end of Gladhouse Reservoir, in a prepared parking area. Watch out for the inevitable notice-board listing dos and don'ts round the loch. Walk to Moorfoot Farm and turn quarter-right, following the hill track leading to Gladhouse Cottage, on the small hill ahead.

Cross the South Esk by the dam and Hirendean Castle is on your left. The track continues up the valley, eventually leading to a ford across the river and a block-built animal-food store. Turn right, away from the Esk, and follow the track which continues uphill over an attractive little bridge to another winter food store.

Just before this last store turn left by a sheepfold and climb the valley, keeping the stream on your left. This will take you out onto the plateau below Dundreich Hill. From the cairn on the top, walk south-west to the spur overlooking Portmore Loch and carefully descend the hill. When you reach the track at the foot of the hill, turn right, northwards, and follow this path round the east side of Portmore to the fishing hut by the dam wall and car park.

The first gate on your right takes you onto the line of the water-pipe. Look over the field and you will see the route as a straight mound leading towards the conifer plantation in the middle distance. The pipe bisects this wood. At the road at Tweeddale Burn, turn right and walk alongside the massive V-walled outlet stream from Portmore to Gladhouse. Turn first right over this stream, back to your car.

11

Romans, Roundheads and Pentland Picts

I T ALL started in Habbie's Howe, thirty years ago. Mildly protesting, yet anxious to please a new girl-friend, I was chivvied from the comfort of the old inn and marched swiftly to the top of the Pentland Hills. I can't even pretend I enjoyed the experience, walking for walking's sake; but it was immediately clear that, if I wished to retain the regard of this beautiful creature, I would have to start enjoying it – pretty damned quick.

Now, more than half a lifetime and four marvellous children later, I still see that special gleam in her eye when she pores over Ordnance Survey maps during long winter evenings, plotting fresh, lung-bursting expeditions; and, I confess, I have come to enjoy it, very much indeed.

Habbie's Howe was our favourite pub, a few miles from

Edinburgh and made famous by Allan Ramsey in his book *The Gentle Shepherd*, published in 1725:

> Gae faurer doon the burn tae Habbie's Howe,
> Where a' the sweets o' spring an' summer grow,
> An' when ye're tired o' prattling side the rill,
> Return tae Ninemileburn, an' tak a gill.

Which good advice I follow, frequently. As starting point, or perhaps more important, finishing point for Pentland walks, Habbie's Howe is ideal. This small hamlet on the road to Lanark was once a busy staging post for travellers and birthplace of George Mickle Kemp, architect of that famous Princes Street monstrosity the Scott Monument.

Romans also walked this way, spears trailing, wearily to Solway, and Nine Mile Burn lies 1½ miles south-west of Eight Mile Burn, but proper, Scottish miles, neither Roman, nor English. The 'lang Scots miles' which Tam o' Shanter, Kirkton Jean and Souter Johnnie ignored in Burns's poem were 1,976 yards, measured from Edinburgh to the Pentland villages. Not the fancy, foreign, metre things we have to contend with today.

Keeping these old roads in good repair was always a problem – so much so that in 1669 by Royal Statute, it was decreed that every man between the ages of fifteen and seventy should give six days work a year on the roads in his parish. The idea worked as well then as it would now and Scotland's roads had to wait for General Wade, Telford and Macadam and their successors before the 'mosses, waters slaps and stiles' of history were finally smoothed away.

The Pentland Hills were my youthful playground, easily accessible from Edinburgh and a popular weekend retreat for the stolid citizens of Auld Reekie. As a boy, the T Woods near Swanson were a regular haunt, where I wickedly bird-nested amongst whins, searching for pale linnet's eggs.

Robert Louis Balfour Stevenson, the author of *Treasure Island*, lived in Swanson Village as a child and I often hung over the garden wall, gazing at windows, watching for my hero's face. Never saw RLS but I did see my first white blackbird in his garden, an albino oddity which chattered about the trees for years.

Sitting in the car park outside Habbie's Howe last July, ready booted, I stared moodily through the rain, wondering if it would stop long enough for a quick dash up West Kip. Selective mist rolled along the hills, giving the Pentlands an almost feminine outline; they appeared and disappeared, embarrassed by fondling clouds. Still, I reasoned, I can only get wet and the rain might pass.

Through the gate at the end of the car park, and on to the track with Cap Law somewhere ahead, the litany of Monks Burn rumbling nearby. I imagined a holy line of closely hooded figures, wraith-like in the mist, squelching up the path. This is the route Cistercian divines followed from their monastery at Newhall, in the woods south of Habbie's Howe, over the hill to Howlets House, 'the house of the owls', once a lonely chapel, now ruins on the north shore of Loganlee Reservoir.

I stopped by Font Stone, the remains of a cross marking the way. A break in the clouds suddenly exposed the small wood at the head of the glen, like a ghostly army marching downhill. Other, less ghostly armies, stalked Pentland in the past. A few miles north, on the slopes of Turnhouse Hill, at Rullion Green, religious intolerance boiled over into bloody murder.

A Royalist force, commanded by General Thomas Dalyell, fell on a group of 900 Covenanters. Men, women and children were indiscriminately slaughtered. Those who survived were hanged, ten at a time, in Edinburgh, or before their own front doors.

The remainder were shipped to the West Indies as plantation slaves. Dalyell was a devoted Royalist. Since the execution of King Charles I he had never shaved his beard, but even he was appalled by the events of Rullion. He retired from the army, and from public life, immediately after this so-called battle.

Those were hard times to be a Christian. Before the Restoration, the Covenanters had committed equally horrifying acts on Episcopalian fellow Scots. In 1661, blossoming freedom from the Solemn League and Covenant produced these heartfelt hopes, inscribed on an triumphal arch in Linlithgow:

> From Covenanters with uplifted hands,
> From Remonstrators with associate bands,
> From such Committees as govern the nation,
> From Church Commissioners and their Protestation,
> Good Lord deliver us.

In 1687, King James II offered religious tolerance, a final, ill-fated attempt at reconciliation that was to cost him his crown two years later. Gilbert Rule, a noted historian of his time, expressed the church's view of religious freedom: 'To accept this toleration is inconsistent with the principles of the Church of Scotland . . . in which we are all bound to extirpate popery.' The Revd Sheilds, a prominent preacher, put the matter in plainer language: 'To engage in bond of living peaceably is to engage in bonds of iniquity with those who are carrying on Babylon's interest, the mother of harlots and witchcraft.'

Past the wood, I puffed up the shoulder of mist-covered West

Kip, a modest 1,806 feet and second highest of the Pentland Hills. The highest, Scald Law, 1,899 feet, lay somewhere to the north-east, shrouded in cloud and rain.

On a clear day the view from the top of West Kip is spectacular, embracing half Scotland at a glance – Edinburgh, arced and protected by Lammermuir and Moorfoots; distant Cheviots; and, westward, tangled Trossach peaks. Perthshire and the Cairngorms crowd northwards. Largo Law in Fife and Lothian's Berwick Law pillar the Firth of Forth, dotted black by Inchkeith, Bass Rock and the Isle of May.

Not today. I could hardly see my hand in front of my face and stumbled along, searching for the path down to Eastside and Eight Mile Burn. With a sense of relief, I found the track and stamped wetly southwards, eventually arriving on the minor road leading to the A702.

The 200 square miles of Pentland are scattered with Pictish remains – indeed, 'Pentland' means 'the land of the Picts' – and on a promontory at the foot of South Black Hill is the prehistoric fort of Braidwood. There is evidence of two separate periods of occupation and construction. The first fort was probably an all-timber structure guarded by a single wall; the second ring, protected by banks and ditches, is 45 feet from the first, but joined to it by a fence.

As they tramped by, along their neat, well-surfaced road,

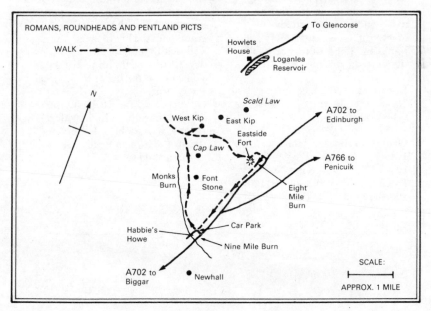

swarthy Roman legionaries must have cursed their luck. What gods had they offended, so badly, to be banished to this last outpost of the Empire, playing watchdog to a bunch of rain-soaked, hair-coated savages? Similar thoughts ran through my mind as I fell in behind a passing cohort and marched back along the Roman road to the car. I left the troop at Nine Mile Burn ad slipped gratefully into Habbie's Howe, to warm my sorrows by the blazing fire.

WHAT YOU NEED TO KNOW

Time and effort All the Pentland Hills are easily accessible from Edinburgh and provide a delightful range of walks, both long and little, strenuous and not so strenuous. The walk described is easy, although sometimes wet, and takes about three hours.

This walk could well be combined with a visit to one of Scotland's most famous places of worship, Roslin Chapel, dating from 1452, and a few miles distant, between Penicuik and Loanhead. The beauty of the Pentland walks is that there is always a quick escape route should the weather turn nasty, and lots of alternative places of interest to visit. Invariably, routes and rights of way are well signposted.

Location Ordnance Survey Sheet 66, Edinburgh, second series, scale 1:50,000.

Grid references Habbie's Howe 178577; Font Stone 175593; Cap Law 175598; West Kip 177605; Eastside 184603; Braidwood Fort 194597; Eight Mile Burn 192593.

Route Drive south-west from Edinburgh along the A702 Biggar road. Park at Habbie's Howe, beside the inn. A gate leaves the end of the car park and the track is signposted, half-left from the gate. Look ahead and you will see the track winding up the hill on the right side of Monks Burn. Half-way up the hill, between Green Law and Broad Law, on your right, is the Font Stone. On the lower slopes of West Kip, go right, round the wood, and on to the summit.

Retrace your steps from the summit and turn south, down the track to Eastside. From here you meet a good, well surfaced road coming up the hill to greet you. Follow this until it takes a 90-degree turn north. Immediately on your right is the site of Braidwood Pictish fort.

Before the little road joins the A702, turn right to Eight Mile Burn. Cross Eight Mile Burn and follow the Roman Road back to the car park and Habbie's Howe.

12

Edinburgh Past
and Present

*I*WAS born and brought up in Edinburgh and wear the 'Auld Grey
City' like a garment round my soul. Thirty-two years separate
me from Scotland's capital, but a small corner of my heart is for
ever Auld Reekie – cautious, reserved, quick to take offence, slow
to forgive, essentially parochial and proud of it.

Worse, I was educated in Edinburgh, at Scotland's oldest seat of
learning, the Royal High School, founded in 1120 under the Abbot
of Holyrood. There I was thoroughly boiled in Bannockburn and
stories of Robert the Bruce and William Wallace, imbued with the
sad, beautiful poetry of Burns and filled with the stirring novels of
our famous former pupil, Sir Walter Scott.

Mathematics and sciences were closed doors, but mention the
Battle of Otterburn, Sir Andrew Wood, Montrose or Bonnie
Dundee and my interest was guaranteed. Burns's poem 'To a
Mountain Daisy' brought tears to my eyes and I laboured for hours
memorising 'Tam o'Shanter' rather than Shakespeare. When I
finally walked through the memorial doors of the old building,
I was about as prepared for the realities of life as King James IV was
for battle at Flodden Field in 1513.

My elder brother, Ian, and I used to roam the streets, from Swanson to Leith. Dangerously bird-nesting in private gardens on Calton Hill. Exploring the endless, narrow, dark, secret lanes off High Street. Pushing buttons in Chambers Street museum, watching, fascinated, as stolid models staggered to life. Buying forbidden winkles, paper-poked-and-pinned, from the huge black-clad lady who sat by John Knox's house.

Edinburgh is one of the most beautiful cities in the world, and a walk through 'The Athens of the North' is always an exciting adventure; but, for me, it is not only a walk through Scottish history but also a walk through green childhood years. What was time then? The distance between the top of Arthur's Seat and the hot chiding waiting when we arrived home late for dinner.

The quick way to school was over Calton Hill and this is an excellent starting point for an Edinburgh walk. The hill is an ancient lava flow, steep-cragged to the south and smoothed by ice to the north – ideal for summer sledging on school drawing-boards. Calton is graced by 'the disgrace of Edinburgh', an unfinished monument of classical proportions, the building of which ended when funds ran out – Scottish pragmatism at its best.

I discovered Schubert on Calton, in 1962 when a limousine of a grand piano was placed on the hill, across from the Royal Observatory car park, and two promising young pianists played to an enraptured audience: Vladimir Ashkenazy and Daniel Barenboim.

The path round the west side of the Observatory, above Leith Street, is also an ideal place to watch the last-night sentiment of the Edinburgh International Festival. Castle lights dim, leaving only topmost turrets illuminated. A lone piper laments. Then the blaze and sparkle as fireworks scatter and burst, brightening dark, star-specked skies.

Nelson's Column crowns Calton Hill, a round, ugly monument to Trafalgar's posthumous victor. The firing of the one o'clock gun from Edinburgh Castle is timed at the Column. As one o'clock approaches, a ball slowly ascends a post to the top of the tower. When it falls, half a mile away, the gun fires. Which is why I never mastered the niceties of algebra. At the window of my classroom I could sit, mesmerized, watching this inevitable daily sequence: rise, fall and bang. Much more interesting.

Steps lead down the hill to Waterloo Place, by vast St Andrew's House, pack-full of government bureaucracy, busily administering Scottish affairs. At the east end of Princes Street stand these grand lumps, the Central Post Office and the North British Hotel. Registrar House, a magnificently proportioned Adam building, eyes them warily from across the street, guarded by a bronze statue of the Iron Duke, horse-mounted, arm outflung, pointing towards supposed danger approaching from Portobello.

I always used to return home this way, and wait outside Elliot's bookshop for a number 9 tramcar. Had to be a number 9: that's the one she took. All I needed was the courage to speak to her, but the High School didn't prepare boys for that either.

Across Princes Street, past Waverley Bridge, squats the Scott Monument, like a huge wedding cake waiting to be sliced. Sir Walter sits serenely under his arches, book on lap, studious hands on marble pages, frequently red-nosed – wickedly painted by irreverent pranksters.

Scotland's National Gallery, a few yards further on, is a favourite stopping place of mine. Not the one fronting Princes Street: the one behind, where admission is free. Could never afford the other, and, consequently, always spent my time round the corner. Raeburn's portrait of Mrs Scott Moncrief, the Rembrandt self-portrait, Monet's poplars, Chardin's flowers and McTaggart are my best-loved residents, and I visit them frequently, like old friends.

A road, known as 'The Mound', leads from the galleries up to Castle and High Street. The Nor Loch used to protect these northern walls, and was formed in 1448 when the east end of the valley was dammed. After it had been drained, the mound was built to give access to the 'New Town', built to ease the crush of tenements clustered down Royal Mile from Castle to Holyrood. The foundations of the first of these elegant squares and terraces were laid out on 26 October 1767.

Edinburgh's earliest inhabitants built a fort on Castle Rock, the most easily defensible promontory amongst marshy forests of pre-history. The present castle evolved from these humble timber beginnings and was much needed throughout the ages. Scots were always 'chronically at war', if not with themselves then with the English – a state of affairs only briefly interrupted by Roman domination and lasting until Bonnie Prince Charlie's disastrous visit in 1745.

A Royal Mile of history leads downhill from the Castle Esplanade, past still impressive tenements, called 'lands' in their days of glory. The higher your station, the nearer ground level you lived; but the same entrance was used by mighty lord and humble servant alike and Scottish social distinctions were much formed by these meetings on the stairs. It was hard to be impressed by your neighbour when you were accustomed to seeing him rolling home, pickled and plain, six nights a week. Sundays were soberly kirked.

An amazing array of intellectual ability flourished in the High Street: Allan Ramsey, founder of the Select Society, a literary elite;

his son, also Allan, the portrait painter, and his pupil, Naysmith; philosopher David Hume; Adam Smith, author of *The Wealth of Nations*; William Creech, publisher of the Edinburgh Edition of Burns's poetry; and Scotia's bard himself.

The High street abounded with private clubs of literary, artistic, political and just good old-fashioned Scots drinking men; the Cape Club, favoured by Scotland's unsung poet, Robert Fergusson; the Pious Club, Spendthrift Club, Salt Herring Club, Ten Tumbler Club, and many more.

However, amidst all the bustle of High Street, my most treasured place is round the back of St Giles's Cathedral – an evening sanctuary of peace and solitude, shadowed and softened by lingering sunlight, watched and guarded by the statue of Corollus Secundus, Emperor of Rome, strangely stirrup-less on his mighty horse.

At the foot of the hill stands the palace of Holyroodhouse, residence of Scottish monarchs until the Union of the Crowns in 1603, surrounded by the well kept acres of Holyrood Park, crowned by the proud 'lion' of Arthur's Seat. The Picts built one of their largest forts on top of the hill, enclosing some 20 acres, and Arthur's Seat is easily climbed from St Margaret's Loch. The ruined chapel on the hill overlooking the little loch was built by King Malcolm Canmore's Hungarian-born wife, the saintly Princess Margaret.

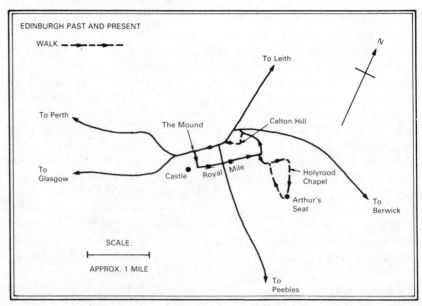

I stood on the lion's rocky head. There was Newhaven Harbour, where Ian and I used to fish; my childhood Edinburgh home; the High School, sad and empty, awaiting the arrival of an ever-absent Scottish Parliament; the hospital, where our first son was born; Jock's Lodge, school playing-fields, where I struggled in winter rugby mud; and, above all, the black-etched castle, rose-hazed and dreamlike, watching carefully over Edinburgh's old grey spires.

WHAT YOU NEED TO KNOW

Time and effort   This walk could take a lifetime, there is so much to see on the way. Do your best to allow at least a full day. The walking's easy, but still wear good stout shoes and carry a waterproof: Edinburgh weather, like the city itself, can be fickle. Prepare yourself before setting off by visiting the tourist information centre on Waverley Bridge. Have a street plan to guide you round and mug up basic information about what you hope to visit on the way. For a walk only, allow three hours.

Location   Ordnance Survey Sheet 66, Edinburgh, second series, scale 1:50,000.

Grid references   Calton Hill 265742; Registrar House 259741; The Mound 255738; Edinburgh Castle 252735; Holyroodhouse 269739; Arthur's Seat 276729.

Route   Park your car on Blenheim Place, adjacent to where London Road and Leith Street meet. Walk up the hill to the church on your right. Steps lead to Calton Hill. A track follows a wall up an easy slope to your left. This leads to Edinburgh's Disgrace, the Observatory and Nelson's Column.

Close to the column, an old brass ship's cannon, on wheels, is 'aimed' towards Princes Street. It also points to the steps which lead down to Waterloo Place. On Waterloo, turn right and walk to the east end of Princes Street. Adam's Registrar House is on the right-hand side.

Cross Princes Street and walk through East Princes Street Gardens to the Scott Monument. If feeling particularly energic, stop and climb the stairs that wind up inside, to the top. If not, pass by and visit the Scottish National Gallery at the foot of The Mound.

Walk up The Mound, bearing right round the railing in front of the Assembly Hall, and up the steep stone-flagged slope to High Street and Edinburgh Castle. After visiting the castle, walk down the Royal Mile and call on Holyroodhouse.

Now, into the park, left along the road, past the wishing well to St Margarets Loch. On the far side of the loch a well marked track leads to the chapel on the hill, and then on to the top of Arthur's Seat. Descend by Hunter's Bog, which returns you to the wishing well.

To return to Blenheim Place, walk through the courtyard of Holyrood and turn right on the main road. Twin tunnels under the railway line. Keep left, up Abbeyhill. At the traffic lights, cross, but don't go downhill to Easter Road. Take the road immediately adjacent to it, uphill to Carlton Terrace. This will bring you back to Blenheim Place.

13

Lomond and Loch Leven

I LIKED it better the old way. A lonely, broken tower. Moss-covered stones amidst alder, willow and tangled briar. An illkept track. Muddy steps into history. Mary Queen of Scots wandering forlornly by the shore, dreaming of a lost crown. What would I say to her when we met? I was sure, one day, that we would meet, in the woods of Castle Island on Loch Leven.

As soon as the long boat berthed by the wooden landing stage, I felt her presence, and after lunch I haunted the tumbled ruins. Through the stillness of summer noons, humming with insects and secret, deep-thicket birdsong, I walked the little island. She never appeared, but she was always there. Now things have been taken in hand. Daily boat trips from Kinross. Grass neatly trimmed and signposted. Cement and mortar. This way to the Castle. Not the same.

As I stood on West Lomond Hill, overlooking Loch Leven and the fertile Howe of Fife, memories of these youthful fantasies flooded back. My companion, George Reid, pointed skywards, breaking the spell. 'Here they come,' he said. A small aeroplane, climbing through cloudless sky, seemed to splutter and stall, dangerously. Tiny black specks fell from the fuselage. Hope it's not bits of wings and propeller. Then, after a seemingly endless plunge, red, blue and orange mushroom parachutes, figures suspended pendulum-like beneath.

Old and new, the story of Fife. Glenrothes not-so-New Town, an established modern technological centre. Declining coal-mining Cowdenbeath, Leslie and Lochgelly. The industrial pall of Dysart and Kirkcaldy. The Pictish fort on East Lomond. Falkland Palace, favourite home of ancient Scottish kings. From the top of Lomond Hills, a glimpse of things past and things to come.

Earlier that morning we had left a dreach Auld Reekie and made the easy road-bridged journey across the Forth into the Wee Kingdom. Speeding northwards along the A90 towards Kinross, I remembered my first journey to Lomond and Loch Leven, made as a boy of twelve, favoured fishing guest of Mr and Mrs Tom Kelly of Edinburgh – the bustle, steam and shriek of early-morning Waverley; the unforgettable hot smell of the station; rattling, smoke-belching, through the red arches of the Forth Railway Bridge; the wonderful sense of excitement on arriving at Loch Leven pier; the kindness of my hosts and the encouragement of our two gillies.

Today, thirty minutes after leaving Edinburgh, we neatly exited at Junction 5, swept round the south shore, past Vane Farm Nature Reserve and St Serf's Island, through Scotlandwell to Leslie. From here, a convenient, twisting, little moorland road cuts through the Lomond Hills between Leslie and Falkland. We stopped on the highest point, at the thoughtfully provided, well ordered Fife County Council car park and information centre.

A long, well made track leads westwards to the top of the highest Lomond hill, a modest 1,713 feet, but with magnificent views on a clear day. Across Perthshire and Angus, range after range lead to the peak of Ben Macdhui in the Cairngorms. Distant Glen Tilt, crowned by graceful Ben Dearg; Ben Lawers, by Loch Tay; over Ochil and Campsie Fells to Loch Lomond; the stub of Largo Law, on the north shore of Firth of Forth; Edinburgh, Pentlands, Lammermuir and Moorfoots.

Below East Lomond nestles Falkland Palace, built mostly during the fifteenth and sixteenth centuries by successive Scottish monarchs. King James II, by royal charter, proclaimed the tower at

Falkland Palace. Perkin Warbeck, pretender to the English throne, was entertained there by James IV in 1495. Probably Perkin's last good meal – he was hanged by his ungrateful peers at Tyburn in London four years later.

At the age of seventeen, James V was held prisoner at Falkland by the ambitious Earl of Angus and eventually died in the palace in 1542, shortly after being brought news of the birth of his daughter, the future Queen of Scots, at Linlithgow: 'Farewell, it cam with ane lass and it will pass with ane lass.'

Cromwell's men knocked Falkland about a bit and felled the beautiful surrounding woods, where Queen Mary used to hunt, in order to fortify the town of Perth. Most of the present building is the work of Bruce of Falkland, who carefully restored the palace during the early years of the nineteenth century. The ghosts of an earlier age survey the scene. On East Lomond, above the village, lie the remains of an early Iron Age fort. Banked and ditched, this fort was probably occupied for more than a thousand years and during recent excavations hollow glass beads were found among the ruins.

They would not have pleased John Knox, Mary's religious arch-enemy. 'Godless frippery,' I hear him exclaim in disgust. Knox visited Fife in 1559, determined to root out the last vestige of Catholicism. 'We reformed them,' he is reported to have said. Which really meant the ruthless destruction of buildings, books and records, and everything else he and his sanctimonious black-gowned band could lay their hands on. Scotland has no fury like a Presbyterian scorned. On the south-west slope of West Lomond, at the head of Glen Vale, a 'step' at the foot of the cliff is still known as John Knox's Pulpit.

George and I plodged on along the soggy track, occasionally skirting the dampest parts. The way is bounded by a drystane dyke, constructed out of huge round sandstone boulders – a major building feat. A few disconsolate grouse rocketed from the heather, past empty butts, and we noticed the marks of Argo-Cat or Snow-Cat. Visions of tweed-clad men and headscarfed ladies heading comfortably uphill in search of sport.

Craigen Gaw and the Split Nose are on the right – a dangerous climb amidst loose, crumbling rocks. Not for us. As the track edges over the shoulder of West Lomond a well marked frontal route leads straight up the east face. Intent upon a photograph, and worried about fading light, I attacked the slope with gusto – for me, quarter of a mile per hour, interspersed with frequent rests.

The summit is topped by a strange camouflaged rectangular sentry-box, surmounted by an aerial. Strange, because there was no apparent way in. Even here, on top of West Lomond, Fife contrast between ancient and modern persists. Scattered over the hill are the remains of a cairn, built three thousand years ago. When or why the cairn was destroyed is a mystery but it still rises in parts to a height of nearly ten feet and measures almost ninety feet round. What minds and hands planned and laboured these stones to this wild, windswept summit? What hopes and memorials lie buried here?

I stumbled back to the track, dark shadows of departing day chasing me down the steep ridged scree and scrub slope. Sunlight shimmered over a cluster of Fife reservoirs, cupped in the horseshoe of the hills: Ballo, Harperleas, Holl, Drumain and Arnot.

Ahead. the sky behind East Lomond blushed pink and red in the evening. Soft winds sighed over the moor as a last clump of parachutists hurtled earthwards. Wonder what Knox and his dusty band of devil hunters would have made of that lot?

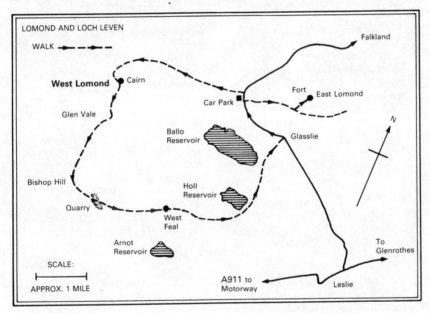

WHAT YOU NEED TO KNOW

Time and effort   It depends upon how much time you have. There and back to the top of West Lomond is an easy couple of hours. Going the other way, the summit of East Lomond is about thirty minutes. If you have a full day, then consider a walk round all the Lomond Hills; from the car park to West Lomond, to Bishop Hill in the south. There is nothing too taxing, providing you follow standard precautions for hillwalking – and choose a good day.

Another good day out may be spent visiting Castle Island on Loch Leven, then Vane Farm Nature Reserve, run by the excellent Scottish Royal Society for the Protection of Birds, followed by a tour round Falkland Palace and a quick dash up to the fort on top of East Lomond. The beauty of the Lomond Hills is that they are so easily accessible and yet wonderfully remote. Back in time for tea.

Location   Two maps needed: Ordnance Survey Sheet 59, St Andrews and Kirkcaldy, and Sheet 58, Perth and Kinross, second series, scale 1:50,000.

Grid references   Leslie 59/ 245015; Falkland Palace 59/255076; East Lomond 59/243063; car park 58/227063; West Lomond 58/ 196066; Glen Vale 58/187059; Bishop Hill 58/185044; Scotlandwell 58/184016; Vane Farm Nature Reserve: 58/160990; Castle Island 58/139018.

Route   In Leslie main street, watch out for a narrow turning on your left, half-way down. There is a notice on the wall, signposting West Lomond, but it is easy to miss. Follow this little road for about four miles, past an interesting-looking restaurant and café on your left, and park in the Fife Regional Council car park. From here, you may strike either right, to East Lomond, or left, to West Lomond. There is an excellent map by the toilet building in the car park and both walks are easy to follow: straight there and straight back.

If you propose a full day's walk, take the track to West Lomond. From the top of the hill, walk due south, keeping as much as possible to the high ground, avoiding the edge of the crags, to Bishop Hill. At the south end of Bishop, look east and you will see an old quarry. A road leads from here, down the hill to West Feal. Walk past the south end of Holl Reservoir towards Ballo and Balgothrie and onto the road at Wester Glasslie, conveniently near the restaurant. Then left along the road, back to the car park.

14

Man Friday in Fife

THE KINGDOM of Fife is a mixture of farming, fishing, mining, heavy industry and some of Scotland's most attractive seaside towns and beaches. I was born in Edinburgh, the wrong side of the Forth as far as Fifers are concerned, but my parents used to take me to Kinghorn for summer holidays. There I learned to love the diversity and dignity of such dissimilar places as Kirkcaldy and gentle Kilconquhar.

I still remember my feeling of excitement upon seeing my first-ever great crested grebe, gracing the calm waters of Kinghorn Loch; and our secret cove, a mile to the east of the town, where my brother Ian and I swam and played with these strange creatures, girls. Days seemed endless then, always sunny, and we quickly befriended the most important people in town: the manager at the local cinema, dispensers of beach-side ice-cream and, our hero, Jake, who ran trips round the bay in a brown clinker-built motorboat.

Fife and golf go together and few areas have so many fine

courses. I have hacked my way round a few, including the 'inner sanctum', the Old Course at St Andrews. Ian, happily ignoring my consistent inability to hit a golf ball with any regularity and frequently not at all, a few years ago invited me to make up a four – all single-figure players. After which I sold my clubs and vowed never again to darken tee or green. My golfing days ended in mortifying ignominy, playing my approach shot to the 18th green from nearly the middle of the main road.

Lower Largo is one of the Kingdom's most attractive towns – well kept cottages lining narrow streets and a tiny harbour backed by a comfortable hotel. The buildings are firmly Scottish domestic architecture in character and appear to have grown, rather than been built. They cluster the shore, leading to a magnificent beach of fine sand that stretches in a golden curve three miles eastwards to Earlsferry and Elie. A relaxing, sea-breeze-refreshing walk; the perfect place to while away a day.

Andrew Selkirk, immortalized by Daniel Defoe as Robinson Crusoe, was born in Lower Largo in 1676. He followed his father to sea and, at the age of twenty-seven years, whilst sailing under Captain William Dampier, was marooned on the island of Juan Fernandez for insubordination. Must have been pretty harsh words to so enrage his captain and merit such cruel punishment.

It takes a lot to keep a Fifer down and Selkirk survived. He was rescued four years later by a passing ship and soon returned to sea, although not under Captain Dampier. Defoe travelled extensively throughout Scotland, as a government agent, or, more accurately, as a spy, reporting the activities and plotting of Jacobites; but it was in London that Defoe met Selkirk and was fascinated by the story of his desert island adventure.

Defoe's masterpiece has captivated readers ever since and a statue of Robinson Crusoe proudly graces Selkirk's birthplace. The figure stands above the door, hand raised, shading eyes, peering endlessly across the street for rescue. Andrew Selkirk died in 1721, in bed, at the tragically early age of forty-five years; but Robinson Crusoe lives on.

I parked my car by the harbour and walked along the quiet main street, past Selkirk's house and up onto the line of the disused railway. Many years had drifted by since I had last passed that way by rail, on gleaming, steam-belching LNER locomotives.

A few minutes' walk left town behind. The long beach, backed by dunes covered in marram grass, was deserted. Square concrete blocks lurched drunkenly from the sand, reminders that Largo Bay was considered a potential landing site for Mr Hitler's happily ill-fated Operation Sea Lion, the invasion of our island fortress during the Second World War. Indeed, the beach was used to rehearse our own soldiers in preparation for the Normandy landings of June 1945.

The dunes play host to a number of rare and beautiful plants, including grass of Parnassus and early purple orchid. They also play host to local sun worshippers, who use the beach for all-over tanning on warm days. The sun was shining brightly, so I joined them, carrying my clothes, bundled under my arm, strolling a couple of carefree miles, naked along the beach.

I stopped to speak to a family, lazing the sun away – two bronzed children, brother and sister, busy with sand castles, watched by relaxed parents. They told me that they used the beach as much as possible during summer months and that many of their friends did likewise. Scotland is blessed with only two official naturist beaches: Lagg at the southern tip of the Island of Arran, and a beach at Saltcoats in Ayrshire. However, there are many unofficial beaches and Lower Largo is one of the most accessible.

At the east end of the beach Cocklemill Burn burbles into Largo Bay and has to be forded – no problem on a hot, clothesless day, but otherwise a long inland detour. There is a large, well ordered caravan site on the other side of the burn at Ford Links, a possible holiday venue, with easy access to the beach.

I followed the track round Shell Bay past Kincraig Point, into Elie, by the golf course – beware of flying balls – and walked through town down to the harbour, a veritable 'Costa', with windsurfing school, instruction in falling in the water, hire of sailboards, sailing dinghies, canoes and pedalos.

In spite of all this activity, Elie is still a working harbour, with local boats fishing for crab, the few remaining lobster and inshore fish. But during summer months Elie is awash with activity and is a popular holiday centre. I sat on the wall by the old granary, used now as sailing club premises, and watched aspiring windsurfers climbing out of and falling into the cold waters of the firth. Cradling a cup of scalding coffee, I pondered man's insanity.

I trudged back through town and headed north, out to Kilconquhar, which has the distinction of being the best kept village in north-east Fife. Looked it, too, and I was almost ashamed to tread the pristine pavements in my muddy boots. No shops as far as I could see, but a fine church and very inviting-looking hotel which offers excellent bar lunches to weary travellers.

The quickest way back to Lower Largo is via the old railway line. This passes close to the A917 Crail–Kirkcaldy highway and from there it is five easy miles home. But, as Daniel Defoe remarked, 'he that will view the county of Fife must go round the coast'. The day was still hot and afternoon sunlight called my soul. Scurrying sandpipers and shrieking oystercatchers dashed and darted in the slow, gravel-tumbling wavelets as I strode the strand, Largo's grey and white houses growing ever larger with every step.

I gave Robinson Crusoe a wink and a nod as I passed – from one lover of quiet places to another. Must find out more about Juan Fernandez; if it was good enough for Andrew Selkirk, it would probably suit me. In the meantime, Largo Bay will do fine – not so far to travel, either!

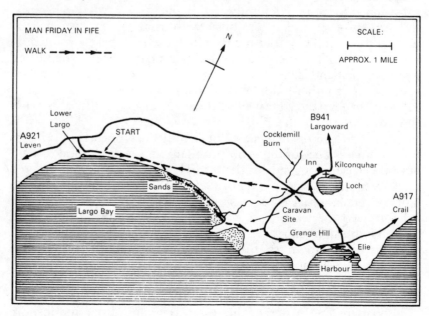

WHAT YOU NEED TO KNOW

Time and effort   Allow a full day for this walk and plan your start, if possible, when the tide is full. As you walk eastwards, the tide should be going out. With luck, on your return you should still have flat, clean sands to stamp along, as the tide comes in. For the full effect, choose a warm summer day; you can linger on the beach, dressed or otherwise, as fancy dictates. The old railway line is stony and rough in places so wear strong shoes if you propose to follow it rather than walk both ways along the beach. To save humping food, aim for a pub lunch in Kilconquhar or Elie.

Location   Ordnance Survey Sheet 59, St Andrews and Kirkcaldy, second series, scale 1:50,000.

Grid references   Lower Largo 415025; start walk 422027; Cocklemill Burn 458008; Grangehill 477002; Elie 492000; Kilconquhar Inn 485020.

Route   Park near the harbour and turn right, walking along Main Street, past Andrew Selkirk's house (small museum a few doors on). Look left and you will see the line of the old railway close by above you on the hill. Once on the railway track, walk eastwards. Clear the town and cut down to the beach. From there, follow your nose along the sands.

At the end of the beach, ford Cocklemill Burn and walk through the caravan site. At the entrance, there is a mini-roundabout. Bear half-right and follow a muddy farm track to Grangehill Farm. Do not go up the hill on the 'no exit' road. This track leads, eventually, down to the golf course. Cross the links and make for the shore road that leads along the front to Elie Harbour.

From the harbour retrace your steps and walk, carefully, up the A917 until you see the minor road which leads straight on as the main road turns sharp left. A few hundred yards and one right turn brings you to the village of Kilconquhar – and the excellent inn.

Return from Kilconquhar by the same road as you entered, but do not turn left down to Elie; go straight on. At the A917 you will see the main entrance to the caravan site. From here, you may pick up the line of the railway – immediately on your right – and make a rapid return to Largo; or walk back down to the beach, through the caravan site, and amble along the sands.

15

Glendevon
and Tarmangie

IKNOCKED on the farm door, wind howling round my bare knees,
rain-soaked kilt chapping rudely against frozen legs. A tall,
red-faced man answered, and stared, unbelievingly, at the sodden
apparition begging permission to camp in his wood. 'I wouldn't
put my dog out on a night like this, son. Come in to the fire.'

Warmth and light, mingled with the smell of new-baked bread,
flowed invitingly from within, but I had to refuse – I was preparing
for my Queen's Scout badge and this journey was the final test. It
had to be completed alone, regardless of weather. So I thanked the
farmer and strode purposefully into the woods to wrestle with tent
and tin-opener.

In spite of the gale, I managed to string main guy-ropes between
two pines and quickly weighted down the sides with accommodat-
ing stones. Wrapped in a blanket, cold-baked-beaned and pied, I
shivered the dark hours away, surrounded by the awful sounds of
night. Later, it seemed a small price to pay for that coveted
certificate bearing the Queen's arms. Then, it was a nightmare.

That was my introduction to the Ochil and Cleish Hills, of
Clackmannan and Kinross, during a rain-filled, stormy two-day

expedition thirty-five years ago. But the experience didn't diminish my enthusiasm for their beauty and charm and I have returned ever since to wander amongst these quiet valleys and gentle grass-covered slopes.

The highest of the Ochils is Ben Cleuch, 2,363 feet, flanked to the east by Tarmangie Hill, 2,117 feet, Whitewisp Hill, 2,111 feet, and King's Seat, also 2,111 feet. They crouch over the River Devon and Forth valley in a long unbroken ridge, guarding the towns of Alloa, Alva, Tillicoultry, Clackmannan and Dollar.

Too close for comfort to Caledonia's political heartland, these lands played a constant, often bloody, part in the shaping of Scotland's story. Constantin, son of Kenneth MacAlpine, was defeated and killed at Dollar by the Danes in AD 877; King Alexander II (1214–49) built a fortified tower at Alloa, visited by luckless Mary Queen of Scots, and where King James IV stayed in 1588. Clackmannan had its own tower, home of the great King Robert the Bruce (1306–29), and, in Dollar Glen, between the Burn of Sorrow and the Burn of Care, Castle Gloom – changed in name by Act of Parliament to Castle Campbell by Colin Campbell, 1st Earl of Argyll, in 1465.

The River Devon rises in the Ochil Hills six miles distant as the crow flies from where it joins the Forth at Cambus, west of Alloa. To get there, however, the river winds its way nearly thirty miles through steep-sided Ochil valleys and gorges, past ancient mills and stark, wheel-spindled pit-heads.

I drove north on the A823, by Yetts o' Muchart and Glendevon, with its tiny church, and parked near Glenhead Farm at the start of the water board road leading to Glendevon Reservoirs, aiming for Skythorn Hill and the summit of Tarmangie.

To the left of the road, the waters of the infant river are stemmed, controlled and directed through a large trout farm. More than fifty well ordered tanks lie by the stream, complete with caravan accommodation for supervisors. Good news for Fife and Kinross trout stocks and anglers.

Ragged heaps of stones litter the fields and a small white farmhouse perches uncomfortably on a plateau by the track. I was greeted by barking sheepdogs as I hurried by, trying not to look too much like a stray North Country Cheviot.

Lower Glendevon Reservoir snuggles in the folds of the hills, more like a Highland trout loch in character than a man-made reservoir. A white notice proclaims that all fishing is by fly only. Bad news for Fife fishermen, who, in my experience, would bait a hook with their grandmother if they thought she would attract more trout.

A first hint of winter lingers over the loch and a flight of mallard rise from the reeds, wheeling across the water, turquoise and white flashes against the sombre autumn browns of Common Hill. Wheatears and meadow pipits flit and dance by comfortably supine cattle – must be going to rain. The burn joining the two reservoirs is bursting with the energy of last night's storms, cascading down the valley in an unbridled froth of white-fringed foam. Upper Glendevon is almost waterless, ringed like a badly scoured bath-tub. Bleak stony banks lie exposed, like a woman surprised in the act of undressing. Someone must have left a tap running somewhere.

Before the dam wall I turned left and followed the road past the narrow, mud-banked southern finger of the loch, up to Backhills Farm, busy taking sheep to market. Broich Burn tumbles down the hill and the road ends abruptly, changing into a muddy, up-and-downer track.

Shirt off, hot midday sun burning my back, I climbed by the fence, up the ever-increasing slope, into the heart of the valley. Dark shadows from Crodwell and Middle Hills enveloped the stream and I stopped by a waterfall to dress quickly. A dipper bobbed agreement from a stone and a curious wren winked encouragingly from a berry-bedecked rowan overhanging a crystal pool.

Head down, now, on the last heart-throbbing stumble to the ridge. Then, reward. A clear blue sky vista, crowded with snow-fringed mountains to the north and the Firth of Forth, like a silver carpet, shining southwards. Ben Alder, Schiehallion and Angus Hills. Hazy Edinburgh, castle-cragged. Berwick Law and the islands of the Firth, sparkling gems, blinking like young girls before first lovers.

I walked over undulating moorlands, stopping on King's Seat, high above the Forth valley, spread map-like below, studded with Scotland's history; Dunfermline, our ancient capital, last resting place of King Robert. The sudden shock of rock-girt Stirling Castle and Wallace Monument, leaping from the plain. The bright ribbon of the River Forth, edged with the industrial tangle of Grange-mouth and Kincardine power station.

Welcome lunch on Tarmangie, then along the edge of the forest that blocks any simple descent to Glen Sherup, other than through the wide fire-break near the dam of Glensherup Reservoir. One day, I fervently pray, my fellow Scots will waken up to the fact that unrestricted forestry is destroying Scotland, and rise up in arms against these desecrators of our scenery.

Sadly through the regimented rows of lodgepole pine and Sitka spruce, down to the dam wall. A flutter of herons dance long-legged in the topmost branches of a proper wood. Must be difficult, organizing all those legs and wings properly, preparatory to landing. Before the traffic, a perfect 'Tam o' Shanter Brig' crosses the golden Devon and I paused, hiding from evening, thinking not a lot – just content to enjoy the last, warm, lazy moments of a happy day.

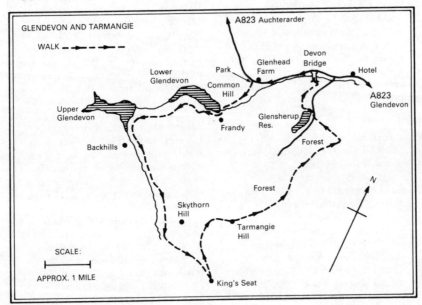

WHAT YOU NEED TO KNOW

Time and effort Took me about five and a half hours, but then I walk very slowly. The first part, on the water board road, is easy. Once you start up Broich Burn the going gets a bit tough. You must wear good walking boots because this path can be very muddy. Once on top, as always, courage and breath return and the rest of the day is just a question of one foot in front of the other over the hill. To have the full benefit of the view from the top, pray for a fine day.

Location Ordnance Survey Sheet 58, Perth and Kinross, second series, scale 1:50,000.

Grid references Glenhead Farm 951053; Lower Glendevon Reservoir 939044; Upper Glendevon Reservoir 914042; Backhills Farm 913036; Skythorn Hill 924013; King's Seat 936997; Tarmangie Hill 942014; fire-break in Glensherup Wood 975037; Glensherup Reservoir 965044; Devon Bridge 966054; Glendevon Castle Hotel 977055.

Route Park just inside the gate at the start of the road up to the reservoirs; there is plenty of room. Follow the road west, past Frandy Farm and Lower Glendevon Reservoir. Just before the dam at Upper Glendevon Reservoir a track leads uphill on your left. Follow this towards Backhills Farm, which is on the other side of the stream feeding the reservoir.

The 'good' track ends here and you now have to try and follow the path south, which climbs up the valley. At times the path is almost too close to the fence by the stream. If this is uncomfortable, there is an alternative path higher up the side of the hill to your left. The sound of water always attracts me so I follow the stream.

Climb out of the valley, onto the shoulder. Still walk south and you see King's Seat ahead. Find your way to the top and then return, north-east, to higher Tarmangie Hill. From Tarmangie, skirt the edge of the filthy forest and, near the end, you will find a wide fire-break. Go down this to the forest road.

As the trees thin out you will see a little track leading down to the dam at the end of Glensherup Reservoir. Cross the dam and follow the road back to the bridge over the River Devon. Turn left here and make your way north along the A823 back to your car. Glendevon Castle Hotel will provide refreshment at the end of your walk.

16

Bad Day on Vorlich

THIS WALK started thirty years ago in Aldershot, where my cousin Bruce Reynolds lived. Big brother Ian and I used to escape there for a few hours each week, a happy release from Her Majesty's cooking and military discipline. Bruce was a small, slightly built boy, much given to television and quick anger if anyone interrupted *Dr Who*, his favourite programme – which, for sheer devilment, Ian and I often did.

In spite of this harsh treatment we remained friends and when Bruce moved to Scotland I was delighted to find that we had a common interest: a love of hill walking. Strictly speaking, Bruce is more a mountain man, infected by the Munro bug, and currently he is attacking Scotland's 3,000-foot peaks with enthusiasm which leaves me speechless. So far he has climbed nearly 200 of the 283 peaks – at great speed and without any sign of the breathlessness which attends my labouring steps up even a modest hill.

Sir Hugh Munro's original list, published in 1891, contained 538 Scottish summits over 3,000 feet, 283 of which were classified mountains in their own right. Sir Hugh climbed all but two: the

Inaccessible Pinnacle on Sgurr Dearg in Skye, which scares the hell out of me, and Carn Clioch in the Cairngorms. Poor Sir Hugh was defeated by bad weather. The first man to surmount the Munros was a minister, the Revd A. E. Robertson, no doubt divinely guided, for he had them all wrapped up by 1901.

Since then, 'Munro bagging' has become a way of life for hundreds of hillwalkers and there is no greater challenge in Scotland. Me, I left it too late. Trout fishing is my excuse. Given a Ross-shire choice between tempting trout in Fionn or life and limb on A'Mhaighdean, the loch always wins. However, pursuit of sport has taken me to some of Scotland's most beautiful mountains, and I honestly admire the determination that drives others up such awe-inspiring heights.

Which is why I found myself, in a blizzard, tramping through Perthshire snow on Ben Vorlich, hopelessly trying to keep pace with my disgustingly fit cousin. Through a mist of pain I longed for the days when it had been possible to 'suppress' him with a single well-aimed swipe. Worse, Bruce was chatting, unconcerned by elements, as though strolling down Sauchiehall Street on a summer evening – and I wished we were.

Earlier that morning, much earlier, Bruce roused me from a warm bed and a particularly comforting dream about a holiday Ann and I once spent on the emerald-green Greek Isle of Paxos, swimming in soft Ionian seas, lazing away blistering days in the shade of olive groves, refreshed by sweet red wine. Snapped to reality, minutes later I found myself shivering out into a grey dawn, muffled and mountainously clothed, Vorlich-bound before I could invent even the glimmer of an excuse.

We drove north from Killearn, through my grandmother's Callander homelands, and followed the long serpentine of Loch Lubnaig to Bonnie Strathyre. The waters of the loch were coloured molten lead and I remembered the last time Ann and I fished Lubnaig. Never caught a thing, other than a shipwrecked bee, floating on a beech-leaf raft. Ann flung him a lifebelt and ferried him safely ashore, where he quickly recovered and buzzed off, presumably seeking swimming lessons.

My cousin and I had ten years of delayed chatter: stories to swop, dreams achieved, grand designs thwarted. Comfortable, relaxing, unimportant bleathers of old friends who had shared baths together as children. Bruce is a member of that famous West of Scotland climbing group The Moray Club – insignia, compass circle, quadrant-filled with ominous words: Hill, Rock, Snow and Ice.

The Moray Club was founded in 1965 by four former pupils of the Moray Outward Bound School and I met some of them during a lecture given by senior Scottish gillie, George Oswald, head keeper on Ben Alder Estate, Inverness-shire. People who walk the hills are nice people – friendly, reliable and patient. Like trout fishermen. I felt instantly at home and welcomed.

When Bruce had a minor accident, falling during a club outing, in an icy car park, not on the hill, he badly sprained his right arm. The offending limb was splinted and strapped in half a ton of white bandage. Nothing daunted – after all, what's a gammy arm to a mountain man – he turned up, slinged and grinning, for the next meet. All the other members emerged from their cars with heavily bandaged right arms, said good morning, and set off up the day's hill.

In 1986, their twenty-first birthday year, Moray Club members travelled the world, exploring distant plains and high peaks. Sheila Fage, three weeks trekking 150 miles in Nepal, climbing 18,000 feet on Annapurna; young Neil Stewart, with the British Schools Expedition to the Yukon; Alasdair Scott, exploring Madagascar highlands; Eric Scott, on Puy de Sancy, the highest point of the Massif Central in France; and a seven-strong team tackling Swiss Alps, Monte Rosa and Matterhorn.

We parked shoreside by Loch Earn at Ardvorlich, where Coire Buidhe burn gurgles past the old house, blushing bride-like under the hump-backed bridge to greet her groom. Bruce and I were greeted less kindly: by bad-tempered wind, glowering clouds and soul-dispiriting, nagging drizzle. Jumpers, jackets, boots, leggings, spare clothing, compass, map, pointless cameras and, most important of all, lunch.

Ben Vorlich, 'the hill of the bay', rises southwards from Loch Earn in a slow shoulder of grassy slopes and jagged outcrops. At the summit, this ridge is joined by three others, crossing to form a welcome plateau, trig.-point-pricked north, grandly cairned south. I had often seen these features from the top of other hills: from West Lomond near Kinross; Tarmangie Hill in the gentle Ochils; and from Pentlands and Arthur's Seat, by Edinburgh.

They looked inviting, from a distance, and I reminded myself of this as I struggled through deepening snow, now falling in thick flakes from mist-grey heavens. Panting like a pensioned cart-horse, I snatched a quick breath from the wind and managed to gasp: 'I suppose you are used to this. One of life's little tribulations.'

Bruce stopped, ear-bending close: 'Are you all right?'

I yelled back, 'Of course I'm all right. I was just asking a question.'

Relief spread across his face. 'I'm so glad. For a moment I thought you were in trouble.'

On a reasonable day, Vorlich is no trouble. Indeed, it is easy to climb and therefore one of Scotland's most popular Munros. Just below the top, for the last few hundred feet, the track does shoot a bit skyward; but with care and caution, and a few rests, the summit is soon reached. So for hillwalkers the ben provides an exciting challenge, magnificent Perthshire views and the pleasure of having conquered a Munro.

However, in bad weather, when icy blasts bustle down the glen, things is different; and, although one travels hopefully, one should always travel prepared. Like the ice axe strapped to Bruce's pack. I wondered where he had secreted the rope. Visions of myself tied to a madman, lost like Mallory and Irvine on their final, doomed assault on Everest.

As far as I am concerned, the actor Vincent Price had it about right when he remarked: 'I once took a climbing expedition as a holiday and found the real reason those mountain climbers rope themselves together. It's to stop the sensible ones going home.' Hiding gloom-laden forebodings, I suggested that perhaps discretion was the better part of valour and our quickest descent was urgently required. 'Thank God,' said my companion, 'I was beginning to think I was climbing with a lunatic!'

As we hurried down the track I cursed the weather, sorry to have missed the summit view and the walk on to Vorlich's neighbour, Stuc a'Chroin. Still, I consoled myself, even the great Sir Hugh Munro had his off days; and there was always another, brighter one, just around the corner.

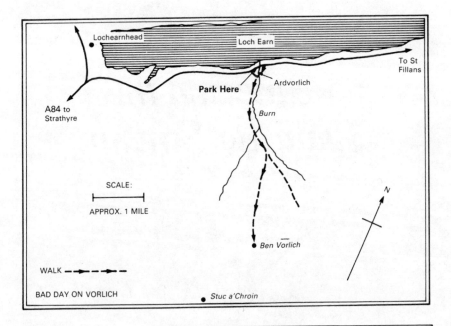

WHAT YOU NEED TO KNOW

Time and effort   In reasonable conditions, Ardvorlich to Ben Vorlich and back will take about five hours. If you intend to go on to Stuc a'Chroin, allow another three to four hours. In bad weather, stay in the car and save your breath for a better day.

Location   Two maps are required: Ordnance Survey Sheet 51, Loch Tay, and Sheet 57, Stirling and the Trossachs, second series scale 1:50,000.

Grid references   Ardvorlich 633229; Ben Vorlich 6299189; Stuc a'Chroin 618175.

Route   Park at Ardvorlich House, by the shore of Loch Earn. There are two drives leading up to the

house and the estate prefers walkers to enter by the east entrance. The track passes the house and leads uphill, with the burn on your left. Once beyond the trees, you see a good path wending upwards.

There is one 'road junction', just past a well made wooden bridge and marked by a massive boulder. Bear right and look out for stumped posts marking the way ahead. A long and, for me, hard slog. The last section before the top is steep and should be tackled with caution.

If you wish to go on to Stuc a'Chroin, follow the fence posts down to Bealach an Dubh Choirein and then scramble up the crags to the ridge by a twisting path. If you anticipate bad weather, give Stuc a'Chroin a miss and stick to well tracked Vorlich.

17

Venue and the Dancing Stream

*I*LOOKED towards the summit of Ben Venue, 'the little hill', and smiled at this glorious understatement. At 2,386 feet, little Venue is not. A great, grey slab, thrusting north from Loch Ard in a slow, unrelenting shoulder; rearing north, twin-cragged above Katrine, guarded by the dark cliffs of Beinn Bhreac, streaked silver and shining with streams rushing to Ledard Burn.

Scots are masters of understatement. Ask directions: 'Oh, just a wee bit down the road, you can't miss it.' Meaning at least six miles and out of sight. What time to meet? 'The back of nine' – any time from five past until just before ten. How's the weather? 'Rare!' Guaranteed torrential rain and gale force winds. Getting an exact answer from a Scot is impossible: which is why they make such good politicians.

I suppose, compared with nearby Ben Lomond, at 3,192 feet, and Perthshire's mighty Ben More at 3,843 feet, Venue is modest – but not on a warm morning, hiking burnside to the first ridge. Least of all for my standard of physical fitness. Nevertheless, I made it, and was rewarded by cloud-scattered blue skies and a panoramic view of mind-numbing beauty.

Ben Venue shares the Trossachs with greater neighbours: Ben Ledi, Benvane, Ceann na Baintgherna and Stob a'Choin. They tower proudly over Scotland's 'Lake District', sweet Katrine, Venachar and Lubnaig, where the road wends lochside northwards, through Bonnie Strathyre to Voil and Rob Roy's grave on the Braes of Balquhidder.

Scotland's grand lake, the Lake of Menteith, lies a few miles east of Aberfoyle, capital of the Trossachs. Here, Sir John Menteith earned himself a hated place in Scotland's story when he captured and betrayed Sir William Wallace to the English in 1305. Battles still rage on the lake, but now, they are between anglers and fish, for Lake of Menteith is a carefully managed and popular Lowland fishery.

Inchmaholme Priory graces Menteith's largest island. Here as a child Queen Mary was hidden after the Battle of Pinkie, before being hurried safely to France. A small boat ferries visitors from Port of Menteith to the ruined priory, founded in 1107 by Culdee Monks. For a number of years this little boat was captained by an old friend of mine, Andrew Mair from Dunblane. We gained our seafaring knowledge whilst serving queen and country in the Water Transport Company of the Royal Army Service Corps, overseas on the Isle of Wight.

Andrew introduced me to Stirling and Perthshire. A gentle man, Scots kindly, he showed me Sheriffmuir, where Rob Roy Mac-Gregor lost the Royalists' battle by refusing to charge at the crucial moment, protecting Clan Gregor's future through masterly indecisiveness. Andrew and I wandered the old streets of Dunblane, arguing constantly from dawn to dusk, about everything in general and nothing in particular, enjoying every heated moment.

The south route to the top of Ben Venue starts at Ledard Farm, by the shores of fishless Loch Ard – fishless, in my opinion, because of the Forestry Commission's badly planned, insensitive and damaging tree planting. Venue was mist-shrouded when I arrived and parked across the road from the farm. I hopped around, heaving on boots, trying to avoid the worst puddles, in a penetrating Trossachs drizzle. Bound to pass.

As I started up the track the rain stopped, leaving the hills freshly laundered, inviting me in. Then I saw the goat: a tuft beard, long jaw, glazed eyes and ungainly horns sticking through the mesh of a fence. I tried a couple of tentative twists, like an ancient patriarch preparing sacrifice to an old god.

The goat grunted and gripped one of my fingers between blunt, chisel-edged teeth. There's gratitude. It took fifteen minutes man-oeuvring before I eased head and horns back. The bad-tempered beast trotted off bleating to rejoin the herd. Never even said thank you. That's goats. I marched on, nursing bruised ego and finger.

Signpost and stile cross Ledard Burn, pointing the way, stealing amongst magnificent oaks, across a forest floor soft with fallen leaves: a startling gold and brown carpet. Finches flit amidst bare branches, and the white burn leaps in a symphonic chorus over moss-covered boulders, through foam-covered pools, down to Loch Ard.

Out on the hill I stopped by a stile and looked back. Mirror-calm water reflected morning hills. Mist wisps hung like smoke over Eilean Gorm. The Duke of Albany's ruined castle glowered resentfully from its little island below green-clad Bad Dearg Hill – a black speck of black history. For years, by fair means and foul, Albany Dukes were Regents of Scotland, on behalf of disastrously infant and absent monarchs.

Whilst James I was King Henry IV's captive in England, Albany allowed Scotland to fall into a miserable state of anarchy. When James returned, one of his first acts was to collect together the late regent, two of his sons and their father-in-law, the Earl of Lennox. He entertained them at Stirling Castle: on the block.

Lingering sprigs of fading heather purpled the track as I tramped on, hot sun baking my jacket. I lumbered upwards like a mobile sauna, half a gallon of Sandison sweat splashing every step. Red grouse rocketed, cackling with laughter at my startled heart-attack spring from their flight path. Ledard Burn, bursting with energy, criss-crossing the damp path, Highland-jigged beside me.

I stopped by a spectacular waterfall, and from a rowan-crested promontory I watched Ledard hurtle outrageously twenty feet over a heathered ridge into a deep, swirling, back-gorged pool. A dipper bobbed in the stream, keeping me company whilst I stopped for coffee. I left him plenty of crumbs.

Stream-crossing needed watching. Under normal conditions, dry-shod passage; but in heavy water, stepping stones are deeply covered and exposed rocks are ankle-breaking slippy. Wrong footing would mean a soaking, at least. After careful consideration, I jumped, fourteen stone of slow motion, and arrived, knee-deep but safe, by the far bank.

The long ascent gradually tamed the bristling burn and, as I climbed higher, Ledard narrowed, but remained a never-ending pleasure, still challenging the steep cliffs and rocky outcrops, and forcing me to scramble up and down the sides of small tributaries, which armied from Creag Tharsuinn to lend support. Eventually, close to the ridge, Ledard faded into the hill and I sat on a stile by the fence, looking warily ahead towards Ben Venue's twin peaks.

Along the hillside lay a magical track, a narrow, close-cut, dark ribbon overlooking Allt Glasahoile stream in its dash to Loch Katrine. Westwards, by Stronachlachar, I saw the white dot of the *Sir Walter Scott* winking amongst russet trees, drawn ashore for its annual overhaul. Ragged Tinker's Loch sparkled on Druim nan Carn and the way ahead beckoned irresistibly.

I felt a complete sense of belonging. I was the hill. My heart and soul were the rocks around me. As though, giant-like, I encompassed time and space. Married to the wind. Held in the arms of eternity. And other daft thoughts only fools and hillwalkers understand.

Until I began to scramble the west peak. Iron railings stabbed bare rocks. Wind screamed over the crest. Narrow, slow, cautious steps. God, its cold. Stumbling to the shelter of the cairn, crouched, shivering, amazed at the wild landscape – wave after wave of mountain-covered crests guarding a blessing, where all things are possible and all things equal, which I never wanted to leave.

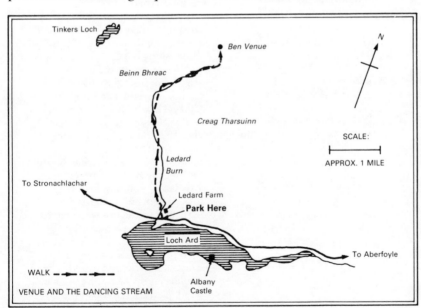

WHAT YOU NEED TO KNOW

Time and effort There and back took me a slow 4½ hours. It's a long haul up to the first ridge and the way is soggy and very wet – even nicer after heavy rain. Be prepared to scramble up and down the sides of a few streams and take great care at the first crossing of Ledard Burn. Otherwise a sprained ankle could ruin your day.

The last hundred feet could be dangerous in bad weather or misty conditions. Even on a good day, some hands–and–knees work is required, but with reasonable caution, and plenty of little rests, you should have no real difficulty reaching the cairn. Always carry extra warm clothing. Be well shod and waterproof.

Location Ordnance Survey Sheet 57, Stirling and the Trossachs, second series, scale 1:50,000.

Grid references Ledard Farm and start point 461023; Beinn Bhreac ridge 462056; Creag Tharsuinn 468049; Venue West Peak 474064.

Route No problem whatsoever, but Ben Venue will be hidden from view until you reach the first ridge. Park across the road from the track up to the farm. There is plenty of room, so make sure you don't block the gate into the field: outraged farmers we do not need. The track passes the left side of the farm buildings and there the way is signposted over an attractive bridge and stile. Say hello to the goats.

Follow the path through an oak wood, with Ledard Burn on your right. Clear the woods and continue up the hill. Look out for the waterfall and make a small detour to the right to view. The first stream crossing requires consideration and caution, particularly after heavy rain. Thereafter, the path crosses the stream several times until you end up walking up the middle of the diminishing burn, on to the ridge.

A fence crosses the path at right angles and from the ridge the track rounds the right-hand slope of Creag Tharsuinn. The twin peaks of Ben Venue can now be seen ahead. Below the summit there is a major 'road junction'. Half-right, downhill, to Loch Katrine. Straight on, slightly right and uphill to the East Peak. You should bear quarter-left, and look for the narrow track that rises steeply to the West Summit.

The last section is very exposed, so in bad weather take great care. The track twists and turns up huge boulders until you come to a small damp plateau. On top of the summit cairn is a strange stone, shaped rather like a hip-bone. You have arrived. Return the same way. You have earned it, and going down is much more sportnik!

18

Bare Bums and Ben Lomond

MANY YEARS ago, my wife Ann and I discovered the joys of naked bathing. Getting dressed to go swimming always seemed the height of lunacy and whenever possible we plunge in birthday-suited. On foreign holidays, we're the luggage-less ones at the airport and since 1978 have been members of the Central Council for British Naturism.

Scotland has its share of sunshine. On hot July days, fishing for wild brown trout amongst lonely hills, I have often waded out, clothesless, to cover rising fish other anglers can't reach; and a summer afternoon snooze on a distant rowan-clad shore is one of life's great pleasures – lulled lazily to sleep by the call of curlew and piping golden plover. However, as in all things, caution is the watchword, and an eye for the weather.

There are a number of official and unofficial naturist sites throughout Scotland and one of the loveliest is on the tree-covered island of Inchmurrin in Loch Lomond. We visited the club. The Scottish Outdoor Club, a few years ago, whilst staying at Rowardennan a few miles north from Balmaha: a perfect holiday which combined marvellous Trossachs walks with lazy, sun-soaked days on Inchmurrin. The name Inchmurrin means 'island of hospitality' and we certainly found kindness in plenty amongst welcoming club members.

Loch Lomond is surrounded by some of Scotland's most dramatic scenery, and some of Scotland's most exciting walks: Arrochar Alps, Cowal and Ardgoil, Crianlarich and Balquhidder. Something for everyone, even sluggards like me. Gentle, lochside strolls along the West Highland Way. The rock-climbing challenge of Cobbler: Gladiator's Grove on South Peak; terrifying Nimlin's and the Chimney Arte on North Peak. Stern stuff. Graceful Ben Lomond towers above all and is favourite with thousands of hillwalkers.

My son Charles and his friend David Martin climbed mighty Lomond from Rowardennan when they were twelve-year-olds, setting the seal on a love of the hills which will stay with them all their lives. My first sight of the Ben was from a less elevated position: afloat on the loch, fishing. Inching over salmon lies round the island-studded south bay: Inchcruin, Inchmoan, Buchin and Tiny Ceardach.

Two friends, Tony Sykes and the late Charles Hodget, had invited me to join them and, happily unsuspecting, I readily accepted. The most productive fishing method is dapping. One angler sits in the middle, wielding a sixteen-foot rod. The cast is made of light floss on the end of which dangles a huge, hairy, artificial fly. This is delicately danced over the waves to attract salmon.

The other two rods fish in the traditional way, with wet flies, from bow and stern. When the man in the middle sees a fish approaching he removes the dap and salmon turn, right or left as the mood takes them, to grab the adjacent wet flies. Which is why I had been invited: all day in the middle, holding a clothes pole whilst they caught the fish.

Loch Lomond is always busy: anglers, sailing boats, canoes, windsurfers, water-skiers – all enjoying the pleasures of this wonderful recreational gem. The *Countess Fiona*, another recreational gem, is owned by Alloa Brewery Company and sails the loch from April until September. An uncle of mine was once the manager of Alloa Brewery, a post I much envied him.

Steaming north, the *Countess* looks as though she had spent all her days plying between Balloch and Inversnaid. In fact, she has had a more chequered career, being tossed about from Loch Awe to Largs during half a century's travel. *Countess Fiona* was built in 1936 for the Caledonian Steam Packet Company and sailed windy Loch Awe under the name *Countess of Breadalbane*.

Dragged overland in 1952, she was set to work in the Clyde, ferrying passengers round Gourock, Holy Loch, Largs and Millport. In 1971 she was renamed *Countess of Kempock* and worked for Mr Roy Ritchie; then for Off-Shore Workboats Ltd, battling up and down the broken waters of the Inner Hebrides between Oban, Mull, Fingle-caved Staffa and holy Iona. Her wandering over, the grand old lady serenely sails over her new home.

The *Countess Fiona*, like her famous colleague on Loch Katrine the ss *Sir Walter Scott*, provides an ideal way of combining the beauties of Lomond with a delightful, rewarding, shore-side walk. Best place to start is from Rowardennan, at the end of the road from Balmaha. The *Countess* will collect you at 11.40 a.m. then glide northwards to the busy village of Tarbet on the west shore; from there, over to Inversnaid on the east, arriving close to the long-distance footpath, the West Highland Way. The walk back to Rowardennan is a distance of eight miles and takes approximately three and a half hours. What better way to spend a summer day?

Some famous names have tramped here: Dr Johnson, dogged by the inevitable Boswell; Robert Burns; William and Dorothy Wordsworth, accompanied by Samuel Taylor Coleridge; Robert Southey and the great Scottish engineer, Thomas Telford. Just as well known, although for less respectable reasons, was Rob Roy MacGregor of Inversnaid.

The MacGregor's exploits – cattle stealing and general skulduggery – caused the government to build a fort at Inversnaid, on the land Rob Roy claimed as his own, half-way between Lomond and Loch Arklet. But the garrison had little luck keeping peace. MacGregor attacked, disarmed the soldiers and burnt the fort. Inversnaid was rebuilt. Rob's newphew, Ghulne Dubh, carrying on his uncle's tradition, sacked the garrison again. It was rebuilt a third time and commanded by no less a soldier than Wolfe, soon to meet his fate on the heights of Abraham.

Sir Walter Scott visited Inversnaid in 1792 and found there was still a 'garrison' at the fort: a solitary veteran soldier, contentedly reaping a sparse crop of barley, who told Scott that if he wanted in he would find the key to the fort under the front door. The MacGregors had little use for keys, but Scott did as bid and rested in the old, battle-scarred building.

My most recent visit to Lomond brought near-disaster and a

sharp reminder that in harsh conditions even the easiest of hills can present a daunting challenge. In search of dramatic, panoramic photographs, I parked one wild November morning by the pier at Rowardennan and buckled on boots and camera. A quick dash for the top, superb scenic shots, back in time for lunch.

The fact that Ben Lomond was cloud-shrouded, barely visible through heavy rain, should have deterred me; but I wanted the photographs badly so I set off through the woods, climbing quickly up first gentle tree-clad slopes. The track is well maintained and I blessed the National Trust for their efforts in easing my way.

But as I rose higher, leaving the shelter of trees, the path ahead became a major river and I was soon soaked, both above and below. I passed two other walkers and as I rested by the gate on the hill I saw them tramping back to Rowardennan. As I turned northwards to Sorn Aonaich, the clouds settled ever lower and I found myself plodding upwards through cold, wet, clinging mist.

Rain turned to snow, blown in on the wings of a freezing north-east wind. My right side was covered in a thickening white blanket and I doubted my sanity in continuing. There was no possibility of a break in the clouds that day; and, therefore, no point in continuing. Frozen strands of hair bumped on my forehead. The higher I climbed the more fierce the storm became and I realized that there was not a moment to be lost in getting off the hill.

I turned and, step by careful step, made my way down,

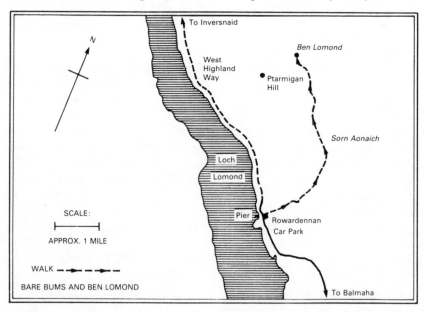

following welcome cairns and my own footsteps, which were fading fast in drifting snow. One slip was all that was required to turn a nightmare into a disaster. What I had done was incredibly stupid, the more so because I certainly should have known better. By luck, rather than by good judgement, I gained the shelter of the woods and safety of the car.

It seemed like an eternity before the effect of the car heater restored some warmth to my limbs and I vowed never to be so daft again. The only comfort I had was my first sight of a rare native Scottish snow bunting, glimpsed fleetingly near the summit. No doubt it was astonished at the stupidity of the human race, walking there by choice rather than of necessity.

WHAT YOU NEED TO KNOW

Time and effort   The sail from Rowardennan to Inversnaid and the walk back takes about four and a half hours and is a pleasant, relaxing way to explore Loch Lomond. However, the walk south down the West Highland Way can be busy, particularly during summer months, and the track is often very muddy. So wear strong shoes and always be prepared for Lomond storms.

The ascent of Ben Lomond is another matter. In good weather it is still a long, stiff walk and the round trip from Rowardennan takes five and a half hours. Always remember that what is easy in good summer weather can be dangerous and difficult at other times of the year. If in doubt, don't. No prizes for breaking a leg on the top and a lot of trouble for others if you do.

Location   Ordnance Survey Sheet 56, Loch Lomond, second series, scale 1:50,000.

Grid references   Inchmurrin 380870; Balmaha 421909; Rowardennan 355986; Tarbet 315045; Inversnaid 338089; Ben Lomond 367029.

Route   Information on *Countess Fiona* sailings may be obtained from Alloa Brewery Company Ltd, Anderston House, 389 Argyle Street, Glasgow. Sailing times may also be had by telephone on a recorded message: dial 041–248 2699. In 1987, a single ticket from Rowardennan to Inversnaid cost £2. The boat has snack bar and licensed bar. At Inversnaid, the West Highland Way is well signposted. Make sure that you turn right, otherwise you might end up in Fort William.

The Ben Lomond walk is also well signposted, from near the pier at Rowardennan. There are excellent car park and toilet facilities. Follow the path through the trees, out onto the hill. It just keeps going, up and up, on to the top. Return by the same route. As an alternative, in good weather, cross over from Ben Lomond south-west to Ptarmigan Hill and come down the shoulder to Rowardennan. But he warned: this is a much rougher and more demanding walk. Lomond midges are rough too, in fact 'man-eating', so take along a five-gallon drum of insect-repellent, each.

19

Autumn Trossachs Tales

TROSSACH rain is the wettest in Scotland. I hunched over the car steering wheel on a cold Stirlingshire morning, parked in Aberfoyle across the street from the newsagent, wondering if they sold boot laces and if I could get there and back without drowning. They did and I didn't, but it was a damned close-run thing.

They don't make boot laces like they used to. My old friends seemed immortal. Now, new pairs come and go with fragile regularity, like snow off a dyke. As if reading my thoughts, the dour Trossach downpour turned to snow, whirling white and wicked through empty streets on the tail of a brash north-east wind. The grey town was soon as devoid of people as Saturday morning kirk.

And I had missed the boat. By about seven days. Moody and miserable, I decided to go on. After all, what's a little rain and snow? My ancestors, Clan MacGregor, would have scoffed at such elements. Indeed, probably welcomed them. Excellent cover from which to mount sharp, cattle-collecting forays on unsuspecting, fire-huddling, soft Lowland neighbours.

The boat I had missed was the ss *Sir Walter Scott*, sailing on Loch Katrine, from Trossachs Pier to Stronachlachar, 4 May to 28

September – £2 a bash or the whole boat on evening charter for £300. Would have been ideal for Rob Roy and his brigands, to hurry them home to Glengyle at the head of the loch, but I very much doubt if he would have parted with any cash for the privilege.

My grandmother, Jean MacGregor, was Trossach-born, in Callander, and I claim rightful kinship with that much persecuted clan, and do so proudly. The lands of Rob Roy lie between Loch Lomond in the west and Loch Katrine in the east – the 'bristling country', of sudden peaks and secret gullies, scanned by mighty Ben Lomond, Ben Venue, Stob a'Chon and Ben Ledi.

Loch Katrine glides through these craggy corries, peaceful and serene, for a distance of eight miles; and the *Sir Walter Scott* rides across summer waters as gracefully as its namesake's creature, the Lady of the Lake, graces the pages of Scott's haunting poem. Dorothy and William Wordsworth visited Katrine on their first tour of Scotland in 1803, when the great English poet was inspired to write that evocative Highland memory 'The Solitary Reaper'.

I turned the engine, and, windscreen wipers working overtime, headed out of Aberfoyle, northwards over Dukes Pass. At the top, by the view-point, snow magically cleared and warm October sun suddenly shone from between rapidly departing clouds. Loch Venachar sparkled west and Ben Ledi, white-fringed and cloud-topped, towered northwards, contrasting brightly with the dark green of stark, tree-covered Ben An.

At the pier, Trossachs Tea Room and Visitors Centre was sullenly shut, the car park deserted, patiently waiting out winter for the bustle and blether of next season's tourists. I unflasked coffee and stood by the car, alone and silent in the fading year, surrounded by the triumphant colours of Trossachs autumn.

Delicate birch dropped silver crystal droplets clinging to precious heart-shaped leaves. Stately pines swayed on rock-girt islands, shimmering fingers of green, mirrored in calm waters. Russet beech scattered last leaves on copper-burnished ferns. Gentle oak sighed, dreaming of long-dead summer days.

Autumn is the best time to visit the Trossachs. By the end of September most tourists have departed and you may enjoy the beauties of the lake in relative peace and quiet. Step on board the *Sir Walter Scott* and book passage to Stronachlachar, five miles' sail up the loch.

From the comfort of the white-painted vessel, enjoy a dramatic journey through some of Scotland's most memorable scenery – and prepare for the walk back. That day, being boatless, I had to content myself with a loch-side walk instead, but you should arrange your visit more carefully, to coincide with the morning sailing which leaves Trossachs Pier at 11 a.m.

The *Sir Walter Scott* is owned by Strathclyde Regional Council and each season the boat is hauled ashore at Stronachlachar, in a small harbour south of the pier, for its regular overhaul: bottom scrape, painting, bilge clean, or whatever else is necessary to satisfy Board of Trade inspectors. So you may board and sail the lovely boat with complete confidence.

Sir Walter arrives in Stronachlachar at 12 noon and as you sail west, two miles before Stronachlachar, on the south shore, watch out for a regal building close to the water's edge, robed in fine woodlands, skirted by neat, well trimmed lawns enclosed by angular, clipped hedges. This striking structure is Royal Cottage, built when Queen Victoria opened Katrine in 1859 as part of the City of Glasgow's water-supply system. Hope she was amused, because in both construction and position Royal Cottage is idyllic.

The road back to Trossachs Pier cuts north, across a tree-covered promontory protecting the mooring, following the shoreline to the narrow head of the loch, where Glengyle Water feeds hungry Katrine. Rob Roy was born in these wild hills and knew every rock and corrie as well as he knew his own name. It was this intimate knowledge of these mountains that saved his life on countless occasions when his arch-enemy, James, Duke of Montrose, pursued him for his life.

In MacGregor's early days, he dealt in cattle – legally, or, at any rate, as legally as one ever could in that notoriously dangerous trade. Rob prospered and became well known for his astuteness and Highland sagacity. However, after a disastrous slump in prices, Rob Roy decided that he had done enough lawful cattle dealing and decamped; he also decamped £1000 of the laird's money.

The infuriated Montrose demanded his capture and, from 18 to 21 June 1712, the *Edinburgh Evening Courant* advertised for his apprehension: 'That Robert Campbell, commonly known by the name Rob Roy MacGregor, being lately instructed by several noblemen and gentlemen with considerable sums for buying cows for them in the Highlands, has treacherously gone off with the money to the value of £1000 sterling.'

Rob always denied having done any such thing, claiming that it was his partner who had vanished with the noble funds. Nevertheless, Montrose visited Glengyle and confiscated Rob Roy's possessions; and made the fatal mistake of turning out MacGregor's wife and children, leaving them defenceless in a harsh, fierce winter. From then onwards, Rob Roy plundered the duke's lands and herds, seeking vengeance for the wrong done to his family and recompense for the wrong done to his sporran.

MacGregor even managed to kidnap the duke's rent collector, Factor Grahame, along with £300 in cash. And, as you walk north up the loch-side, you will see the island where Rob Roy incarcerated the unfortunate man, known to this day as 'Rob Roy's Prison'. MacGregor politely asked the duke to ransom Grahame, but the noble lord refused. So, after keeping Grahame uncomfortably frozen for a week in the middle of the loch, Rob allowed the factor home, unmolested, but rentless.

The MacGregor house still stands at Glengyle, initials 'GM' and date 1704 on a lintel above the door, at the foot of Meall Mor. Urgent, silver streams cascade down savage crags, tumbling into Katrine by the MacGregor graveyard, where Rob Roy's mother lies buried amongst kilted kith and kin. MacGregor himself, against all seeming odds, died in his bed and sleeps life's endless sleep in the old churchyard overlooking Loch Voil, on the Braes of Balquhidder, flanked by wife and family.

The long walk along the north shore of Katrine, back to the car park at Trossachs Pier, is an endless delight, through a constant flutter of red and brown falling leaves and awesome views across the loch to towering Ben Venue. It is easy to imagine how in days past lawlessness reigned amongst these trackless hills, how they were both home and refuge to hunted men whose wayward actions polite society deplored.

But I never pass Brenachoile, near journey's end, without

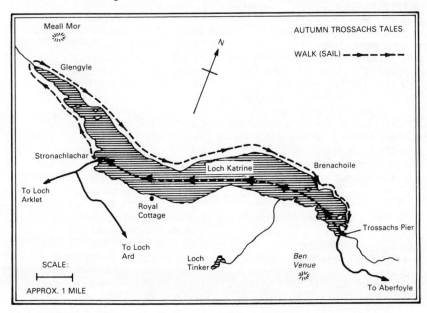

wondering who were more civilized: the untutored men of northern glens or King George's grand ministers in London. For it was at
Brenachoile that fate and government soldiers caught up with
Doctor Archibald Cameron, brother of Cameron of Lochiel, out
with Prince Charlie in the Forty-Five.

Doctor Cameron's only crime was that of tending the wounded
after the slaughter of Culloden. For this 'crime' he was branded a
rebel and hanged at Tyburn in 1752. No Highlander would ever
have been party to a dirty deed like that; and, least of all, Rob Roy
MacGregor.

WHAT YOU NEED TO KNOW

Time and effort   Great effort
required for the first part of this
journey: arriving at Trossachs Pier
on time for the boat, climbing on
board, watching the water slip by,
walking round the deck to enjoy
the views, remembering to
disembark at Stronachlachar.
Exhausting stuff.

However, the walk back, round
the top of the loch and down the
north shore, is about ten miles and
could be tiring. Certainly, there is a
good road all the way; but still wear
strong shoes and take along
waterproof clothing.

Because of sailing times, it is best
to sail up the loch and walk back.
The other way means that you
must arrive at Stronachlachar Pier
at 12 noon, for there is only one
sailing back to Trossachs Pier and if
you miss that it's a long walk
home.

Sail first, walk later. Then you
can amble back at your own pace.
Remember, there are no Saturday
or Sunday sailings to and from
Stronachlachar, so this must be a
weekday walk.

Location   It is almost impossible
to get lost, given that the master of
the *Sir Walter Scott* knows what he
is doing and where he is going –
which he most certainly does. From
Stronachlachar, follow the road
north, round the loch. It's the only
game in town and there are no
branch roads. However, maps are
comforting and they help identify
hills and places of interest. You
need two: Ordnance Survey Sheet
66, Ben Lomond, and Sheet 57,
Stirling and the Trossachs, second
series, scale 1:50,000

Grid references   Trossachs Pier
496074; Ben Venue 478061; Royal
Cottage 423091; Stronachlachar
403102; Glengyle Water 380136;
Gregor MacGregor's Cottage
386135; Brenachoile 478099.

Route   Full details of sailing times
from Trossachs Pier may be had
from Strathclyde Regional Council
on 041-336 5333. Ask for Steamer
Enquiries. 1987 charges were: adult
£1.20 and child £0.60 for the single
journey. There is an excellent tea
room and visitors centre at the pier.
Refresh the body and inform the
mind before setting out.

Once at Stronachlachar, simply
walk north along the narrow road,
round the loch and back to
Trossachs Pier. As they say, you
can't miss it!

20

Dunkeld Fires and Forests

ONE VICTORY doesn't win a war. Bonny Dundee's Highlanders scored a notable success at Killiecrankie in July 1689, but a few weeks later their kilts were badly singed at the Battle of Dunkeld. Graham of Claverhouse had been killed at Killiecrankie and command of the wild men of the north was now in the hands of the appropriately named Colonel Cannon.

His force of 5,000 Highlanders, with murder in their hearts, marched north intent on a bloody visit to the cathedral city of Dunkeld, ancient Scottish capital, centre of learning and holy bishopric. I suppose the frightened inhabitants of the little town by the banks of the River Tay were used to it, for this was not the first time they had been visited with fire and sword.

King Kenneth McAlpin saved them from an approaching Viking force in AD 845. Sixty years later, Dunkeld was not so lucky when the Norsemen broke through and ravaged the town. They returned in 1027 for another courtesy call, leaving most of the town a smouldering ruin. Very careless with matches, Vikings.

During the religious wars of the sixteenth century, the old

cathedral didn't stand an earthly. Built between 1318 and 1501 and one of Scotland's most beautiful places of worship, it was 'reformed' in 1560: only the nave was left, semi-intact.

In 1689, with the Highlanders advancing, many of the townsfolk must have instantly packed children and belongings and fled. The Cameronians, under command of William Cleland, poet and divine, stayed. It is ironic that, rushing to meet him, broadsword sharpened, was his namesake, Ewen Cameron, wolf-killer of Lochaber – as staunch a Royalist as Cleland was a Covenanter.

Cleland's force of 1,200 Lowlanders, the embryonic Scottish Rifle Regiment, held the centre of town and fought furiously. Cleland soon died, as did his second-in-command, and it was left to Captain Munro, thrust into unexpected authority, to save the day. At the dark hour of midnight, he dispatched a band of desperate men with instructions to lock the unsuspecting Highlanders in their lodgings. Then the Lowlanders passed round the matches.

Few of the attacking force survived the flames; those who did decided that enough was enough, and scampered off, no doubt smouldering, northwards into the night. When dawn broke over sweetly flowing Tay all that remained of Dunkeld were the two dwellings so bravely held by dead Cleland and his powder-stained, weary men. The rest of the town lay utterly ruined.

Dunkeld today is the product of the faith, hope and hard work that rebuilt the town after the battle. The famous 'Little Houses' between Atholl Street and the cathedral all date from this period and are now safe in the caring hands of the National Trust for Scotland.

The Trust has laid out a well planned walk round town, starting at a visitor centre and exhibition near the fountain in High Street. Although the walk is not very long in distance, it is long in content, encompassing all the most notable places of interest: Bakehouse Cottage, Old Smiddy, Stanley Hill, the famous Dunkeld Larches, Cathedral, Dean's House, Ell House, Telford's Bridge and others.

My mother-in-law's family, the Blairs, come from Dunkeld and I first visited the town many years ago, whilst camping as a Boy Scout at Inver Park, just outside town on the banks of the Tay. Sadly, the place where we pitched our tents is now covered by the A9 highway, but I never pass that way without remembering the lumpy nights I slept there, lulled by the sound of the river.

There is something special about this glorious part of Perthshire: the scent of pine trees mingled with wood-smoke; the broad, confident Tay, huge autumn salmon leaping upstream; September browns, reds and russets as leaves turn to winter; the amazing blaze of heather-clad hills; soft-spoken, welcoming people.

From camp at Inver, we marched, Sunday-self-conscious, to the cathedral for morning service. Even the most boisterous were sobered by the sombre magnificence of the grey stones. The first church at Dunkeld was built around AD 570 by Culdee Monks and expanded by Kenneth McAlpin in 848. King David I designated the building a cathedral in 1127. The sanctimonious reformers of 1560, alight with righteous indignation, destroyed one of Scotland's most significant religious monuments 'For the greater glory of God'. He must shake His head in despair.

As boys we ranged wide and wild throughout the magnificent woodlands surrounding Dunkeld, stalking the course of the River Braan to the waterfalls and the deep pools below the Hermitage, where we swam in the clear, tumbling waters.

The Hermitage is easier approached today and the walk starts from a well ordered car park one mile west of town along the A9. The path wends through wonderfully mature, tall trees, alive with birdsong, to an ornate folly, built by the 2nd Duke of Atholl in 1758. Perched high above the Black Linn Fall, there is a balcony overlooking the sparkling, brown-tinged waterfall and even now I still look down expecting to see boys swimming below.

Ossian's Cave is a small, much-reduced building, further up-stream – our headquarters in a day-long game and site of a famous battle between the rival troop patrols of Otter and Beaver. Ossian would have approved, being much given to the Gaelic sport of battle. Legend has it that he was lured away after being defeated in a fight in AD 293 by the Daughter of the Land of Youth, where he spent three hundred years in happy, presumably youthful, exile.

From Hermitage I often walk on through the woods by the Braan to Rumbling Bridge, a little arch where the river is forced spectacularly through a narrow cleft in the rocks. For best effect, make the visit after heavy rain when the Braan is in spate, angry with spume and spray.

Braan meets big brother Tay just upstream from Dunkeld Bridge, where I almost drowned whilst riding a home-made raft downstream in heavy water. We had decided, Viking-like, to give the craft a decent send-off before we returned home to Edinburgh, but when my friend and I found ourselves in the middle of the river, gripped by a fierce current, we threw caution to the winds and dived overboard, striking hopefully shorewards.

I remember the feeling of absolute panic as I struggled in the peat-stained brown waves. More by good fortune than by good sense we both survived, but we had been swept from Inver almost to below Dunkeld Bridge before we reached dry land. Sheepishly, red with embarrassment, we climbed the steps up to the road, swimming-trunk-clad, laughed and pointed at by passing tourists. That was even worse than our dip in the Tay.

The bridge over the Tay at Dunkeld, built by Telford in 1809, was financed by the Duke of Atholl. Not unreasonably, there was a charge for crossing. However, when there was no sign of the toll ever being lifted, in 1868, the good citizens of Dunkeld decided to take matters into their own hands. In the ensuing riots a troop of soldiers had to be rushed from Perth to restore order. Which they did, and the toll stayed until 1879, when the county council finally took over responsibility for the bridge.

Another bridge, much loved by me, is a more modest structure over the Braan at Inver. As a Senior Scout, I was allowed the luxury of an evening stroll by myself once the little ones had been safely tucked up and lashed down for the night.

Watching the moon glinting over Craig a Barns from a blue-black star-specked sky, I recovered from the day's labours: bridge building, knots and lashings, instructing in 'birds and trees', my speciality, which I fondly imagined I knew something about, and the general turmoil of camp cooking.

Neil Gow, that most marvellous and famous of all Scottish violinists, was born at Inver in March 1727; and I know that it sounds ridiculous, but I could almost swear that, sometimes, I heard the haunting strains of his magic fiddle, closely accompanying the soft music of the burn.

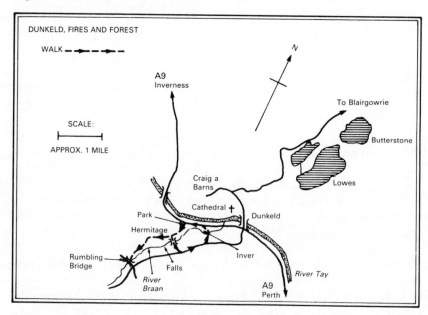

WHAT YOU NEED TO KNOW

Time and effort   This walk would make a super break on a journey north or south along the A9. You can follow the Dunkeld Heritage Trail, round town and about an hour and a half; or you can combine that walk with a visit to Black Linn Fall, Hermitage and Rumbling Bridge, which makes a round trip of about four hours. There are no worrying heights to be scaled, just a gentle, peaceful walk along well made paths, amidst glorious woodland and mountain scenery. Stop at the tourist information centre in High Street and obtain copies of their excellent guide.

Location   Ordnance Survey Sheet 52, Aberfeldy and Glen Almond, second series, scale 1:50,000.

Grid references   Dunkeld 027426; Inver 007423; Hermitage 999418; Rumbling Bridge 997413.

Route   Turn off the A9 into Dunkeld and cross the bridge. Half-way down Bridge Street, turn left into High Street. Park here, or, if this is full, there is additional parking at the end of Atholl Road, which is a continuation of Bridge Street. The tourist information centre and exhibition is just opposite the fountain in High Street. Obtain a plan of the Dunkeld Heritage Walk and follow the marked route, round town, a distance of two miles; slightly further if you branch off to visit the Dunkeld Larches.

The Heritage Trail ends at the north of Dunkeld Bridge. Either walk (there is a wide grass verge) or take the car one mile north along the A9 until you see the Hermitage route signposted, from a good car park. The National Trust has an automatic 'booklet dispenser' in the car park and this will furnish you with information for your walk. The track passes under the railway line and leads up the River Braan to Hermitage. From Hermitage, walk upstream to Ossian's Cave and thence on to Rumbling Bridge.

Return to Hermitage and cross the bridge to the south bank of the River Braan. Follow this track to the A822 down the hill to Neil Gow's birthplace, the small forestry village of Inver. Walk through the village to the A9. Turn left and the car park is 100 yards distant.

21

Jam Doughnuts and Brandy

NORMAL people don't have my trouble. They climb straight to the top of a hill. Not half-way up, back to the bottom then up again; followed by three-quarters of the way up, half-way down, then back up again. An assault course, not a walk. However, normal people don't have Jean or Heathcliff. Which is where I went wrong on the Braes of Angus.

There were seven of us, parked by the South Esk at the head of Glen Clova. My wife Ann, and her constant companion – not me, but a rag-haired, black-snubbed Yorkshire terrier called Heathcliff; eldest son Blair and his wife, Barbara; second son Charles and small daughter, Jean.

On either side of the glen mountains tower two thousand feet above the teenage stream and our day's purpose was to explore them. Walking eastwards up Green Hill (2,854 feet), round the horseshoe corrie and down to Loch Brandy, cupped below sheer cliffs, where we planned to have lunch – and, perhaps, a cast or two at some of Brandy's hard-fighting little brown trout.

This is Ogilvie country. In 1432, Sir Wallace Ogilvey, Treasurer of Scotland, was granted permission by King James I to fortify his Tower of Eroly, site of the present Castle of Airlie. James had returned after eighteen years captivity in England, determined to break the power of Lowland nobles and Highland lairds who had ruined Scotland during his absence.

King James paid the customary price for his efforts. On 20 February 1437, as he settled to sleep in the Dominican monastery at Perth, three of his relations – the Earl of Atholl, Sir Robert Stewart and Sir Robert Graham – called to say goodnight, permanently. Catherine Douglas, a lady-in-waiting, barred the door by thrusting her arm through iron clasps, but the murderers snapped it like a twig and defenceless James was dirked to death.

Could never get away with doing that to Heathcliff, although I often feel like trying. What stops me is the sure and certain knowledge that I would meet the same fate as King James's assassins: soundly tortured, pinched wiith hot irons, then hanged. Without mercy.

I looked at the invitingly open door of Ogilvie Arms Hotel whilst the gang got ready. Time for a quick one? 'Boots on, Bruce, I know what you are thinking and the answer's no.' Ann, a true Scot, though Yorkshire born, has a strong streak of Protestantism: labour first, pleasure later, perhaps. 'Have you got my jam doughnuts?' inquired Jean. It was going to be one of those days. My daughter can only be tempted uphill by promise of reward at the top. In this case, half a ton of jam doughnuts – which I was expected to carry.

There are numerous notices at the foot of the hill warning walkers to keep proper control of their animals, presumably dogs and children. One notice explained that keepers had instructions to shoot stray dogs on sight. What about stray kids, I wondered. Bang first, questions later? Traditional Highland welcome.

Sunlight warmed our backs as we fell into line behind Ann, who is the only one who can read a map – at least that's what she says. Making our way past the little school, we followed the narrow track, climbing steeply between Ben Reid and Rough Craig. Grouse-shooting country, dogs too. Early July heather begged to bloom, covering the hill in a dark-green purple-specked carpet. Twin streams chortled busily by. A good-to-be-alive day.

Then I remembered the camera, which I had left on the car roof. In the turmoil of packing and pleading with Jean to behave, I had forgotten the other purpose of the walk: capturing award-winning photographs from the top. By this time, the fit members of Clan Sandison had disappeared over the first ridge. I had been detailed to bring up the rear, which meant helping and encouraging Jean – no mean feat of persuasion, threats and downright violence.

I instructed my complaining daughter to wait and, fingers crossed, set off back down the hill, hoping that the camera would still be there. Thankfully, it was. Grabbing a few lungfuls of air, I hastened hillwards, anxious that my little charge hadn't come to any harm. She hadn't, but was most resentful when I suggested continuing up the track.

We found the others having a leisurely coffee break and I

immediately noticed that Heathcliff had managed to persuade Ann to slip his lead. Would never have happened if I had been there. Just as I opened my mouth to complain, a hare broke cover and bounded over the moor, long antennae ears laid back for greater speed. Heathcliff gave a joyful yelp and set off in pursuit.

I had a vision of a dozen twelve-bore shotguns being raised to twelve tweed-clad shoulders. What would life be like if Ann lost Heathcliff? Could our marriage survive the shock? Throwing down undrunk coffee, I sprinted after the brute, screaming blue murder at him to stop. It was like talking to the wind, or a parliamentarian – complete waste of breath.

The dog had vanished. I stopped on a ridge, panting, heart pounding, covered in sweat. In the distance, a small group of black-faced sheep grazed peacefully. Heathcliff couldn't be anywhere near them. I searched for signs of movement, parting heather, swaying twigs, anything to give me a clue. Failure to find the dog would mean a ruined day and a ruined life. Ann would be broken-hearted.

As I wandered over the moor, calling 'Heathcliff! Heathcliff!' like a hirsute Cathy in search of her Yorkshire lover, my spirits sank lower and lower. Had he gone back to the car? By this time I was half-way down anyway, so I trekked on, fingers once more crossed. No luck. No dog.

Wearily, I started uphill for the third time. All I wanted was a quiet midsummer stroll amongst restful Angus glens. I should be so lucky. The sound of voices raised my eyes heavenwards. The final call? My sinking soul ready to meet my maker? The family lined a ridge, Blair waving. Heathcliff was clutched in his grasp, half-circling overhead.

My worry changed to outraged fury and I increased pace, planning exactly what I would do when I laid hands, feet and anything else lying about on his misbegotten, misshapen body and fog-filled head. Women know these things. When I finally panted up, Heathcliff and Ann were a quarter of a mile ahead. The theory being that by the time I caught them anger and I would be too exhausted to do anything. Which was true.

We laboured up The Snub and stopped to admire our achievement. Glen Cova and Glen Doll lay mistily below. Esk, like a silver ribbon, twisted and turned through small, fertile fields. Driesh, most easterly Scottish Munro, reared west, protected by the jagged scar of Winter Corrie and tumbled rocks of The Scorrie. Sheer hundred-foot cliffs surrounded Loch Brandy and we followed the track, carefully, round Green Hill, down a slow spur to the loch.

With lunch spread and waiting, as if by some devilish command clouds hurtled into the corrie. Rain mixed with sleet drove in horizontally as we rock-huddled, sheltering from the sudden storm. Ann pulled Jean closer. 'Now then, Jean, isn't this fun?' she announced brightly. 'What about my jam doughnuts?' came her angry reply. I had the answer. They were still in the car where I had left them. Nor was I offering to dash back either. Enough was enough for one day.

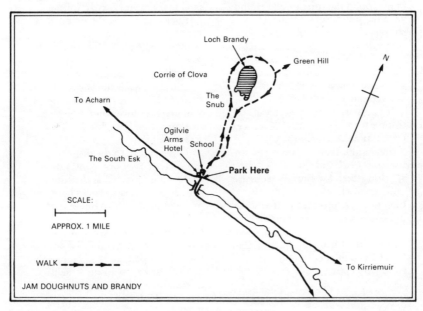

WHAT YOU NEED TO KNOW

Time and effort Five hours if you are normal; ten if you have Heathcliff or Jean. Either way, this walk should not be undertaken lightly. The way is steep and the crags round the top of Loch Brandy are a dangerous place to be if sudden clouds obscure the route. Regardless of weather, stay well away from the edge and take great care. In winter this route should be attempted only by experienced walkers, in good weather.

If you wish to try your hand fishing for Loch Brandy trout, seek permission first from the Ogilvie Arms Hotel. Don't expect 'one for the glass case'; indeed, don't expect anything at all for Brandy trout are notoriously fickle. Just cross the fingers and keep casting. If you must take a dog, keep it on the lead.

Location Ordnance Survey Sheet 44, Ballater, second series, scale 1:50,000.

Grid references Ogilvie Arms Hotel 326732; Corrie of Clova 326755; The Snub 335755; Green Hill 348758; Loch Brandy 340755; Driesh 271736.

Route The B955 rectangles round Glen Clova and the Ogilvie Arms is at the north end. Park by the hotel and walk past the little school onto the hill. The track is well marked and easy to follow – just very steep. On the first ridge bear left. Ahead, you will see Corrie of Clova and The Snub vee together, with Loch Brandy's horseshoe cliffs east.

The track leads up The Snub and then circles the top of the corrie. As you begin to turn south you come to a path junction. Bear left for a scramble up to the top of Green Hill and then return to the original track. This eases you gently down to the loch, arriving at the south end. A scattering of rocks here provide shelter and a lunch spot.

Follow the path back down the hill to the Ogilvie Arms. If you have your timing right, the doors should be open, and Sid Stephen behind the bar, waiting to help refresh the thirsty inner man and woman. You will have earned it.

22

Panting Round the Knock

THERE WERE nineteen people in the photograph, including Ann's Yorkshire terrier Heathcliff, which she insists is a person. It was taken in woods above Crieff Hydro, Perthshire, outside one of the Hydro's excellent self-catering chalets where Clan Sandison had gathered for a family weekend – Mrs Sandison senior and three daughters-in-law; brother Ian with two of three boys; brother Fergus with two smashing little daughters; my married son, Blair, and his wife; married daughter Lewis-Ann and her husband; Charles, Jean, cousin Bruce Reynolds, Heathcliff and me.

We called the photograph 'the family grope' because, at the critical moment, an unspecified sister-in-law shoved a hand where she shouldn't have, between an unsuspecting husband's legs, causing much merriment to everyone except Mrs Sandison senior, who was very definitely not amused. Still, its a super, happy snap and I treasure it.

Which is more than I can say for some of the memories of that weekend, or rather assault course. The attraction of Crieff Hydro to more youthful Sandisons was splendid recreational facilities: swimming pool and sauna, tennis, table tennis, squash, badminton, golf, riding and billiards. Younger brother Fergus, who is good at things, mapped out a programme of events whereby everyone did everything all the time, and by the end of the first day I felt as though I would never walk again.

I had anticipated a relaxing weekend, striding through old woods on Knock of Crieff, imparting words of wisdom here and there, about birds and trees, to those intelligent enough to listen. Should have known better, much better. My sister-in-law Liz, Fergie's wife, is a keen, fit runner. Come crack of dawn the door of our chalet burst open and we awakened to the sound of a boiling kettle.

Moments later: 'Tea. Outside in five minutes please. We're all waiting. Can't let the side down. Come on, Bruce.' What side? So I'm getting on in years. What do I have to prove to a bunch of fitness freaks? God, its barely light, let alone morning. Never at my best, mornings. 'Come on Uncle Bruce, Auntie Liz is getting cross' from a platoon of nieces and nephews surrounding the bed. Which is how I found myself running, rather than walking, through Creiff woods on a sharp September morning, first frosts of winter ridging the track ahead.

Our bunch set off at the gallop, thankfully downhill towards the stables. Then left. Up a long, slow, wet climb into trees, Liz leading, closely pursued by a brace of teenagers, chattering away as though ambling along Princes Street. Me, I knew I was going to die.

Liz Sandison is an amazingly fit lady. Fell running in the Lake District, several marathons to her credit and seaside runs down the Northumberland coast from Bamburgh Castle. In fact, looking round, they all seemed in good shape and as I found my second breath I hoped I could keep up and not make too much of a fool of myself. Elder brother Ian fell in step beside me and we conversed in convulsed gasps.

'How is it that Ann and Isobel (respective wives) aren't here?' he inquired.

'You're asking me? How should I know? Perhaps they had more sense. Save your breath for running.'

He persisted: 'And what about Fergie? He organized the run and he isn't here either.'

'That's why I'm saving my breath,' I replied. 'I'm going to kill him if I ever get back.'

Jean and Charlie joined us. 'What about a breather?' asked Charles. We crashed together in sudden halt, like a motorway pile-up.

Seconds later, downhill came Liz. 'That's where you all are. On your feet, you lot. Get a move on.' She was running on the spot. 'Think of the good this is doing you. Left, right, left, right, that's it, come on.' Hell hath no fury. We lumbered on.

Knock of Crieff is a gentle wooded hill to the north of the town, criss-crossed by paths, 911 feet in height. Trees vary in type from monotonous conifers topside to magnificent beech, oak and ash on lower slopes. That autumn morning, as the sun sidled up over Mound and Keillour, the world seemed frozen in time and space. Deep wisps of mist valley-lazed below Kate McNieven's Craig and Culcreiff Farm. Dewdrop diamonds sparkled on green larch branches; September golds and browns shaded lingering leaves.

Sounds of awakening Crieff floated upwards, cars busy with early-morning office-bound drivers. The small town lies uneasily between Gaelic-speaking north and anglicized lowlands and was the hub of the Highland cattle trade during the seventeenth century, when southern Scottish and English buyers gathered to argue prices with kilted northern men. As many as 30,000 beasts were bought and sold. More furious arguments raged in 1716 when Jacobite forces set fire to Crieff, destroying every building – no doubt settling a few old cattle-dealing scores in the process.

Like a scene from *Chariots of Fire* we arrived, more or less together, at a heather-clad clearing. I grabbed the concrete pillar at View Point for support and everyone gathered round to squabble over which hill was which. Grampian mountains lay north in faint, distant outline. Eastwards across Strathearn were the Ochil Hills, King's Seat and Tarmangie, resting shadowed in sunlight shafts.

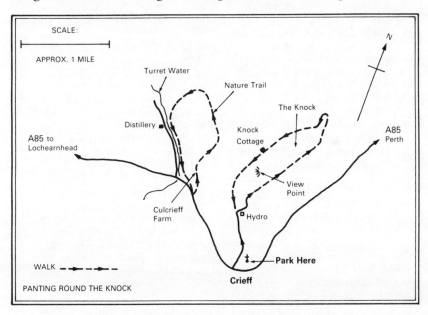

Liz was checking the map. Good grief, I thought, was it that bad? We jogged to the highest point of Knock then turned homewards, down the wide path past Knock Cottage and the Hydro's private gold course. A hopeful golfer, half-way through his swing on the first tee, gave a startled glance as we burst in a baying pack from the trees, and missed completely. Roars of impolite derision and offers of help didn't help. We clattered into the chalets, collected swimming gear and trotted down past tennis courts to the pool. Never had warm water been so welcoming.

Later that afternoon, during a brief lull in hostilities, mother dropped her bombshell. 'You know,' she announced ominously, 'we have enough people to make up two Scottish country dance sets after dinner. Won't that be fun!'

I thought longingly of the high tops of Foinaven and Arkle in darkest Sutherland, and agreed.

WHAT YOU NEED TO KNOW

Time and effort First thing you need to know is that running is not obligatory. Three miles walking takes you round the Knock and it is a delightful journey. The track can be wet at times, awash after heavy rain, but the views from the two high points are worth seeing. In spite of best efforts, giving directions is difficult since there are a number of paths within the woods. Still, you can't go far wrong and they are all pleasing.

As an addition to a walk on the Knock, consider also following the Crieff Nature Trail, one and a half miles in length, well signposted and starting from the car park at Culcrieff Farm. This walk has been prepared by members of the Scottish Wildlife Trust and a useful booklet is available to guide you round. Personally, I haven't seen much of the trail, but I have run round it.

Location Ordnance Survey Sheet 52, Aberfeldy and Glen Almond, second series, scale 1:50,000.

Grid references Crieff Hydro 865224; Knock View Point 867229; summit of the Knock 875235; start of Crieff Nature Trail at Culcrieff Farm 861234.

Route Walk starts from St James Square in the village. Go up Knock Road, through the gates leading to Crieff Hydro. At the stables, bear right and follow the path up into the woods with Crieff Gold Course on your right. This path leads up to the highest point of the Knock. From the top, bear left through the trees and the track brings you back down past Knock Cottage and the Hydro's private nine-hole golf course to the stables.

For the Crieff Nature Trail, leave Crieff by the A85 to Lochearnhead. Just outside the town, turn right along a minor road which leads to Culcrieff Farm. After swatting up local wildlife, trot north to the distillery near Hosh and sop up something else. A guid day deserves a guid end.

23

The Smooth Slope of Rannoch

Mᴏʀᴇ ᴛʜᴀɴ 1,800 years ago Claudius Ptolemy, Greek geographer and astronomer, author of the *Almagest*, a thirteen-
volume work of scientific 'knowledge and explanation', marked the
position of Schiehallion on the first map of Britain. Sixteen
centuries later another astronomer came to Sidh Chaillean: in 1774
Dr Nevil Maskelyne, Astronomer Royal, conducted his famous
experiments there in order to determine the specific gravity and
weight of planet Earth.

The only substantial difference in the landscape during the
intervening years resulted from the great depredations amongst the
forests of pine and oak that once covered Perthshire hills and glens.
Ancient trees were felled to make safe the traveller's way: to give
security from attack by thieves and robbers and protection from

wolves which ranged the woods.

Tree were burnt to make charcol for iron smelting, timber was in constant demand for shipbuilding and sheep cropped regenerating young plants. But there was also great concern for the fast-vanishing forests and in 1579 the death penalty was imposed upon those convicted of destroying trees or broom.

To small effect. All that remains of the Caledonian Forest are woods which line the south shore of Loch Rannoch from Finnart to Bunrannoch – the Black Wood of Rannoch, a magnificent open forest clad in silver birch, alder, rowan, juniper and stately pine, where the Forestry Commission is making valiant efforts to recreate the old forests in the lands of Clan Gregor, the children of the mist.

In 1603 the Privy Council in Edinburgh passed an Act ordering the 'extermination of that wicked, unhappy and infamous race of lawless lymmaris call it the MacGregors'. Men were hunted down like animals, woman branded on the forehead and children trans-ported to camps in the Lowlands and Ireland to serve as cattle boys.

But some escaped to carry on their traditional pastime of relieving softer southern neighbours of anything not nailed down. And two of their descendants climbed Schiehallion's smooth slope in the mid-1970s when my brother Ian accompanied our late father, John MacGregor Sandison, on his last long walk, to the summit.

To reach Schiehallion, follow the winding wooded road west-wards from Pitlochry, 'the road to the isles', past Queen's View. No, not unamused Victoria, but a more earthy, Scottish queen. Luckless Mary gave the name, when she visited the rocky promon-tory in 1564 and was reported to have been very amused with the noble view up Loch Tummel.

In more recent times others less earthy have been just as captivated by that gentle scene. William Wordsworth and his sister Dorothy tramped by during their tour of the Highlands. Alfred Lord Tennyson sought inspiration amongst the tree-lined banks. The great Liberal prime minister, William Gladstone, and Baden-Powell, hero of Mafeking, founder of the Boy Scout movement, both came here to pay silent homage to the beauty of Perthshire.

Ann and I pay homage also and return frequently to Tummel, Rannoch and Laidon to walk the hills and fish clear waters for wild brown trout. Schielhallion, an old favourite, dominates the long glen – a dreamlike, fairy-tale peak, snow-capped, graceful and always welcoming. A friendly mountain.

During recent visits we have stayed in the splendid comfort of lodges at Loch Rannoch Hotel – a far cry from mountain bothy or damp Highland cottage but, after a long day on hill or loch, marvellously relaxing. The lodges are carefully landscaped into mature woodlands and all have magnificent views over Rannoch to Schiehallion. There is an excellent restaurant and, best of all, a swimming pool and sauna complex. Aching joints ease and cold bodies quickly warm in mind-numbing, all-enveloping heat.

Last time, before saying hello to Schiehallion, we took a boat from Moor of Rannoch and sailed up Loch Laidon, across Rannoch Moor, 'the watery place', a desolate plateau a thousand feet above sea level. Laidon lays a silver scar across the moor – horizon crowded west with Black Mount and Glencoe peaks, Black–Corrie north, and bounded south by wild empty moorlands rising to Glen Lyon mountains. We parked the boat three miles down the loch and spent the day hillwalking with only fox and wild cat for companions.

If you have time and relish geographical tricks, sail down Laidon to Tigh na Cruaiche and the north shore bay protected by Eilean Iubhair. Beach the boat and follow up Allt Lochain Ghaineamhaich burn. After a few hundred yards, at streams cross, you may stand in three counties at once, Perthshire, Argyll and Inverness-shire. Presuming, of course, that you have three legs; otherwise, I should imagine you would have to jump about a bit to get the full effect.

A narrow hill road leaves Kinloch Rannoch south to Schiehallion, past shallow, flooded Dunalastair Reservoir. I remember, one cold Easter morning in the early 1960s, going aground in the middle on a barely submerged tree-stump. Whilst Ann gave directions, I stood, waist-deep and freezing, trying to push the boat free.

Our more sensible companions had retired to the pub to roast in front of a blazing fire. Before they had lowered a quarter of their first pint, the door of the bar burst open and a local exclaimed: 'Here! You will never believe what I have just seen. There are a couple of idiots wading in the middle of Dunalastair!' Our friends expressed amused interest but nothing else. We caught nothing.

The tortuous hill road climbs Meall Dubh then falls to Braes of Foss at the edge of a plantation of new trees. The broad shoulder of Schiehallion rises west, still snow-capped in May. Her sister Munros, Carn Gorm, Meall Garbh, Carn Mairg and Creag Mhor, symphony south and the long skirts of the smooth slope cradle tumbling waters of Allt Kynachan stream, pointing the way upwards.

Resting by the summit cairn with Scotland spread before me, I often think of father, labouring up the cairned path to the top, no doubt mightily encouraged by Ian. It was a clear day when he made that last climb. A wonderful memory to sleep with.

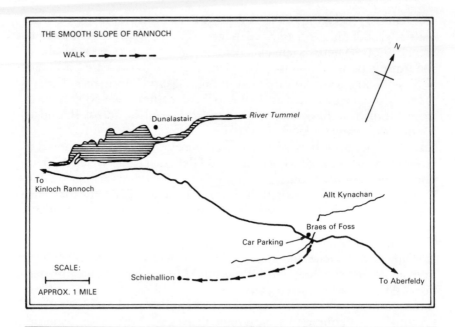

WHAT YOU NEED TO KNOW

Time and effort Be prepared. Although this is an easy walk, in bad weather even Schiehallion can turn nasty. The distance there and back from Braes of Foss is about five miles and you should allow three hours for your journey. The summit is a Munro at 3,547 feet and you will climb nearly 2,500 feet to reach it.

Location Ordnance Survey Sheet 51, Loch Tay, second series, scale 1:50,000.

Grid references Braes of Foss and parking 750559; Schiehallion summit 714548.

Route From the car park at Braes of Foss, to east of the house south of the road, a path leads up a broad valley, on the left-hand side of a small burn. Once you leave the moorland heather habitat and climb higher up the shoulder, a line of cairns marks the way to the summit. On top there is a trig. point and substantial cairn. Return to the car park the same way.

24

Gilbert, Gow and Marble

HE CASTLE at Blair Atholl was built in AD 1269. Oliver
Cromwell, that great seventeenth-century demolition contrac-
tor, knocked it about a bit in 1653 and the scarred building had to
wait until 1872 before being restored. Earls and Dukes of Atholl
played a prominent part in Scotland's turbulent story throughout
the ages. Much given to royalist tendencies, Atholl dukes and sons
were supporters of James Francis Edward Stuart, the Old Pretender, and Charles Edward Louis Philip Casimir, known to his
family as Carluccio and to history as Bonnie Prince Charlie.

The dukedom was created when the 2nd Marquess of Atholl fell
in with William of Orange in 1688 and was elevated for his pains.
Proper pains came later. Like many Scots before and after, the
prospect of a Scottish king and expected benefits made the
embryonic duke change horses in midstream: from 1703 onwards,
Atholl sympathies were pro-Jacobite.

Three of his sons were 'out' in the 1715 rising. The most famous,
Lord George Murray, was later pardoned, but failed to profit from
such surprising leniency. In 1745 he joined the Young Pretender on
his abortive, disastrous bid for the crown of these sceptred isles and
was certainly the best of Charlie's rag-bag of generals.

Murray advised against the ill-fated night march to Nairn, before the final battle on Drumossie Moor, and begged the Prince to choose another, more easily defended site. Should have saved his breath. The stubborn Stuarts were incapable of taking advice. Which is how they had got themselves into such a mess in the first place.

Atholl fortunes brightened considerably when the 2nd Duke inherited sovereignty of Isle of Man in 1736. This was sold to the British government in 1765 for £70,000, and in 1828 the 4th Duke parted with his remaining Manx rights for the huge sum of £417,000. A good day's work if ever there was one. The white castle at Blair Atholl is more peaceful now, although more thoroughly besieged by tourists than Cromwell could ever have mustered troops to batter the ancient walls.

Our eldest son is named Blair, his grandmother's maiden name. The family came from Dunkeld and we consider this beautiful part of Perthshire second home – next to Edinburgh, where I was born; the Borders, where my wife was brought up; Caithness, my grandfather's birthplace; and the Trossachs, where Jean Mac-Gregor, my grandmother, lived. Suppose that's more than two, but you know what I mean.

A long track leads north-east from Blair Atholl, knifing thirty-one miles through Glen Tilt by Falls of Tarf and Geldie Burn to White Bridge and Linn of Dee. This is a dramatic, magnificent walk past some of Scotland's grandest scenery, but organizing time and transport is complicated and difficult. The journey takes twelve hours, one way. So you have to rely on public transport at one end or make the walk in conjunction with friends, passing mid-way and picking up cars at the finish. Overnight accommodation for tired feet may also be required.

A good alternative is to do this walk in two parts: from south and north, returning down the glen the same way. Even then it is a long walk, but you can walk as far as you like and the scenery along the path is well worth the effort. Beinn a'Ghlo dominates the eastern slopes of Glen Tilt, hiding from Blair Atholl behind Carn Liath. Munro country. Braigh Coire Chruinnbhalgain, Carn nam Gabhar and Airgoid Bheinn, sparkling white with spring snows, strewn with rough, ankle-twisting boulders.

Deep in the hills (crushed between Coire Cas-eagallach and Meall Reamhar) lies one of Scotland's remotest trout waters, Loch Loch, a narrow ribbon of silver water, shores hour-glassed together. Northwards, Grampian peaks rear skywards: Beinn a'Chait, Braigh nan Creagan Breac, Carn a'Chlamain and Conlach Mhor. In the valley, sweet River Tilt tumbles southwards to its meeting with Garry at Blair Atholl.

Queen Victoria stayed at Blair Castle in September 1844 and fell in love with Glen Tilt:

> We drove along Glen Tilt, through a wood overhanging the river; and as we left the wood we came upon such a lovely view – Ben-y-Ghlo straight before us – and under these high hills the river Tilt gushing and winding over stones and slates, and the hills and mountains skirted at the bottom with beautiful trees; the whole lit up by the sun, and the air so pure and fine. But no description can at all do it justice, or give an idea of what this drive was.

Knew a thing or two, did Queen Victoria, amused or otherwise. Each morning a jug of water was placed at her bedside, drawn fresh from a spring high up the glen where she and Prince Albert always stopped to drink and known to this day as a Queen's Well. Little bridges cross the Tilt, each graced by a morsel of history: Gilbert's Bridge, guarded by wonderful beech trees, and named after William Gilbert Robertson, who was 'out' with his laird in the Forty-Five. Near by is Tom na Croich, the hanging hill, last used to dispatch one John Stewart, convicted of murdering a shepherd on Beinn a'Ghlo.

Gow's Bridge, near Marble Lodge, is where marble was quarried and rocks are still chisel-marked where they were struck to split the stones – 'twenty-one shillings a cubic foot, delivered Edinburgh' at

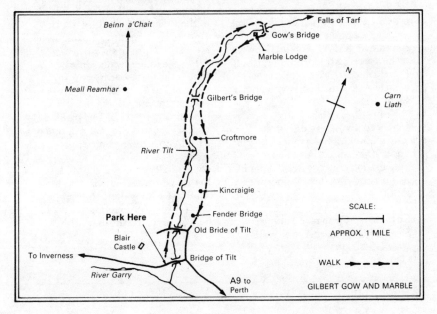

the end of the nineteenth century. Blairuachdar Wood to the north of Old Blair, stands witness to Atholl dukes' pioneering forestry work. James Murray, the 2nd Duke, brought the first larch trees from the Alps to Atholl in 1727 and the 4th Duke became known as 'the planting duke', establishing more than 10,000 acres of forest over a period of sixty years.

Sir Walter Scott, in *The Fair Maid of Perth*, wrote: 'Amid all the provinces of Scotland, if an intelligent stranger were asked to describe the most varied and most beautiful, it is probable he would name the county of Perth.' Spend a day walking in Glen Tilt and you will know why.

WHAT YOU NEED TO KNOW

Time and effort   As long and as much as you want. I suggest two alternatives: a walk of about 6½ miles, from Blair Atholl to Gilbert's Bridge and back; or a longer walk of 10½ miles, on from Gilbert's Bridge to Marble Lodge and Gow's Bridge, then back to Blair Atholl. No hardship in either of these walks.

For the hardy, tramp on to Forest Lodge and Falls of Tarf, which is near the half-way mark to Deeside; but allow a good ten hours for the round trip. Shorten this walk by seeking permission from the Atholl Estate office to use their private vehicle access road on payment of a small fee.

Your trip will be greatly enhanced if you buy one of the information leaflets available at the caravan site office. Also seek information concerning stalking in August and October. Who wants shot?

Location   Ordnance Survey Sheet 43, Braemar, second series, scale 1:50,000.

Grid references   Start point from car park at Blair Castle 866663; Blairuachdar Wood 876684; Gilbert's Bridge 881701; Marble Lodge 898717; Forest Lodge 933741; Falls of Tarf 983797.

Route   The start point is at Blair Atholl caravan site and you exit by the first gate to the riverside footpath. Turn left and follow it up through the woods on the left bank of the River Tilt. At Gilbert's Bridge, cross to the east bank of the river and return to the car.

For the longer walk, simply follow the track northwards up Glen Tilt to Gow's Bridge, cross and return south down the east bank to Blair Atholl. The paths are well signposted and you will find it hard to go wrong – unless, of course, you are like me, and congenitally prone to getting lost. In case you are tempted into a little Munro-bashing along the way, don't forget compass and map and be well prepared for the weather.

25

Linn of Dee
and Tarf Falls

THE MAN and woman stopped on the banks of the river and took off boots and socks. They were a handsome young couple, bronzed from the hills, laughing in warm September sunlight. Back-packed and barefooted, they stumbled hand in hand across shallow, sharp-rocked Dee. We spotted them an hour since, a splash of white and red amongst heather, inching down from Carn Liath by corries of Dalvorar burn and Carn an Leth-allt.

Obviously, they had tried to shorten their long journey through Glen Tilt by cutting east over Buachaille Breige and Carn Liath to pick up the stalker's path to Inverey. And missed. Not difficult to do in these wild, remote lands. The rough tramp seemed to have dampened only their feet, for as they walked off down the sand-packed road to Linn of Dee happy laughter filled the air.

I was in a Land-Rover, with a Swiss and a Skye man, parked by the side of the river, watching autumn-red salmon surging to upstream spawning grounds beyond Chest of Dee, where silver Dee rises between mighty Ben Macdhui and Cairn Toul in fierce Cairngorms before cascading through Royal Deeside past Balmoral Castle seawards to Aberdeen.

My hosts were from Mar Lodge, a few miles down the glen near Braemar. Mar Lodge was a royal hunting lodge, built in the late nineteenth century by Queen Victoria for the Duke of Fife and Princess Louise, daughter of Edward VII. Nice to be near granny, but not too near.

Great deer drives were held on Mar, hundreds of beasts being driven before the muzzles of expectant royal guns – a tradition going back centuries in the mountains between Blair Atholl and Braemar. Deep in the glen, where chill waters from Loch Loch rush down An Lochain burn to Tilt, the Earl of Atholl built a hunting lodge in 1529 for King James V. More than a thousand men herded deer down from the corries of Beinn a'Ghlo for the king's pleasure. His daughter, Mary Queen of Scots, was similarly entertained in 1564, before she became the hunted one herself.

Today the estate still boasts some of the finest stalking in Europe and Beinn a'Bhuird has a red deer population of 5,000. The ballroom of Mar Lodge is adorned with the heads of 3,000 stags and in days gone by the Mar employed two full-time taxidermists. Grouse on the moor, salmon in the river, stags on the hill. What sportsman could ask for more? Apart from the wherewithal to pay.

Walking is less costly and far less dangerous to fish, fowl and beast. I prefer walking and the only time I interfere with nature is when I attempt to remove a few wild brown trout from their natural habitat, an infrequent occurrence. But I would never begrudge another man his pleasure for it is not my business in life to dictate how others should enjoy themselves. Authoritarian pre-scription scares the hell out of me. Live and let live – just too bad if you happen to be born grouse, salmon or stag.

Dramatic Linn of Dee is the start of the 31-mile walk to Blair Atholl. The river roars through a narrow defile, cut over centuries by the force of the stream. Dark waters swirl below secret ledges where resting salmon lurk. Cliff-tops are spread thick with pine needles and the smell of resin lingers in mist-fine spray.

A splendid road leads westwards, faced by peaks of Glenfeshie Forest to White Bridge, where the Geldie burn gathers in all the waters from Cnapan Mor and Scarsoch Bheag, sending them chortling to Dee. New trees bunch by the stream as the path climbs slowly past the ruins of Bynack Lodge to the birthplace of the River Tilt.

Loch Tilt lies to the west of the track, hidden from view. In 1769, Thomas Pennant, that caustic Welsh observer of things Scottish, passed that way and described Loch Tilt as 'swarming with trouts'. Pennant had little good to say about Scotland or its people. Further south, he castigated Lowland scenery with his usual brashness and further north he was soon describing the natives of Sutherland as little more than worthless, idle savages.

In the meantime, resting by Loch Tilt, he observed of his journey '. . . the most dangerous and the most horrible I have ever travelled; a narrow path so rugged that our horses often were obliged to cross their legs in order to secure place for their feet.' Welshmen take a lot of pleasing. Unlike Pennant, Queen Victoria enjoyed the trip and wrote in her journal: 'This was the pleasantest and most enjoyable expedition I ever made; and the recollection of it will always be agreeable to me, and increase my wish to make more!' Takes all sorts.

South from Loch Tilt, the infant river is christened Allt Garbh Buidhe, 'the boisterous yellow burn', and the track feints and fades through a long narrow pass, sheer-sloped by Meall na Callich Buidhe. Tarf Water, Tilt's principal companion, slides in a snake-like silver thread from the north, leaping three, final, mighty, waterfalled strides into the waiting arms of Tilt.

A sad bridge was built here nearly forty years after Victoria's merry party trotted by, the Bedford Memorial Bridge. 'This bridge

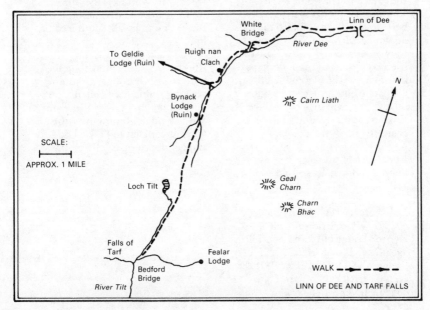

was erected in 1886 with funds contributed by his friends and others and by the Scottish Rights of Way Society Ltd to commemorate the death of Francis John Bedford, aged 18, who was drowned near here on 25th August 1879.' Crossing rivers can seriously damage your health.

Blair Atholl lies ahead, but, unless you have been lucky enough to make arrangements with friends to leave your transport there, turn and retrace steps to Braemar. If you feel very unhappy about turning back, brighten your walk with three of the Munros on the way. A track leads eastwards to Fealar Lodge and you may navigate across the hills to Carn Bhac, Geal Charn and Carn Liath.

Pick up the stalker's path south of Carn Liath summit and follow it down to Inverey. Don't worry too much about getting lost. Head north and wade across the shallow, sharp-rocked Dee. I'll be the guy in the Land-Rover, waiting to greet you on the other side.

WHAT YOU NEED TO KNOW

Time and effort This a long, tiring walk and you should choose the best possible day before getting involved. The total distance is in the order of sixteen miles, there and back so think in terms of an early start and a full day out. High summer with longest days is the best. If you strike east into the hills on your return, make sure you are fully equipped and know how to use a compass and map. Perhaps best to make the high hill walk into a separate outing. Depends upon how fit and experienced you are. Whatever you do, don't take chances.

Location Ordnance Survey Sheet 43, Braemar, second series, scale 1:50,000.

Grid references Linn of Dee 062897; White Bridge 019886; Bynack Lodge 001856; Loch Tilt 993827; Falls of Tarf 983797; Fealar Lodge 009799; Carn Bhac 041828; Geal Charn 032833; Carn Liath 035867; Inverey 086892.

Route From Braemar, follow the minor road west by the side of the river which loops at Linn of Dee. Park here and walk west along the north bank of the Dee. This is an excellent road and takes you smartly to White Bridge, three miles from your start point. Cross the bridge and walk south into the hills.

The main path turns west after Ruigh nan Clach cottage, up the burn to Geldie Lodge. Continue walking south. Tarf Falls are on your right, about five miles from White Bridge. Return the same way, or turn left to Fealar Lodge and get out compass and map.

26
Avoiding Aviemore

I REMEMBER once hearing a lecture by Professor Colin Buchanan on the subject 'Can Man Plan?' Visit the nightmare village of Aviemore on Speyside and make up your own mind. Set amidst some of God's most glorious scenery, this once attractive village has been devastated by mass tourism.

Lord Fraser of Allander, a principal promoter of the development, was much given to referring to scenery and wildlife as 'the merchandise'. With friends like these, Aviemore never stood a chance and the best thing that has happened to Aviemore in recent years is the bypass which excludes its ugliness from view. In my opinion, Aviemore is a fearful monument to man's insensitivity to his environment.

The graceful Cairngorm Mountains have been opened up to allcomers and development is the new god. Conservationists and wildlife bodies are ridiculed when they express concern and nothing must be allowed to stand in the way of commercial exploitation or profit. Those who complain are branded as crackpots, trouble-makers standing in the way of progress.

Wonderful once-remote corries and summits have become easily accessible by ski-lifts and a trip to the high peaks in summer is no less daunting a prospect than an afternoon amble down Oxford Street – and often just as crowded. Ease of access means despoliation: notice-boards, signposts, keep out, private, don't, must and the malignant growth of bureaucracy.

It was not always like that. As a teenager, my wife, Ann, used to visit the Cairngorms during the late 1950s, when Aviemore was just a Highland Blackpool gleam in the developer's eye. She stayed at Carrbridge and each morning a party of young people would set off by bicycle on the fifteen-mile journey to Coylumbridge or Loch Morlich.

From there, they spent their day trout fishing in crystal-clear lochs, scrambling by White Lady Shieling to the summit of Cairngorm, or walking in the Lairig Ghru. But it will never be the same again and something beyond human price has been destroyed for ever.

I first visited Speyside in 1950 as a tenderfoot Boy Scout when the troop camped at Creagdubh near Newtonmoor in the lands of Clan MacPherson. I was homesick, too, but we were kept busy building bridges, hiking into hills, swimming in the little lochans nearby. My interest in trout fishing probably dates from that time. What made those strange, mysterious rings on the calm surface of the loch?

By the time Ann and I met, nine years later, I was a confirmed fisherman and used to boast youthfully about my supposed skill – until one evening, with a quiet smile, she produced from her handbag a photograph of a magnificent two pound trout.

There could be no argument either, because a ruler had been placed above the fish. 'Where did you catch that?' I asked, through gritted teeth. The fish had been caught during one of her days walking in the Cairngorms and was all the more remarkable for having been taken from a tiny mountain stream.

When our children were little we brought them to Speyside and stayed at Nethy Bridge, far from the madding crowd of Aviemore. The old village still retains its ancient charm and we found a perfect cottage close to the banks of gurgling Nethy Burn. The stream rises on Cairngorm's saddle above blue Loch Avon, stumbling down from high peaks between Cnap Coire na Spreidhe and Stac na h-lolaire to the west and A'Choinneach and Bynack More to the east.

King Edward of England, the 'hammer of the Scots', paused at Nethy Bridge during one of his endless forays north to quell unruly neighbours. Claverhouse and Montrose camped here and General

Hugh MacKay of Scourie, defeated at the Battle of Killicrankie, passed by on his way to disaster.

Communications throughout these wild lands were much improved by that great soldier road-builder General Wade. Between 1725 and 1733 he constructed no less than 250 miles of new ways throughout the Highlands, including the tortuous route over Corrieyairack Pass, employing 500 men in order to do so.

Wade's instructions, as commander-in-chief of government forces in the north, were 'to reduce the Highlands to obedience'; but it takes a 'lang spoon' to sup with a Highlander, as the rebellion of Forty-Five proved. Butcher Cumberland was less delicate in his methods after Culloden and completed the task of subjugation without mercy.

Swiftly flowing Spey meanders past Nethy Bridge in an urgent, silver thread, collecting Nethy Burn and Allt Mor waters into its turbulent arms. One evening after heavy spare, I offered to baby-sit while Ann went to fish where Allt Mor and Spey meet. After an hour or so I began to worry – not so much for Ann's safety, but rather because I suspected that she might be catching lots of fish when I wasn't.

Carrying daughter Lewis-Ann and taking small kilted son Blair by firm grip, we set out through another rainstorm to investigate. We arrived at the river just in time to see Ann landing a lovely trout of about a pound and a half. 'Look, children,' I said, 'isn't Mummy

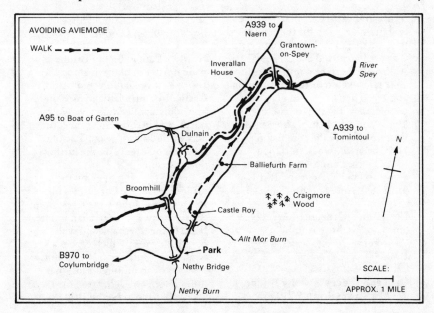

clever. She's caught supper.' Then I looked again and noticed a tear in the corner of her eye. 'What on earth's the matter?' I asked.

'Put it back please. I couldn't kill it. It fought so well.'

I did, but will never understand why.

The Spey is one of Sctoland's finest salmon rivers and a perfect walk leads northwards along the river bank to Grantown and the old arched bridge. One cold night, full of hope, Ann and I fished for sea trout under the bridge. After an hour with nothing to show for our efforts other than freezing faces, we retired under the arches with my hip flask, thoughtfully charged with cherry brandy, and left the fish to get on with it undisturbed.

To complete a memorable Speyside walk, cross the bridge and return to Nethy down the north side of Spey. The banks are busy with salmon fishers and the river busy with fish avoiding them. Above the forests of Craigmore and Abernethy, Cairngorms rise majestically in a mighty shout of mountain triumph.

Before the last ice age, mammoth, musk ox, Arctic fox and lemmings used to haunt these old hills. Ice there still is in plenty, but the only animals haunting hills now are hordes of human lemmings. Wonder if there is any chance of them following the example of their furry, four-legged counterparts?

WHAT YOU NEED TO KNOW

Time and effort Total distance is about nine miles for the round trip and the only obstacles along the way are fences and dykes. Easy walking but can be damp underfoot after rain. Avoid disturbing salmon anglers. They have enough problems as it is and do not take kindly to rocks being hurled into the pools where they are fishing. Have been known to hurl them back. During your day try and fit in a visit to Loch Garten and RSPB-protected osprey nesting site.

Location Ordnance Survey Sheet 36, Grantown and Cairngorm, second series, scale 1:50,000.

Grid references Nethy Bridge 001206; Castle Roy 006219; Speybridge 035268; Old Spey Bridge 040264; Broomhill 995225,

Route Park in Nethy Bridge and walk north out of town along the B970. Past Balliemore and before Castle Roy, turn left and pick up line of dismantled railway. Walk north, and in three miles meet the new bridge across Spey. The old bridge is quarter of a mile further downstream.

Return crossing Spey by the new bridge. Just at the north side, turn sharp left and follow the track along the river towards Inverallan House. Keep to the riverbank and walk beside the Spey, which curves and twists past Dulnain to Broomhill, a distance of about three and a half miles. At Broomhill, cross the river and walk back to Nethy Bridge.

27

Bennachie, the Don and Paradise Wood

IN 1078 Malcolm Canmore, the one who did for dastardly MacBeth, rested at Monymusk whilst on his way north to quell yet another Morayshire uprising. Using his spear, he marked on the ground an outline of the church he marked on the ground an outline of the church he would build if granted victory over the rebels. He quelled the uprising – a quaint Scottish euphemism for wholesale slaughter – and the church he built still graces the old-world charm of this grey-stoned Aberdeenshire village.

A better-known pattern commemorates the delightful Strathdon hamlet today and is traced on the ground by the feet of Scottish country dancers as they weave and smile their way through the intricate measures of the dance 'Monymusk'. We Scots have always been great ones for dancing. As children, Ann and I were given compulsory lessons in the ancient art. She, more Highland; I, less taxing Lowland shuffles.

One of Scotland's most important relics came from the House of Monymusk, ancestral home of the Grant family since 1712 – the Monymusk Reliquary, a seventh-century casket said to contain a bone of St Columba. Must have been bad news, being an important religious figure. The moment you snuffed, the world beat a path to your corpse, knives poised to cut off bits and pieces for posterity.

The Monymusk Reliquary was at Bannockburn in 1314 inspiring the troops of Robert the Bruce, and can still be seen in Edinburgh at Queen Street, in the Scottish Museum of Antiquities. Another important Scottish antiquity is my mother, Mima Sandison, a wonderful, sparkling octogenarian who still dances three nights a week and is a walking encyclopaedia on Scottish country dancing. Eight people together, anywhere, means one thing to my mother: enough for a Scottish country dance set.

Aberdeenshire's two mighty rivers, Dee and Don, ride the county together, from the heights of the Grampian mountains to the cold waters of the North Sea by the honest Granite City. Both are famous for their salmon runs and yet they are entirely different in character. The Dee is essentially a spate river, much given to variations in water level, whilst the gentle Don flows serenely through fine farmlands in unhurried calm. Aberdeenshire farmers, in clipped, sing-song voice, claim: 'A mile o'Don's worth twa o' Dee.'

Bennachie, a smooth range of forested hills, rises quietly over softly flowing Don. Oxen Crag is the highest peak, 1,733 feet, courtiered by Mither Tap, Hermit's Seat, Black Hill and Millstone Hill. The Forestry Commission has laid out a series of pleasant walks through woodlands and across open hills, varying in length from one to eight miles. But, before visiting Bennachie, walk to Paradise, my favourite Strathdon forest, enfolded in a crook of the river by Woodhead and Tilliehashlach.

Paradise Wood is a proper wood, not like today's commercial plantations – dark, impenetrable, sterile deserts. Paradise borders the Don and was beautifully planned and planted by Lord Cullen in 1719. Last year, Ann and I parked the car near the ruined mill on the south bank and walked by the river through a dappled day of sunlight and shadow, amidst friendly old oak and beech, where tall pines swayed sweetly in the breeze and the air was bright with woodland birdsong – Frederick Delius and a 'Walk to the Paradise Garden'.

During that visit I had a close look at the Don. Unexpectedly, dangerously close. I had been fishing Dam Pool, near Forbes Castle. Deep water, clear and slow-moving, alive with summer insects, bordered by high reeds, tree-backed on the north bank – fish-stalking water. Half awake in warm sun, I was taken completely by surprise when a monster fish grabbed my fly. Stepping forward in fright, I performed a neat dive straight into the river.

Fully equipped – waders, fishing jacket and tackle bag – under I went, thinking 'Well, this is it. Wonder what it will be like.' But I managed to struggle upright, head barely above the stream and struggled shaken and dripping ashore. Lost fish, dignity and very nearly life. When I told the family of the near demise of their father I received scant sympathy. 'Not safe to be let out alone.' 'Get your eyes tested.' 'Where did you say the hip flask was? 'How big was this fish supposed to be?'

The climb to the summit of Bennachie is a popular walk and starts from a parking area near Maiden Castle. When we arrived the car park was busy with people preparing for an afternoon stroll. There is an information centre at Don View where a guidebook is available, along with toilets, children's playground and picnic area. The route to Mither Tap is along a well worn track, stamped flat by thousands of feet.

At Pittodrie, on the low east slopes of Bennachie, is a small Pictish fort. The remains of the protecting wall can be clearly seen, enclosing an area 80 feet long by 60 feet wide and there is evidence of further defences, a rampart and ditch. Mither Tap also has hill-fort remains but you may be excused for walking by without noticing for they lie scattered amongst the granite and felspar boulders described in the 'Guide to Prehistoric Scotland' as:

> The outermost wall, about 15ft thick, runs round the bottom of the tor for nearly 100ft below the summit; several stretches of its

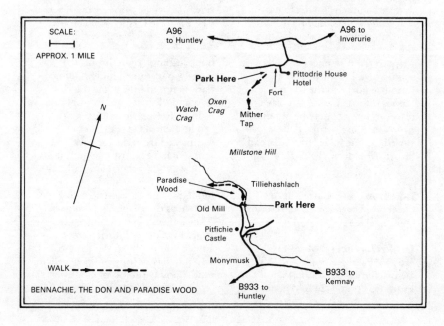

faces can be distinguished, and there are suggestions of a parapet in one place. A second wall encircles the interior of the enclosure thus formed about half way up towards the summit.

A more recent pillar has been erected on Mither Tap, brass-plate-engraved with lines pointing to surrounding peaks. On that fine day, 128 miles north, our Caithness mountains of Morven and the Scarabens were clearly visible whilst the vast bulk of Ben Macdui, Braeriach and Cairn Gorm reared westwards. Patchworked fields, rivers and forests flowed east to Aberdeen.

At the 'back of Bennachie', by the side of a quiet minor road, stands one of Scotland's most beautiful Pictish symbol stones, the Maiden Stone. An ancient slab of red granite, ornately carved front and back with early Christian symbols. On the front, in relief, a man is shown between fish monsters. As I gazed at the elaborate interlace of carvings, a distant bell rang in my mind: I had seen one of these fish somewhere before. Then I remembered. Underwater in Dam Pool on the River Don. Wait until I tell the family.

WHAT YOU NEED TO KNOW

Time and effort Mostly time. The walk up Bennachie, there and back, is only three miles and about a couple of hours' easy stroll; but there is so much else to see nearby that really you should plan a whole day out, driving between various sites.

Apart from Bennachie walk, you should visit Paradise Wood, Pittodrie Fort and the Maiden Stone. Information about other places of interest may be obtained from Gordon District Tourist Board, St Nicholas House, Broad Street, Aberdeen. Tel: (0224) 632727.

Location Ordnance Survey Sheet 38, Aberdeen, second series, scale 1:50,000.

Grid references Monymusk 685154; Paradise Wood 675185; Bennachie car park 691245; Pittodrie Fort 694244; Maiden Stone 703247; Mither Tap 683224.

Route For Paradise Wood, drive north from Monymusk on the west bank of the River Don. Where the minor road turns right to cross the river at Pitfichie, drive straight on past Pitfichie Castle, which is on your left. A mile further, the road bends sharp left. Directly ahead is a track leading down through woods, past ruined mill buildings. Park here and follow the track down to the river and through the woods. Return the same way.

The Bennachie walks are signposted from the car park and you will have no trouble finding your way to Mither Tap. Although often busy, Bennachie is well looked after by a team of men known as the Bennachie Rangers. They are very helpful and will supply whatever information and advice you may require. I suggest you purchase a copy of the excellent guidebook before setting out.

28

Gairloch, Fionn and Fisherfield

During summer months, Gairloch in Wester Ross is a busy, bustling tourist centre. Thousands of visitors flock to the world-famous Inverewe Gardens, begun in 1865 by Osgood Mackenzie, now containing some 2,500 species of plants from around the world. Children bucket and spade on shining white sands or splash in clear waters warmed by the Gulf Stream. There are excellent restaurants, hotels, museums, craft centres, golf courses, pony trekking, sail-boarding and Highland safaris. Something for everyone.

But the shores of the Short Loch were not always so peaceful; nineteenth-century famines and evictions brought ruin to the north. When Lowland granaries were full, Highlanders starved. People went barefoot, clothed in meal bags, whilst Free Church ministers appealed in vain to London for help. Lord Napier, leading a royal commission in 1882, reported: 'A state of misery, of wrong-doing, and of patient long-suffering, without parallel in the history of our country.'

The open-air pulpit of the Free Presbyterian Church is a reminder of these sad times, when sheep and profit took preference over people; when young and old alike laboured for Destitution Boards or accepted the blandishments of Emigration Societies: bible-blessed with a pound and packed overseas like cattle. Today, a new wind of hope blows throughout the Highlands and the sympathetic development of Gairloch as a major tourist centre is evidence of respect for the past and renewed hope in the future.

North-east from Gairloch is one of Scotland's most beautiful and remote lochs, Fionn, the 'white loch', deep in the heart of turbulent Fisherfield Forest – 180 square miles enfolding thirty-five mountains, eighteen of which tower more than 3,000 feet: a 'thunder' of Munros; a hillwalker's paradise and gamefisher's delight.

In his book *A Hundred Years in the Highlands*', Osgood Mackenzie describes the most famous basket of brown trout ever taken from Fionn: 'There were four beauties lying side by side on the table of the small drinking room, and they turned the scales at 51 lb. The total weight of the 12 fish caught that 12th day of April by trolling was 87 lb 12 oz.'

Fionn trout are of more modest size today and average half a pound, but there are few more delightful places to fish and the last time Ann and I assaulted Fionn we were rewarded with a dozen brightly marked, sprightly trout. She caught twelve and I managed to catch the rest. Salmon and sea trout also lurk in Fionn's deep waters, making their perilous journey from the sea past anthrax-ridden Gruinard island and up Little Gruinard River to the loch.

There are several fine walks out to Fionn – from the east, from Drumchork near Aultbea, by Loch Mhic 'ille Riabhaich, named after a sixteenth-century outlaw who terrorized the surrounding countryside; from the north, by long climber's path from Corrie Hallie near Dundonnell on Little Loch Broom; and from the west via Poolewe, Loch Maree and Kernsary.

Our favourite approach is from Poolewe, along the banks of the river, where there is always the chance of spotting salmon surging upstream to Loch Maree. Sometimes, surging downhill, come perspiring humans, for this is the line of a fun-run, from Dundonnell, by An Teallach (3,484 feet), Sgurr Fiona (3,473 feet), round Loch na Sealga, down by Ruadh Stac Mor (3,014 feet), past Fionn, then into Poolewe. Twenty-nine miles through Strathnasheallag and Fisherfield forests. Fun?

The road turns north-east at the west end of Loch Maree and climbs the hill to cross Kernsary stream at a high, locked gate. The National Trust for Scotland owns land to the north-west, crested by Meall an Leathaid Dharaich and Carn an Eich Dheirg, and as you hike past new woodlands at the top of the first rise Loch Kernsary sparkles below, spread over the moor in long silver fingers and crooked bays, offering magnificent westwards views to Loch Ewe and the stormy seas of the North Minch. When we passed last summer, a graceful hind, belly-deep in yellow flag and sweet meadow grass, drank from the outlet burn surrounded by clumps of purple heather and backed by the vivid silver-blue loch. An unforgettable moment.

As the broken road twists and turns past Kernsary Lodge, climbing ever higher, majestic mountains bid you welcome. Spidean na Clach, Beinn Airigh Charn and Martha's Peak. Martha was tending cattle on high summer grazings when she dropped a spindle of thread. In attempting to retrieve it she fell to her death and the peak has been known by her name ever since.

A short distance past Kernsary, the track divides and we follow the right hand fork, up the line of Allt na Creige burn, skirting north slopes of mountains, by the forbidding sheer cliffs of Beinn Airigh Charn, past a series of inviting lochs and lochans: na Moine, nan Clach Dubh and finally, Beannach Mor and Beannach Beag. This was the route to the old fishing hut, before things were sited upmarket at north end of Fionn, and it is still known as Old Boathouse Bay. A bustling stream empties into Fionn, a favourite salmon lie.

Climb the headland above Beannach Beag and look east up Fionn. The end of the loch is gripped by seemingly inaccessible, frighteningly steep slopes; Ben Lair leading to Slioch; A'Mhaigh-dean and Mullach Mhic Fhearchair; Ruadh Stac Mor and Beinn a' Chaisgein Mor. Challenging, difficult climbs and best left alone by unfit, novice, or just plain hillwalkers like me.

A two-mile bankside stumble along the rocky south shore of Fionn leads to New Mooring Bay, protected by scrub-covered Eilean an Eich Bhain. Across the windy loch, in the bay below Beinn a' Chaisgein Beag, is the site of one of Scotland's remotest shops, on the line of a long-dead drove road. As Highland herdsmen cursed lowing black cattle through Fisherfield, the welcome sight must have brought warmth to their hearts and a new spring to their step. For us, a downhill slog to Poolewe before such luck – but wonderful memories to carry on the way.

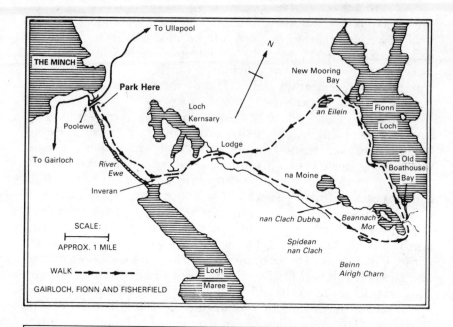

GAIRLOCH, FIONN AND FISHERFIELD

WHAT YOU NEED TO KNOW

Time and effort Allow a full day for this long, beautiful walk; and choose a good day to do it in. Total distance, there and back, approximately 13 miles. No serious climbs or problems other than the weather and weary legs towards the end. The section along the south shore of Fionn is tiring as there is no real path and the going is rough. Take it easy.

Location Ordnance Survey Sheet 19, Gailoch and Ullapool, second series, scale 1:50,000.

Grid references Poolewe and start 858808; Inveran 874786; Kernsary 894804; fork in track 897803; Old Boathouse Bay 945779; New Mooring Bay 928810.

Route Ample parking space in car park on north side of River Ewe near the school. The road leads south-east from here, along the banks of the river, turning north-east at Inveran. Follow the road uphill to the gate over Kernsary Burn. There is a stile. From there walk on past Loch Kernsary to the lodge.

Past Kernsary Lodge the track forks. Go right. As you climb, the path becomes faint but with common sense and compass and map you will not go far wrong. Keep the large lochs on your left and, immediately past the little loch on your right, bear down to Fionn and Old Boathouse Bay. Follow the south shore, left, to the north end of Fionn, where you will arrive at New Mooring Bay. A good track leads back to the fork in track and Poolewe.

29

The Mountain of the Birds

*B*EINN AN EOIN in Wester Ross is strictly for birds and lovers of wild places. Indeed, the Gaelic name means 'mountain of the birds' and this 2,801-foot peak is home to some of Scotland's most beautiful and elusive species.

Golden eagle nest amongst high corries in nearby Beinn Eighe Nature Reserve, delicately feeding snow-downed chicks on carefully sized morsels of rabbit, hare and anything else stupid enough to move below their fierce gaze. Greenshank flit and pipe over hidden valleys. Dippers dash and splash in shallow, tumbling streams. Snow bunting, dotterel and ptarmigan haunt high tops. Peregrine and raven engage in endless territorial battle. Golden plover dance along the tracks and the hills are loud with the song of curlew, snipe, and sandpiper.

But the grandest prize of all was spotted on 23 June 1970, the first recorded instance of great northern diver nesting in the Highlands of Scotland. Nethersole-Thompson described this historic moment: 'While fishing among wooded islands on a loch in Wester Ross, Eric Hunter saw a large diver with a black head – in sharp contrast to the grey head and hind neck of the black-throated diver. Hunter took no chances. He watched and noted: 'The birds were undoubtedly great northern divers.' This strange diver had two young, which often dived and were hard to see against the background of loch and shore scrub.

Ann and I weren't so lucky when we tramped out into the magnificent wilderness but everything else was perpetual pleasure and for once the weather was spectacularly well behaved – long, cloudless, summer days, warmed by July sun, cooled by soft southerly breezes from the Atlantic. On a calm morning I parked by the hut near Loch Bad an Sgalaig and fell in the troops: Ann, Breac, Heathcliff and me. Our destination, Beinn an Eoinn, Poca Buidhe and Loch na h-Oidhche, 'the loch of the night'.

Civilization lay ten miles distant at Gairloch, where we were staying in one of Harry Davies's cottages at Creag Mhor Hotel. For the time being, however, we were alone amidst a mountain and moorland wonderland, Loch na h-Oidhche is cradled between Beinn an Eoinn to the east and Baosbheinn, 'the wizards' mountain' to the west. From the road, their dark slopes look intimidating. Both are substantial mountains, just below 3,000 feet; but, beside overbearing neighbours, they become mere children.

Slioch spears northwards above the blue waters of island-clad Loch Maree, backed by a mad thrust of Fisherfield peaks. Climbing southwards into the hills, Torridon Mountains line the horizon in splendid array: Beinn Alligin, 'the mountain of beauty'; Beinn Dearag, 'the great rocky peak; Carn na Feola, 'the hill of the flesh'; and, rising above all, the sheer, black, north face of Liathach, 'the grey one'.

Full of hope, we crossed the little wooden bridge over the outlet burn of Am Feur Loch and struck southwards. Well, Ann, Heath-cliff and I crossed the bridge. Breac dashed straight into the stream and had to be dragged protesting from his early morning swim. Heathcliff stayed close to heel; he has a long memory and ingrained distrust of water. Can't say I blame him either, given his Scourie experience.

We caught second breath as the stony path climbed between Meall a Ghlas Leothaid and Meall Lochan a'Chleirich to edge round Meall na Meine. Wet, rough going, down the slope to the valley of Abhainn a'Gharb Choire, the outlet stream from Loch na h-Oidhche. We rested, watching the black and white flash of a dipper darting amongst tiny waterfalls. Breac resumed his interrupted swim and charged upstream as we walked on, Beinn an Eionn now tamed in height by our rising approach.

A final valley and slow climb brought us to a flat, boulder-scattered plateau and shining levels of the loch: a narrow, wind-filled channel, one and a half miles long by almost half a mile wide.

Crystal-clear waters lapping a soft, sandy northern bay. Loch na h-Oidhche contains perfectly matched, beautiful wild brown trout which weigh approximately 12 ounces and fight like the devil. High-summer fishing at its finest.

The slopes of Beinn an Eoin rise steeply from the shores of the loch and a path runs down the east shore; but, to fully appreciate this mystical land, climb the north shoulder and walk along the wide ridge to the summit at the south end. Beyond 'the mountain of the birds' lie Gorm Loch Fada and Gor Loch na Beinne: promontories, fishy corners, sandy bays, tempting weed beds – an angler's delight.

But the most startling aspect of the view is the sudden shock of first sight of Ruadh Stac Mor (3,309 feet), Sail Mor (3,217 feet), and the famous Triple Buttress of A'Chonneach: an amazing, uncompromising howl of mountain pleasure, scarred and screed to the shores of lonely Loch Coire Mhic Fheachair, cupped in its bosom. Beinn Eighe, Liathach, Slioch and Fisherfield summits crowd round with golden moorlands brushing their feet, ribboned with silver streams, specked blue with secret lochans – a Bach-like cathedral world of spire and steeple; a glorious hymn of praise to nature.

Descending from Beinn an Eoinn, we spent the night in the bothy at Poca Buidhe, at the south end of Loch na h-Oidhche, by the yellow stone. In days gone by the hollow below this huge boulder used to provide shelter for 'fishers, stalkers and other liars'; now there is a comfortable, well equipped cottage instead.

The following morning we walked south from Poca Buidhe, across wide granite pavements, over rough, trackless moors. For two hours we tramped in solitude, broken only by startled herds of stately red deer, south to a tiny water between Sail Mor and Carn na Feola called Loch nan Cabar, where we caught lunch. Bearing out prize back to Poca Buidhe, we cooked the small fish and ate royally.

In warm afternoon sun, with rising trout stippling the surface of Loch na h-Oidhche, the sense of peace was a tangible, living thing. You feel small and insignificant; yet, more surely than words can ever explain, you know that you also are an important part of this timeless beauty, with as much right to be there as raven, deer or wild cat. If the hills and mountains of my native land mean anything, that is what they mean to me.

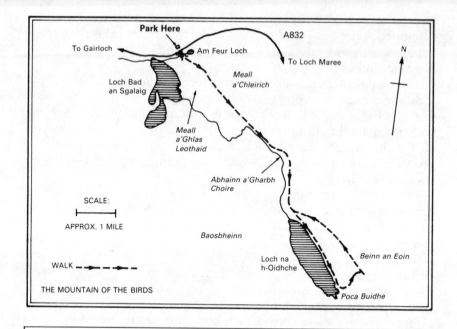

THE MOUNTAIN OF THE BIRDS

WHAT YOU NEED TO KNOW

Time and effort   This is a long, rough walk along a stony, often wet track. The total distance from Loch Bad an Sgalaig via Beinn an Eoin to Poca Buidhe and back is approximately thirteen miles and you should allow six hours. Apart from the long slog and the possibility of bad weather, nothing to worry about. If you plan to walk further south from Poca Buidhe, allow another three hours.

Location   Ordnance Survey Sheet 19, Gairloch and Ullapool second series, scale 1:50,000.

Grid references   Loch Bad an Sgalaig 854713; car park and start point 856721; Loch na h-Oidhche 890887; Beinn an Eoin summit 905646; Poca Buidhe 899644.

Route   Follow the A832 from Gairloch to Loch Maree and about quarter of a mile past Loch Bad an Sgalaig there is a hut on your left. Park here. On your right you will see the wooden bridge that crosses the outlet burn of little Am Feur Loch. Cross this bridge and follow the well marked path south. When you reach Loch na h-Oidhche, climb the north shoulder of Beinn an Eoin and walk south to the summit.

Descend carefully from the top, down the west slope, avoiding the crags at the south end, to Poca Buidhe. From here, either walk further south to explore the moorland between Beinn an Eoin and Liathach, or follow the lochside track northwards, back to the car.

30

Black Isle Fossils and Saints

THE BLACK ISLE is a fertile finger of farmland dividing the Cromarty and Moray firths in north-east Scotland. One explanation of the name is the fact that during harsh northern winters the gentle peninsula is often snow-free when surrounding hills are blanket-white.

A Pictish tribe, known to the Romans as the Decantae, settled and worked the land, blissfully unaware of the turmoil the legions of Rome were causing their southern neighbours. The Roman advance of AD 79 stopped short of Ross-shire, on the south shores of the Moray Firth, and the Picts were left largely to their own devices, to flourish, struggle, and eventually perish at the hands of invading Norsemen. However, these stern Vikings soon succumbed to the persuasive ministrations of the infant thrusting nation of Scots.

One of the Black Isle's most famous sons was Hugh Miller, a stonemason and self-taught geologist of extraordinary ability. He was born in 1802 in the little village of Cromarty, once a busy fishing port, now a cluster of neat houses and holiday homes lining the far north-east shore of the Isle. Hugh Miller's thatched cottage is cared for by the National Trust for Scotland and is now an orderly museum, depicting the life and work of this well-loved humble man of Ross.

Hugh Miller discovered and explored the fossil fish of the Black Isle Syncline, rocks of the Old Red Sandstone period, 350–400 million years old, and described his findings in a book, *The Old Red Sandstone*, published in 1841. I visited the neat cottage to prepare myself for a walk to Hugh Miller's fossil beds, and came away head ringing with strange names but with a clearer picture of our ancient lands and a better understanding of what I hoped to see by the wild shores of the Moray Firth.

On a warm, autumn day, I parked at Eathie Mains Farm and walked back up the road to the end of a mixed plantation of new conifers and old hardwoods. The locked gate is crossed by a wooden stile and a track follows the side of the wood, red-soiled and muddy. Golden barley, heads drooping for harvest, waved and rustled in a soft breeze.

Stately foxgloves lined the woodside bank, watched by lazy bluebells sleeping amidst roots of gnarled oak. The wind whispered through friendly beech, brown with winter's coming. Tiny yellow-headed tormentil peaked at my passing from purple heather and that ultimate botanical survivor, rose-bay willow-herb, grew in profusion along the track.

The sad stones of a ruined croft lie tumbled in a field close to a reed-fringed pond, alive with the hum and buzz of insects, and at the next gate a notice reminds me to 'beware of young trees'. Attacked by bulls and angry farmers, yes, but young trees? I stopped at the gate to munch a good Scots pie, watched closely by a brightly dressed chaffinch, waiting hopefully for crumbs.

The track winds to the top of the cliff where there is a first glimpse of water – the Moray Firth, shimmering, heat-haze-hung to the distant outline of Inverness-shire. Larks twitter and a female corn bunting bustles by, busy with something or other in yellow-flowered whins. On the silver-blue sea an oil tanker heads ocean-wards, small and insignificant against the horizon, and the track plunges down the cliff by heather banks and clumps of orange-yellow ragwort. Butterflies dance in afternoon sunlight amidst gossamer spider webs and the deep throb of the tanker's engine reverberates underfoot.

Black-backed gulls raise noisy protest as I reach the shore by Eathie Fishing Bothy. Southwards, the finger of Chanory Point, crowned by white lighthouse, reaches across the firth to the gaunt symmetry of Fort George, completed in 1769 and used ever since as military barracks. The oil-rig construction yard at Ardersier throws up dark steeples of steel, stark against green and gold Nairnshire fields.

A narrow track runs along the edge of the stony beach, through banks of meadowsweet and tangled rose-hip bushes. Stumbling time, eyes down, watching for pitfalls. After a few hundred yards I am forced onto the boulder-strewn shore. A family of pied wagtails flit and dart welcome on the rocks. Suppose they are being taught the rudiments of feeding; seaweed-covered rocks abound with insects for practice. The parent birds work hard, encouraging their youngsters to ever greater efforts.

Now a different sound of water, and I discover Eathie Gorge, with the old stream chattering down the narrow glen to the sea. More than one hundred years past, Hugh Miller searched for fossils here. I sit on a rock, looking out to sea, surrounded by millennia of history.

Wild, ancient rocks; jagged, red, black, blue, white and grey. Finely weathered into fantastic shapes and patterns, as old as when our world first burst from the darkness of limitless space. Strange marks scar their surface, painting a picture of gasping life struggling from the ocean: 'calcareous shales, containing hard limey nodules with occasional fragments of primitive armour-plated fish'.

The sides of the gorge are a monstrous tangle of birch and bracken, specked yellow with patches of fallen sand, wrenched from the raised beach that runs the length of the south shore. The burn sings softly and I feel a presence: people watching. I turn, expecting to see them, these fantasy figures of my mind, as Hugh Miller saw them – the fairies of Eathie Glen.

I walked eastwards, across the awesome saw-edged rocks, and arrived at a single grass- and daisy-covered stack, linked to the shore by a tide-washed stony causeway. Just the place for lunch, sheltering in the warm lee, lazy lingering. Sleep comes easy here. Too easy. I awoke with a start to find the waves washing the stones and had a wet mad scramble back to the shore.

Round the next headland, where massive rocks have been torn from the cliff and tumbled onto the shore, lies my goal – St Bennet's Well. An inquisitive wheatear guides me through the boulders, white-tailed, bobbing ahead. Then the final bay, watched by a half-hidden ruined shoreside shack, full of dust and old fishing nets.

Alder, birch and willow and waist-high ferns hide the site of the well. I stumble through the tangle until I almost fall into a soft, mossy, emerald-green pool, where the saintly Bennet no doubt stooped to drink. Me, I'm just wet. Retreating to the shore, I sit on a throne-like rock in evening sunlight, tide at my feet, brown-edged waves smoothing wrinkled sand. Fulmers cruise by, stiff-winged. I watch, like some ornithological king presiding over his screaming, squabbling, myriad sea-gull courtiers.

Hard to leave – to start the shore-side stumble, past the fantastic fossil beds, back to Eathie Bothy and up the cliff. On the stiff climb, an anxious lizard scurries across the dusty path. Drops of sweat splash at my feet, I rest. Northwards, the mountain circle of Ben Wyvis colours and changes as clouds throw endless shadows scudding from corrie to summit. A robin, bright-eyed and cheerful, speaks from the stile, keeping me company through the last moments of my sea-walked fairy-spell day.

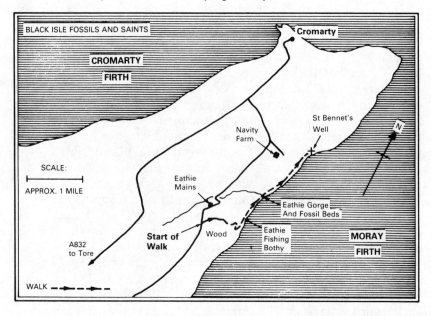

WHAT YOU NEED TO KNOW

Time and effort Visit Hugh Miller's Cottage in Cromarty first, 17½ miles east of the new roundabout at Tore on the Black Isle. Turn eastwards along the A832. This is a National Trust property, with museum and video display of Hugh Miller's life. Open to the public from Easter to 30 September, Monday–Saturday, 10 a.m. to noon and 1–5 p.m.; Sundays 2–5 p.m., June to September only. Choose a good day for the walk and try to avoid a south wind, blowing onto the shore. The only real effort required is going up and down the cliff. This should be taken gently. Wear stout shoes. The track can be muddy and the shore is rocky. The walk takes four hours, allowing for time to stop and stare.

Location Ordnance Survey Sheet 27, Nairn, second series, scale 1:50,000.

Grid references Cromarty 787675; Eathie Mains Farm 771639; Eathie Wood 769636; Eathie Fishing Bothy 777635; Eathie Gorge and fossil beds 784641; St Bennet's Well 792651.

Route Park the car at Eathie Mains Farm, making sure that you first ask permission to do so. Turn right out of the farm and walk back up the road to the small wood on your left. There is a red-painted gate with a stile over. This is the start of the walk. Follow the track over the field and, eventually, down onto the beach. Turn left and walk on to Eathie Gorge and St Bennet's Well. Return the same way.

31

Stac Polly Saga

ANN AND I arrived late. The drive from Caithness to Assynt had been difficult – busy, fog-blanketed roads crowded by motorists with little experience of driving on single-track northern highways. The concept of using passing places to allow overtaking was beyond them. Darkness had fallen by the time we reached Ledmore Junction and turned down the thankfully wide A836 to Elphin.

The old school building at Elphin is used by parties of young people, accompanied by their teachers, as a base from which to explore the surrounding area. This time there had been difficulty in getting a female adult to join the group, in order to keep tabs on the two girls present. I could understand why this was necessary because one of the young ladies requiring tabbing was my daughter, Lewis-Ann.

Ann had been roped in to help – much to Lewis-Ann's discomfort. She had been looking forward to a weekend off the lead with her love of the moment, a large, lanky, speechless boy much given to nose picking and occasional grunts. I tagged along to provide moral support, and to introduce a few of the gang to the fine art of fly fishing.

This was our first visit to Assynt and I rose after a near-sleepless night on a near-springless bed to introduce myself to our new surroundings. Stumbling outside, cursing the weak moment when I had agreed to come, I rubbed sleep from my eyes, and gawped!

Mountains crowded round, startlingly near. I reached out to touch them. Early morning sunlight etched their graceful shapes in a cloudless blue sky. I had never seen anything so magnificent. Which was the start of our love affair with Assynt, Inverpolly and Coighach. We have been returning ever since to walk and fish amidst this awesome mountain and moorland wilderness.

Stac Polly is an old friend: 2,009 feet of crazy peaks and pinnacles. The view from the top is one of the finest in Scotland: island-studded Loch Sionascaig, wandering seventeen twisting miles round hidden bays and dark headlands; a glimpse of tiny Lochan Dearg a'Chuil Mhoir, nestling in the corries of Cul Mor. That great Scottish poet Norman MacCaig, in his poem 'Musical Moment in Assynt', said of Cul Mor: 'And God was Mozart when he wrote Cul Mor.'

Northwards, Suilven, the Vikings 'pillar mountain', thrusts its grey saddled bulk skywards; Suilven's crown, Caisteal Liath, the 'grey castle', towers over desolate, tree-less moors. Quinag and Ben More Assynt line the horizon and the gentle shoulder of Canisp strides by Veyatie and crooked Loch Cama.

Southwards, above the blue and silver of Loch Lurgainn, Ben More Coigach praises the heavens, knifed by the sandstone edge of Sgurr an Fhidhleir, Sgurr Tuath and Sgorr Deas. Across the golden Summer Isles lie the mountains of Harris and Lewis, abed amidst Atlantic haze, Skye Cuillins and majestic An Teallach guarding 'destitution road' at Dundonnell.

One of our favourite walks starts from the old quarry by Linneraineach, on the road between Drumrunie and Achiltibuie. The track follows a fence line, leading gently over the west hip of Cul Beag and down to Loch an Doire Dhuibh, then round little Loch Lon na h-Uamha and up the north face of Stac Polly. A glorious introduction to the delights of Inverpolly, climaxed by a panoramic view from the summit.

However, recently, I made a quicker visit to Stac Polly. In fact three quicker visits, all in pursuit of the photograph which adorns the front of this book. After a meeting in Lairg concerning the damage being done to the north by mass afforestation, I dashed westwards hoping to zip up and snap a gripping sunset. My only companions were Breac, my golden retriever, a self-focusing camera and a tripod.

Littered like a *War of the Worlds* combatant, I approached Polly from the large car park where Lurgainn narrows and struggled up the hill, tripod banging awkardly, Breac bounding ahead, panting to the rocky promontory below the crest on the east flank. Me panting, not the dog. Late afternoon sun was sinking, so, ignoring a growing gale, I set to work with gusto. Position camera, adjust tripod, mark my spot, call Breac to heel, press self-timer, dash to mark.

On the basis that only one out of every hundred photographs I take is usable, I had brought along five million films, and I danced around the rocks, grimacing and leering from all possible angles. Just before shot number 35 of the first reel, whilst I was adopting a particularly dramatic stance, peering eyes shaded into the distance, disaster struck.

The look on my face turned to one of horror as I watched the tripod collapse, blown over by the wind. Tripod and camera hit the deck and the camera back flew open, ruining an hour of jaw-breaking smiles. Worse, the camera was badly damaged, so there was no possibility of starting again. Unsure whether to laugh or cry, I did both and shuffled sadly downhill to face the 130-mile drive home.

My family are very supportive. They can be relied upon to rally round when things go wrong – as they frequently do with me. First, however, I had to keep my hands from their heads as they fell about laughing when I described what had happened. New plans were laid. Ann would accompany me the following morning and take charge of the situation. I was to do nothing other than what I was told, pretty damn quick, no arguing.

Off early at 4 a.m. to catch sunrise. Dawn broke as we reached the car park. So did the weather. Torrential rain, thick mist and not even a finger in front of your nose to be seen, let alone Stac Polly. We sat in the car, sipping coffee. After all, it is well known that west coast weather changes quickly. It did, and got worse. After four hours we abandoned hope and drove home: another wasted 260-mile round trip.

Plan B was then activated. We decided that at the first hint of a good day we would drop everything and dash. Three days later we awoke to a perfect morning, not a cloud in sight and the promise of hours of highly photogenic weather. Within minutes we were in the car, speeding south over the Ord of Caithness, hell-bent for Stac Polly.

Everything went superbly and there were no accidents. I did as I was told and Ann did the camera work. Hard, keeping my mouth shut for such a long time. Hard also keeping warm, whilst we waited for the sun to move along Coigach and Inverpolly crests in order to capture the best shots.

Still, as with most things, Ann had the answer. In between taking photographs, we warmed ourselves by going up and down Stac Polly, like yo-yos. I lost count of the number of times I stumbled up the broken muddy track on the north face. 'Come on, Ann, give it a rest, for goodness sake. I'm knackered.'

Her reply was predictable: 'No arguing I said and no arguing I meant. Stop moaning and get a move on.' By the end of the day I knew every inch of the hill; but I was as warm as toast. When we reached home that evening, for the first time ever Breac was really exhausted – a stone-like golden heap of mud-bespattered dog. I joined him, just as stone-like, and slept the sleep of the just. As we professional photographers say, it was 'in the can'.

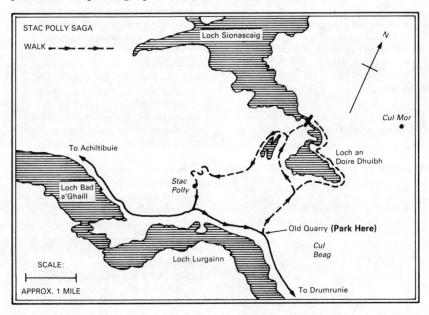

WHAT YOU NEED TO KNOW

Time and effort   The walk from
Linneraineach Quarry, round Loch
an Doire Dhuibh, then up and over
Stac Polly, takes about four hours.
You may extend this by turning
right at Doire Dhuibh and going
round the north shore, crossing the
stream by an old bridge just before
the river flows into Loch
Sionascaig.

This is an easy walk with a good
track most of the way, but the hike
over the moor to the north face of
Stac Polly is rough going, so be
well-shod. The hike up Polly is a
brief, fierce, stiff climb. Take it
easy. No prizes for being there first.

If you do this walk in winter,
remember that the north face of
Stac Polly is hidden from the sun
for most of the day. Consequently,
ice will still cling to the rocks,
making them very dangerous. The
greatest care is advised in all your
movements.

Location   Ordnance Survey
Sheet 15, Loch Assynt, second
series, scale 1:50,000.

Grid references   Drumrunie
166055; Linneraineach Quarry
126090; Loch an Doire Dhuibh
135107; Loch Lon na h-Uamha
128109; Stac Polly 108106; Stac
Polly car park 108096.

Route   Park in the old quarry and
walk up the hill, following the
fence line. The track is well
marked. As you come down the
flank of Cul Beg, which is on your
right, a track branches off left. Go
straight on if you want a slightly
longer walk. If not, bear left and
follow the track between the two
lochs. Walk round the north end of
the small loch and head straight up
the hill towards Stac Polly. As you
near the rocky summit, look out for
small cairns which line the narrow
path up to the top. This path is
rough but well defined and it leads
you in a gentle series of zigzags to
the crest.

Descend from Stac Polly down
the steep south face. Descend with
maximum caution. The slope is
spread with loose rocks. Once off
the crest, a wide, soggy track takes
you downhill to the car park. At the
car park, turn left and walk along
the road back to the quarry.

32
Salmon and Suilven

A FEW MILES north from Inverpolly National Nature Reserve
near Inverkirkaig, Ross-shire and Sutherland meet. A narrow
road crosses Aird of Coigach, twisting and turning towards
Sutherland past deep roadside lochans, reaching the sea at Loch an
Eisg-brachaidh – a bay of tide-marked rocky islands, alive with
Atlantic waves endlessly threatening to tear the little road from the
hillside.

Ann and I left early that morning, packing lunch and dogs with
urgent speed, bound for Kirkaig river, Fionn Loch and Suilven. But
the sudden sparkle of sea at Eisg stopped us and we were happy to
watch awhile as curlew and sandpiper went about their business.
Oystercatchers poked moodily amongst seaweed-covered stones
and a seal popped up to say hello. It was the sort of morning when

you knew that all was right with the world.

This was a special day, our silver wedding anniversary, and we planned to celebrate it properly, on Caisteal Liath, Suilven's rounded western peak. Vikings called the mountain Sul-fjall, the pillar mountain, for, as they edged their longships cautiously down Assynt's rocky coast, they saw only the huge bulk of Suilven's west face, rearing above Loch Inver Bay in a mighty sandstone tower.

Suilven is one of Scotland's most dramatic and most inaccessible mountains. You have to work hard to get there. It hearts Glencanisp Forest and no matter how you approach there is a five-mile moorland tramp before reaching the lower slopes. The mountain is only a modest 2,399 feet in height and yet, seen from a distance, towering over a loch-sprinkled landscape, Suilven is a lordly masterpiece of ancient Lewisian gneiss and Torridonian sandstone.

There are four principal lines of attack: from the east from Ledmore Junction and round Cama, the crooked loch; from the north-west, via the estate road and the beautiful Glencanisp Lodge; from the south by following the Kirkaig river; and, perhaps easiest, up the long ribbon of Loch Veyatie by boat. For us, all routes are dangerous because they skirt superb trout lochs, and we find it hard to resist the temptation to stop and fish, getting nowhere fast in the process.

Which is why we planned our visit in April, when only the most foolhardy fish rise and only the most foolhardy anglers brave biting cold to catch them at it. Highland April fanfares spring. Days fight and squabble over whether or not to be reasonable or wild. Sunny mornings change suddenly to nightmare storms. Good weather is a matter of luck and nothing is predictable – other than that you are going to be wet, dry, hot and cold probably several times each day.

Our base was at Achiltibuie in the Summer Isles, where we had rented a comfortable, well equipped cottage for the duration. During summer months this is a busy, popular tourist area but, in early April, delightfully deserted. Days were spent walking in Coigach and Assynt; evenings, relaxing, reading, and watching Turner sunsets from the panorama window overlooking the bay. After a quick dash to the pub.

Before setting off up Kirkaig, Ann and I visited Achins bookshop at the end of a little track leading from the bridge over the river – surely the remotest bookshop in Britain. Alex and Agnes Dickson preside over a stock of 15,000 volumes and have built up the business to include a library service and an excellent range of woollens and tweeds, deerskin, hornware, pottery and paintings.

The path to Suilven follows a good track along the north bank, past deep, silent pools where salmon lie. They run Kirkaig from

March onwards and fishing for them requires strength, skill and feet like a mountain goat's. Near the head of the river are spectacular falls, plunging sixty feet into a dark, sombre, cliff-crowded pool. Instructions for landing salmon from the pool are as follows:

'Slide down to the right-hand side of the fishing stance, and onto a ledge. There is a rope attached to the rock as a handhold. When the fish is gaffed, both gaff and fish are handed up to the angler, who must take care not to let the fish off the gaff and drop on the head of his gillie!'

During the long, slow climb Suilven is hidden from view and it is not until you reach Fionn Loch, the white loch, that Suilven's full majesty is revealed. From the boat mooring bay, across smooth blue waters, the bulk of Caisteal Liath, the grey castle, challenges you to climb him. Skirt loch and at the little sandy bay on the north shore stride across rock-strewn lower slopes to do so.

A wide, steep gully leads upwards to the centre of the mountain, Bealach Mor. No matter what anyone says, a gut-busting scramble. From Bealach Mor a broad ridge points to the summit of Caisteal Liath – sheer round three sides, unexpectedly grassy and sparkled with quartzite boulders on top. More hardy souls than I traverse eastwards along the narrow crest to Meall Mheadhonach, which requires great care and a head for heights.

By the time Ann and I reached Fionn Loch the weather had turned nasty, and decided to stay nasty. We huddled frozen, sheltering by a peat hag, surveying wind-lashed waves screaming down Fionn. Over rims of steaming mugs of coffee, we watched Caisteal Liath disappear in a flurry of snow. Clouds crept down Bealach Mor and soon the whole mountain was hidden from view. To attempt the climb in these conditions would be courting disaster. Discretion and valour time.

But it was hard to leave that wild place and we lingered, thoughtful, silent. Two thirty arrived, the hour when we were hitched near Tron Kirk in the old grey city of Edinburgh.

'What are you thinking, Ann?' I asked.

'You know,' she replied, 'some people would think it madness to spend their wedding anniversary freezing in a snow storm on the shores of a Highland loch.'

I paused, wondering. 'Do you?'

'Of course not, there is no place I would rather be. Happy anniversary, dear.'

Calling dogs to heel, we turned our backs on Suilven and tramped down to Kirkaig. The champagne was on ice, ready waiting at Achiltibuie.

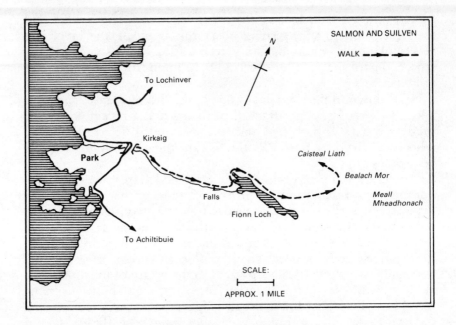

SALMON AND SUILVEN

WALK ▪ ➤ ▪ ➤ ▪ ➤

N

To Lochinver

Kirkaig

Park

Caisteal Liath

Bealach Mor

Meall
Mheadhonach

Falls

Fionn Loch

To Achiltibuie

SCALE:

APPROX. 1 MILE

WHAT YOU NEED TO KNOW

Time and effort   A full day's
time and effort. The Kirkaig
approach to Suilven is an easy,
rising walk. Bealach Mor will test
your fitness and stamina, but there
is no need to hurry so take your
time and enjoy the climb. Treat the
summit of Suilven with respect.
Reaching Caisteal Liath is simple
and safe; Meall Mheadhonach
requires caution and is best left
alone if you are inexperienced.

Location   Ordnance Survey
Sheet 15, Loch Assynt, second
series, scale 1:50,000.

Grid references   Loch an Eisg-
brachaidh 073176; car park 086194;
Kirkaig Falls 121179; mooring bay
on Fionn 124177; Bealach Mor
158181; Caisteal Liath 154184;
Meall Mheadhonach 165178.

Route   There is a good car park
near the bridge at Kirkaig river.
The Fionn–Suilven track leads
eastwards from the bridge, through
a gate on the north bank of the
river. Follow your nose. You have
to divert right from the path to
view Kirkaig Falls. Take care in wet
weather.

   By prior arrangement, shorten
your walk by rowing across Fionn
to the north shore. Permission to
do so from Culag Hotel in
Lochinver. Otherwise, tramp
round the west shore and then angle
towards Bealach Mor, which is
easily recognisable. From there on
in it's up. The view from the top is
worth every gasp.

33

Canisp and
Inchnadamph Caves

CANISP is a lady. Mature, gentle, serene and welcoming. Her neighbours are more brusque: the sudden, male shock of Suilven 'one sandstone chord that holds up time in space'; masculine Ben More Assynt, long-ridged and pinnacled; the triple sweep of Quinag and corried Cul Mor. Eleven miles of Assynt mountains, none of which falls below 2,000 feet.

Ann and I parked at the roadside by Loch Awe, a tiny shadow of its famous Argyllshire namesake but none the less beautiful – shallow, clear waters, bursting with bright, red-spotted brown trout and an occasional surprise of salmon. Seven scrub- and tree-clad islands scatter Awe, protected by Cnoc an Leathaid Bhuidhe to the west and Beinn an Fhuarain to the east.

Above Loch Awe, Canisp's grey, boulder-strewn shoulder lies like an old dun-coloured skirt; patched purple with heather, silver-threaded by sparkling streams. The walk to the summit (2,779 feet) is an easy three-mile couple of hours' stroll. Indeed, most climbing books describe Canisp as nothing more than a good viewpoint from which to survey surrounding peaks, which is less than true and completely false on the day we chose to mount our assault – mid-April with winter snows covering tops.

Assynt forms the southern boundary between Sutherland and Ross-shire and many years ago the exact boundary line was disputed. In an attempt to end argument, two senior Ross-shire citizens, having first been reminded that their 'feet were on oath', were instructed to walk the marches. They did so, claiming never once to have left Ross-shire soil. Nor had they, for they had filled their shoes with earth from Balnagowan in Easter Ross.

This Highland astuteness is commemorated in the name of the hotel that used to stand at the county boundary on the A837 from Bonar Bridge to Ledmore Junction, Altnacealgach, 'burn of the cheat'. The hotel was once famous throughout Scotland for quality of food, service and sport; but it declined badly and was ravaged by fire in 1985. The last time I passed, even these sad, blackened ruins had been demolished and all sign of the once happy hotel gone.

As we sat in the car by Loch Awe, Canisp looked a daunting prospect. Spring storms raged across the loch, tearing water to shreds, flinging a fine, wet spray over chill moors. The snow line was ominously low. If we wished to reach the top, then we were in for some cold, rough tramping.

Nevertheless, from time to time sun broke through encouragingly and we were prepared for the weather. So, light of heart, we dragged on boots, wrapped up, crossed the outlet stream from Loch Awe and set off uphill, dogs bounding ahead, excited, through the heather.

A faint path pointed the way past lead-grey lochans and, as we climbed, heather receded, giving way to patches of bare, slippery sandstone rock. Weather didn't recede and we were soon walking into the teeth of a howling blizzard. Even the dogs became subdued and we sheltered together, huddled in an untidy human-animal heap. Sunshine again. On up the slow, never-ending slope. Glimpses through the storm of our goal, snow-crowned, shining on the horizon. Then more biting wind-driven sleet.

At about fifteen hundred feet, an amazing tree – someone has planted a little rowan. The infant is protected from Canisp storms by a well built circular wall. Wonder if the tree will survive? Into snow now, hard-packed, thin-crusted over hollows. Every step ever-increasing effort. Summit is cloud-blinded. I feel my body freezing. The animals are miserable. Two thousand five hundred feet. Conference time. We turned back.

Skirting Meall Diamhain we picked up the line of Allt Mhic Mhurchadh Gheir, a long name for such a little stream, the principal feeder burn of Loch Awe. With wicked inconsistency bright sun broke through grey skies and we quickly peeled off heavy layers of clothing, basking in welcome spring warmth. The dogs recovered their spirits and Breac splashed downstream, in and out of crystal-clear limestone pools.

If ever you seek a secret, beautiful place for a family picnic or quiet summer laze, then the upper reaches of this magical burn will provide that location. Even little ones should manage the walk and I know of few more delightful spots in all the Highlands. We arrived back at the car with time to spare and decided to adopt plan B – a visit to Inchnadamph Nature Reserve, a few miles north-east of Loch Awe.

Inchnadamph Hotel is the best centre from which to explore Assynt, a whitewashed fishing and climbing hotel peering west-wards down a wild loch. Willie Morrison presides, greeting guests and visitors alike with old-world Highland charm. Inchnadamph is surrounded by massive limestone outcrops which provide an ideal habitat for rare alpine plants such as sawwort, hawkweed and purple and mountain saxifrage.

Behind the hotel, up Traligill Burn, are the famous Inchnadamph Caves, deep underground passages some five hundred yards long filled with rushing waters. Traligill is the Norse name for Troll's Gill, or Giant's Ravine, and it is believed that mesolithic man inhabited these caves more than six thousand years ago.

We gratefully inhabited one of the caves that afternoon, shelter-ing from another storm that drove huge snowflakes into our numb faces. Then, suddenly, threatening clouds departed, sun shone and

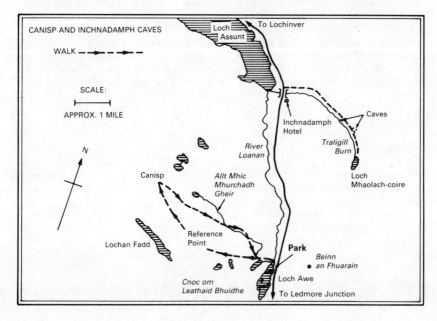

glorious Assynt sparkled before us – the same view hunter-gatherers of old must have blessed and cursed during their endless search for food.

To the north-west the Torridonian bulk of Quinag, snow-capped and glistening, guarding the head of Loch Assynt; graceful, unclimbed Canisp towering to the south-west; whilst above us corries and crags of Conival and Ben More Assynt crowded round. Every step of our day-long snow-swept journey was made worthwhile by that single, stunning, humbling vision. We knew we had found something precious: another wonderful memory for the dream bank of the mind.

WHAT YOU NEED TO KNOW

Time and effort In reasonable conditions, this is an easy, delightful walk offering spectacular views from the summit. Seven miles there and back; about four hours. However, take care in bad weather and always go with compass and map. North-east and south-west sides are very steep near the top and, in misty conditions, dangerous.

The walk to the Inchnadamph limestone caves is without problems, other than making sure that you find them all. Ask Willie Morrison in the hotel for additional directions before setting out. Allow about three hours for the round trip.

Location Ordnance Survey Sheet 15, Loch Assynt, second series, scale 1:50,000.

Grid references Park at 249158; Loch Awe 246154; Reference point on hill 229168; summit 204188; stream 232172; Inchnadamph Hotel 251216; limestone caves 272207.

Route There is ample car parking space, off the road, by Loch Awe. Cross the outlet burn at the north end of the loch and find your way up the broad, wide shoulder of the hill. From the top, descend the same way, but angle left to find Allt Mhic Mhurchadh Gheir burn. Follow this back to Loch Awe and the car.

For Inchnadamph limestone caves, park by the hotel and follow the good track that borders the Traligill Burn. There are signposts and you should have no problem finding the caves. One cave is actually in the riverbed. The others are on the south side of Traligill, by the track that leads out to Loch Mhaolach-coire, known locally as the Gillaroo Loch.

34

Seals and Sandwood

THE GREAT fleet sailed south. One hundred warships sparkled with long lines of shields, oars dipping in unison, powered by fierce, merciless men. Men to whom murder came easy. Their leader was old, in a time of youth when survival was chance and old age remarkable. King Haakon of Norway surveyed his force with eagle eyes: eight thousand men, battle-hardened from a hundred fights.

But this was to be Haakon's last battle. Within a few weeks, many of these ships would lie wrecked off the coast at Largs, destroyed by September gales and the cunning of a mere boy – the 22-year-old Scottish monarch, Alexander III. Viking power was broken and Haakon died in Orkney, shepherding the shattered remnants of his fleet home.

When I walk the wild hills and cliffs of the Parph Peninsula I imagine I see this mighty fleet, sailing past Sandwood Bay to meet its doom. Parph means 'turning point' and in August 1263, the year of the Battle of Largs, the Vikings rested weary arms in the long finger of Loch Inchard, close to where the busy fishing port of Kinlochbervie now stands.

Two longships had foundered in heavy seas off A'Chailleach and

Am Bodach – the 'old man' and 'old woman', twin stacks guarding the way south from Cape Wrath. Survivors tried to climb the 300-foot cliffs and the marks of their desperate axe strokes still scar the crags. Six others were killed earlier, when a foraging party was ambushed at Loch Eriboll by clan MacKay, sending Vikings scurrying foodless back to their ships.

The Parph is edged by huge cliffs; 850 foot Cleit Dubh, the 'black cliff', is the highest on mainland Britain. A rutted road wends over desolate moorlands to squat, whitewashed Cape Wrath Lighthouse, completed in 1829. The building stands 370 feet above the sea and its light can be seen from a distance of almost thirty miles. Southwards, Fashven, Creag Riabhach and Farrmheall rise gently from peat-covered moors, and the only way in is by foot.

Sandwood Bay is the most beautiful bay in Scotland. Almost two miles of golden sand, washed clean by long, wind-fringed, blue-green Atlantic breakers born a thousand miles away, sweeping across the ocean to caress desolate Scottish shores. Rocky outcrops, black, sea-sprayed promontories, strut aggressively into the middle of the bay, challenging the elements in an endless battle of surf and thunder.

Northwards, sands mingle with emerald slopes that stride upwards in an amazing array of jagged, dark, stark cliffs, marching to Cape Wrath. South, the slim stack of Am Buachaille, 'the herdsman', breaks the waves in their rush to greet Druim na Buainn. Behind Sahara sand dunes, Sandwood Loch sparkles in summer sunlight, surrounded by green fields specked white with grazing sheep. This is a special, wonderful place. The birthplace of silence. Where time stops and life begins.

This remote corner of north-west Sutherland is one of our secret retreats, frequented by piratical skuas, presided over by golden eagles. When slings and arrows beleaguer flagging spirits Ann and I escape to the Parph, and nothing ever seems so bad when we return. Walking refreshes bits thinking can't reach and there are few finer walks in Scotland than from Oldshoremore to Sandwood.

The road from Laxford Bridge, the A838, turns and twists northwards through a wilderness of heather-clad moorlands, past tiny lochans glimpsed with red-throated divers and hungry grey heron. It climbs, single-tracked, by tumbling, rocky torrents to Rhiconich at the head of Loch Inchard. Turning west to Kinloch-bervie is a cultural shock. One moment, wild Highlands; the next, dual carriageway and heavy industry.

Kinlochbervie, packed with piers and boats, is the most important port in Sutherland. Heavy lorries trundle off, loaded with the best of Scottish sea harvest bound for European markets. Those prawns, shrimps and lobsters we gobble greedily whilst on holiday probably passed this way, edging you off the road in the process. Wagons return crowded with Spanish tomatoes and other Continental fruit and vegetables.

Past the port Highland life returns to normal – narrow road bounded by empty hills, sudden clusters of cottages and a heady smell of peat smoke in the air. There are a number of fine, sandy bays along the way; by the crofts at Oldshoremore and Oldshore Beg and just after Blairmore, a notice points north to Sandwood.

Foolhardy or high-wheelbased motorists drive the first two miles of the track leading to Sandwood. Since our last damaged radiator, we park on the road and hoof it. Much more enjoyable, and much less costly. There are tracks and tracks. Some quickly wear you out; others bore you with blank vistas. But this track is the perfect gentleman of all tracks.

A chain of seven shining lochs line the route and the path threads by them. Loch na Gainimh, complete with inviting rowing boat for attacking hard-fighting, red-speckled wild brown trout; delightful a'Mhuilinn, where the track spills onto the sandy east shore, begging you to abandon Sandwood and follow its margins into the hills. My golden retriever, Breac, likes this loch best of all: he swims along, parallel to our progress, and has to be sternly ordered out at the end.

From the highest point of the track the white speck of Cape Wrath Lighthouse blinks above green-brown hills. Reay Forest mountains, bare, scree-scattered, grey peaks, uncompromisingly climb to billowy clouds – the razor-edge of Foinaven and bulky Arkle. Soft winds blow from the dark-gashed gully of Bealach Coir a'Choin, calling you in.

Suddenly, Sandwood Loch, watched by a shepherd's cottage, surrounded by sheepfolds and old stones. Moorland becomes lime-rich pasture, blushing with wild flowers. Then, the glorious, breathtaking, golden sweep of the bay. Footprintless, virgin sands, washed by green seas, surging onto an empty beach.

This is where Sandy Gunn saw his mermaid, sitting on a rocky ledge, gazing wistfully out to sea. At least, that's what Sandy, a local shepherd, reported later; and I believe him. Ann and I were resting on these same rocks last October, watching the endless ballet of dancing, sparkling waves, when a movement in the surf caught our eye. It seemed to be human and, remembering Sandy Gunn's experience, I fumbled for my camera. This would be the photograph of the century and I wanted to be ready.

A young seal was playing in the breakers, surfing to the shore and then swimming out again to repeat the ride. It splashed and

turned, clearly enjoying a moment of most un-seal-like irresponsi-
bility. We watched, transfixed, as the graceful beast turned and
tumbled in the foam.

A large wave washed the seal almost onto the sands and, unaware
of our presence, he flapped ashore in a series of ungainly shuffles.
We could see the whiskered face and bright, black, intelligent eyes
as he settled on the sands to while away a comforting moment in
warm afternoon sun.

After a while, we put the dogs onto their leads and walked
towards the sleeping seal. From about twenty-five yards, he saw us
and decided the sea was a safer place, although we wished him no
harm. We waited as he struggled afloat. The dogs were breathless
with excitement and I slipped Breac. He dashed to the shore,
sniffing furiously, then plunged in. Not a chance, old fellow, I
thought; though I'm sure that they would have been great pals,
given the chance.

A dark head appeared above white foam and we responded with
a cherry wave, thankful for the pleasure he had given us. Then we
turned sadly from the beach to begin the long walk home. The
hardest part was leaving, and we lingered at the top of the hill,
looking longingly back to lovely Sandwood Bay.

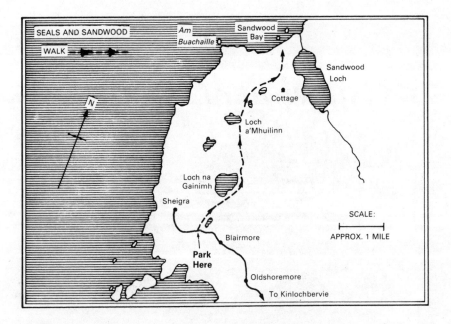

WHAT YOU NEED TO KNOW

Time and effort There and back, this walk is a distance of eight miles along a well defined, easy track. How long it takes depends upon how long you choose to stay at Sandwood Bay. Be warned, once you have seen Sandwood, that could be for ever.

The track is rough so wear stout shoes. Also, be prepared for some muddy splashing after wet weather. Because the walk is relatively simple, it is possible to lug along more than one would perhaps normally carry. Include camera, binoculars and sketch-pad; water colours would be nice too.

Location Ordnance Survey Sheet 9, Cape Wrath, second series scale 1:50,000.

Grid references Laxford Bridge 237468; Rhiconich 255524; Kinlochbervie 220565; Oldshoremore 209585; start of track 195600; Loch na Gainimh 204614; Loch a'Mhuilinn 207630; Sandwood Bay 220650.

Route Drive west from Rhiconich, through Kinlochbervie and Oldshoremore to Blairmore. A few hundred yards past Blairmore you will see a signpost to Sandwood Bay on your right. Park off the road and follow the track. Simple as that. Can't go wrong, but take the map anyway, just in case.

35

Sinking at Scourie

THEY TOOK me for my first real walk when I was six months old. Ten trackless miles across Sutherland moors. I have learned since that puppies should not be exposed to such rigours until at least a year old, but it didn't harm me. Other, that is, than instilling a fear of water – and that was my own fault anyway.

Yorkshire by heritage, I was born and brought up in the old, grey city of Edinburgh. Early days were spent happily under the dining room table, playing with brothers and sisters – a boisterous lot, always ready for a bit of bite-and-tumble. I suppose, being terriers, that's understandable.

Liked the big fellow the moment he appeared in the room, and I rushed round, giving of my best, trying to impress. You see, I heard him say that his wife was a Yorkshire lass and I knew immediately this was the family for me.

My sisters backed off, growling, sensing that silk cushions and fancy ribbons would never be achieved in a home ruled by Him. But who needs ribbons? Should I want to be a canine poof? Great-grandfather Bert, miner's pal all his life, would turn in his grave. So I scuttled to the huge feet and flashed a bright, 9-carat, ear-splitting grin, which secured my future instantly.

That first walk, however, was something else and I confess that there were moments when I wondered if I had done the right thing. Inexperience. After all, coming from Edinburgh, how was I to know the mallard wasn't really injured? She flapped about as though in big trouble. Naturally, I ignored fledglings and chased after her. What would you have done?

Which is how I found myself eyeball-deep in freezing water being blown down the middle of a Scottish loch, whilst the bloody bird made a miraculous recovery, cackling skywards in derision. Cold! Believe me, it was cold. The few scraps of hair I possessed did nothing to protect vital parts and I was certain my last moment had arrived.

It nearly had, and the only reason I'm here telling the tale is because His son, Blair, stripped off and waded after me. Grateful I was, but in retrospect there was no need for Blair to hurl me, like an underdone Yorkshire pudding, twenty yards up the bank. Bruised me something awful. By the time I had recovered and found the scent, the damned birds had flown.

We were staying at Scourie Hotel, which was very comfortable. Every evening, after They went down for dinner, a considerate girl brought me a hot-water bottle. Carefully covering it with blankets, so that I wouldn't be burnt, she gave me a friendly pat, then put the lights out. A real treat, curling up on top of that warm hump. True Highland hospitality.

If I had known then what I know now, they would never have got me out the car. Ben More Assynt, snow and all, I don't mind; even the gut-bursting last hundred feet up the south face of Stac Polly. But Sutherland moorlands are the worst imaginable place for Yorkshire terriers – soggy, bog-filled, heather-humped and tick-ridden.

They walk ten miles. I do forty, at twice their speed. Just to keep up. Do they care? No. It's 'Heathcliff, heel' and 'Heathcliff, come' and Heathcliff do this and Heathcliff do that. First sight of sheep, they have instant apoplexy, particularly Him. Lead-lashed, I find myself being hauled through black, stinking peat hags like some soulless bit of fluff.

We parked that morning by a little lochan, unnamed on the Ordnance Survey map, three miles east along the A894 from Scourie. At least that's what He said. I have come to understand that He couldn't map-read his way out of a paper bag, unless it had hole in the middle and a pint at the end.

Apparently, the proposal was to walk out the Gorm Track (renamed by me 'Gorm-less'), spending the day bird-watching and fishing for something called 'brown trout'. There were six of us: Master and Mistress, Blair and his wife, Barbara, Stanley Tuer, a retired schoolteacher and amazingly fit walker, and me.

The first loch up the hill has one of these funny Gaelic names which I find impossible to pronounce, Loch a'Mhuirt. Apparently it means 'murder loch' and Stan told its story as we tramped by.

Many years ago, a man and his wife lived on one of the islands in the loch. When the Lord of Reay came to stay at Stac Lodge, tenants took him presents. The man sent his wife down to the lodge with a fine hare, but Lord Reay had other ideas about presents and demanded that the woman become his wife. She replied, 'Never, as long as my husband is alive, never.' Reay sent two of his henchmen up the hill to the loch. Seeing them coming, the husband rushed inside and bolted the door.

Flaming arrows set fire to the cottage thatch and when the man ran out they shot him dead. Rowing across, they cut off his head and returned with it to Lord Reay. Bearing the grisly object on a platter, Reay presented it to the woman: 'Madam, your husband is no longer alive and you will be my wife.' Made my skin creep, that story, and I stayed close to Him as we passed the island where the unfortunate man met his doom.

After my escapade with the mallard, I decided to give up swimming and He kept me on the lead all the way to Gorm Loch. Imagine my horror when they piled into a small boat and asked Barbara to lift me aboard. Well, I struggled, of course, but there wasn't much I could do about it. Managed to nip one of His fingers, which made me feel a little better. The next moment we were off, completely surrounded by the cold, dark, awful stuff and escape was impossible.

To this day He claims it was an accident. I know different. He has a nasty streak, usually hidden but sometimes all too obvious. His fishing bag was lying on the stern seat and I had been having a look – you know, just nosing about, chewing the odd glove and reel of nylon, something to do. As He cast, his arm came back and caught me a cracking blow on the side of my head. Next minute I was overboard, fighting for my life again – the second time in two hours.

'Did you hear that fish rise?' He exclaimed. Fish be damned, it was me, going under for the third time. The harder I tried to reach the boat, the further I seemed to drift away. She grabbed the oars and set off after me. 'Hold on, Heathcliff, I'm coming!' She would be too late. My strength was being sapped by freezing water and I knew another ten seconds in the loch and that would be that.

As I sank below the waves my whole life flashed before my eyes: mother's warm tummy, the rag I used to chew, hot milk before the fire. Then, miraculously, I felt myself being lifted to the surface. He had me in his landing net and I was deposited in the bottom of the boat, gasping like a well hooked fish. Fortunately, She is medically qualified and banged and massaged me back to life; but it was a close-run thing.

You would have thought, after such an experience, that the day would have been abandoned, that They would have hurried me home to bed. You would have thought wrong. They asked me if I was all right, tied me to a seat and carried on fishing. I'm dying and they ask me if I'm all right! I will never understand human beings. Sunshine and smiles one moment, drowning you the next.

The rest of the day was spent walking, in pouring rain, and I have never been so cold and miserable in all my life. He must have sensed it because he bent down and, plucking me from the middle of a particularly large clump of sopping heather, stuffed me into the game pocket of his jacket. Thus warmed, I travelled the next three miles, and that rest enabled me to regain sufficient strength to make it back to the car.

In spite of everything, I suppose I really did enjoy the day. The scenery was spectacular: sheep, grouse, deer, ducks and some utterly fascinating smells. The highlight was when I followed one of these scents into a straggle of boulders and came face to face with the most enormous cat I have ever seen.

Cruel yellow eyes blazed from a snarling face and I realized that I would need some help to deal with this fellow. I trotted back and

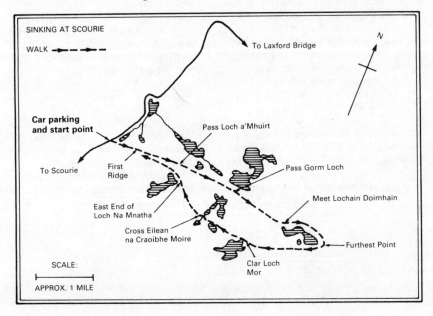

SINKING AT SCOURIE

WALK

To Laxford Bridge

N

Car parking and start point

Pass Loch a'Mhuirt

To Scourie

First Ridge

Pass Gorm Loch

Meet Lochain Doimhain

East End of Loch Na Mnatha

Cross Eilean na Craoibhe Moire

Furthest Point

Clar Loch Mor

SCALE:

APPROX. 1 MILE

SINKING AT SCOURIE

told Him but he just carried on fishing. I decided that I would have a go anyway, but by the time I got back the cat had escaped. Lucky for him, I thought.

When we arrived at the hotel that evening I was so tired I could hardly eat dinner. My feet were killing me. But She sat beside me, stroking my head, telling that I had been a good boy. I explained about my fear of water and She seemed to understand. That night, when the maid brought my hot-water bottle, I grunted thank you, and was sound asleep before she hit the lights.

WHAT YOU NEED TO KNOW

Time and effort This is a dramatic walk through magnificent scenery surrounded by mountains, lochs and moorland. Although there are no steep gradients, it is a long, hard walk, particularly in wet weather. The round trip takes about five hours, longer if you wish to have a few casts on the way. If fishing, obtain prior permission from Ian Hay at Scourie Hotel (Tel: 0971-2396).

To follow the route, a compass and map are essential. Even in good weather, it is easy to get lost in this vast landscape. A useful marker in times of trouble is to turn your back on Ben Stack and walk in a straight line. This will, eventually, bring you to the main road. To avoid having to do so, brush up on your map reading.

Location Ordnance Survey Sheet 9, Cape Wrath, second series, scale 1:50,000.

Grid references The references given follow the route of the walk

from the main road and back again. Start point and car-parking place 185451; first ridge 190449; pass Loch a'Mhuirt at 200445; pass Gorm Loch at 211439; Meet Lochain Doimhain at 222431; furthest point 231427; Clar Loch Mor 214427; cross Loch Eilean na Craoibhe Moire at 205434; east end of Loch na Mnatha 199441.

Route There are few tracks over the moor so you will have to depend upon accurate map reading to stay on route, which makes this walk a bit of an adventure. Ben Stack is the dominant peak facing you. North-east lie Foinaven and Arkle. So getting your bearings should be easy.

Sometimes, however, it is not; for, apart from the dozens of lochs marked on the OS Sheet, there are others which are not. Nevertheless, with care and caution, you should be able to find your way round. The only steepish part of the walk is when rounding Lochain Doimhain to begin the return journey.

176

36

The Winds of Hope

GAUNT Dun Dornaigil Broch glowers by the tortuous track through green Strath More in Sutherland. These defensive towers were built by Picts during the final pre-Christian years, sited along fertile, sheltered valleys, close to water and grazing for animals. In wilderness lands, unpenetrated even by the might of Rome, Dicaledonae tended crops, hunted red deer and netted salmon-rich Strathmore River. When danger threatened, families hurried inside and bolted the door.

Brochs were massive structures – drystone built, circular in plan and up to fifty high. Fifteen-foot-thick walls enclosed a space measuring forty feet in diameter and often the marks of timber lean-to dwellings are found inside. They were virtually impregnable, which was just as well, given that the nearest policeman was some two thousand years away.

Strath More is enfolded by graceful Ben Hope, at 3,042 feet Scotland's most northerly Munro and one of the easiest to climb. Westwards, lesser hills rise in tangled ridges to Reay Forest peaks: Cranstackie, Foinaven, Arkle, Creagan Meall Horn and the pinnacle of Ben Stack. Lady Hope towers above all, her craggy cairned head majestically cloud-crowned.

I became interested in Ben Hope, the 'hill of the bay', whilst fishing the loch she guards, one of Scotland's finest sea-trout fisheries. Sea trout and salmon rush short Hope River to the six-mile silver-ribbon loch from May until September; they linger close to shore, scenting gravel spawning beds, freshly washed by winter snows, waiting for egg-heavy, urgent females.

Visitors come from all over the world to battle with the silver inhabitants of Loch Hope, and, to help them find the best places to fish, row the boat and tie on flies, they seek the services of a Highland gillie, the sporting 'gentleman's gentleman'. Even today, many northern gillies speak more Gaelic than English, and prefer to do so; for, in spite of all the efforts of so-called 'improvers' during the eighteenth and nineteenth centuries, the old Celtic tongue survives.

After the taming of the clans, at the terrible carnage of Culloden, in defiance of defeat, Gaelic poetry flourished; and close to the old Pictish tower of Dun Dornaigil is the birthplace of one of the most famous Gaelic bards, Robb Donn, the 'Bard of Sutherland'. Robb Donn, along with others such as Alexander MacDonald, John MacCodrum, Duncan Ban MacIntyre and Dugald Buchanan, created a great lyrical Gaelic history of immense beauty, as alive today as when written two hundred years ago.

Ann and I climbed Ben Hope on a wild October morning. Seeking an early start, we stayed the previous night with Paul Panchaud, at Altnaharra Hotel. Altnaharra is an excellent centre from which to explore the surrounding area and the hotel, at the head of Loch Naver, is one of the oldest in the north – a comfortable, well managed haven, playing host to fishermen and walkers for more than a century.

We parked by the grey broch in torrential rain, wondering at our sanity in even considering an ascent. But the rain passed, tempting us from the warmth of the car. Eager to be off, dogs bounded down to the river, splashing through wet grass, instantly muddied – in Breac's case, being a retriever, up to his middle; Heathcliff, his smaller companion and a brash Yorkshire terrier, just muddy all over.

The keeper's house at Alltnacaillich was busy. Six legs extended from under a sad-looking truck, bits of engine scattered round. Risking rebuke, I checked that a climb on Ben Hope was in order and would not interfere with any stalking parties. Half-Gaelic grunts confirmed we could climb.

Seeing the intense mechanical activity reminded me of the

English visitor whose car had broken down along a wild, lonely stretch of Highland road. After struggling fruitlessly for an hour to restart the engine, the man stopped a passing local riding by on a rusty old bike, chased by a rusty old sheepdog.

The local had a quick look under the bonnet, fiddled a bit and then requested that the stranded motorist turn the ignition key. Magically, the engine fired healthily to life. 'Thank you,' said the visitor. 'You must be a mechanic.' The local paused, considering this statement, then replied: 'Oh, dear me, no. I'm a MacKay from Strathnaver.'

Wind howled as we found and followed the track up behind the house onto the hill. Summer-bleached grass flattened in the gale and Allt na Caillich burn, 'the old woman's burn', rushed white-foamed between steep boulder-strewn banks. The path was soft with autumn rain, marked by deer and sheep, and we struggled upwards, heads bent, shoulders into the storm.

The proud, sheer flanks of Leiter Mhuiseil loomed ahead, thrusting the stream over its ridge in an astonishing sheet of pure silver. Water sprang from rocks, dancing, sparkling droplets, brightening the dark bowl of the corrie. At the foot of the hill the matchbox house seemed an isolated island of calm amidst fierce, timeless elements.

On the exposed ridge, the strength of the wind was an almost animal force and we huddled behind an outcrop of boulders, sipping welcome coffee, assessing our position. The spectacular ridge of Ben Loyal, jagged and knife-like, rose east. The moor shone with lochs and lochans: Meadie, an Dherue, Haluim. West-wards, an azure carpet of Loch Hope; the tiny speck of Loch Bealach na Sgeulachd on Lean Charn; and, beyond, the long finger of sea-Loch Eriboll.

Ahead, the ridge rose gently between Creag Riabhach and the steep cliffs of Leitir Mhuiseil, rearing quickly towards the summit. We walked on for a further quarter of an hour and then decided to abandon the attempt. If the ridge was so exposed and windy, then the summit would be downright dangerous.

Ben Hope is topped by a small, grassy, trig.-pointed plateau, buttressed on three sides by steep cliffs. It would have been impossible to stand there in safety and madness to try. Reluctantly, we turned back down the ridge, promising ourselves that we would return again another, milder day.

As we stumbled, defeated, down the hill, rain fell in solid sheets; the waterfall cascaded endlessly over the cliff. Clouds began to settle on the summit of Ben Hope and we quickened step, anxious to be off the hill before they reached us. Sheep huddled, sodden mournfully, backs against the storm which now raged furiously about our ears.

Back at the broch we leapt, booted, into the car and boosted the heater. The damp smell of wet dogs assaulted our senses. Two tired panting heads thrust between ours, instantly steaming windows. As we drove past Alltnacaillich Cottage I noticed six legs still sticking out from under the truck. Obviously, what they needed was a Mackay from Strathnaver.

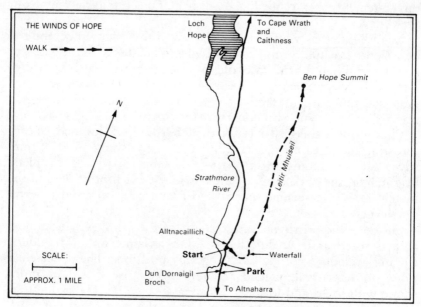

WHAT YOU NEED TO KNOW

Time and effort   There and back takes about four hours – a lot more on a hard, windy day. I find the first hike, from the road up to the waterfall, tiring. Maybe its just me, for there is a good track all the way. Anyway, take it easy and take your time.

From the waterfall onwards the route is long but undemanding. Apart from the final assault on the summit, which should be treated with caution, there is nothing much to be concerned about – other, that is, than enjoying yourself.

Location   Ordnance Survey Sheet 9, Cape Wrath, second series, scale 1:50,000.

Grid references   Dun Dornaigil Broch 458450; Alltnacaillich 459456; waterfall 465455; Ben Hope summit 478502.

Route   A word of warning before you start climbing. The little road from Altnaharra to Loch Hope is a very dangerous place, perhaps even more so than the mountain itself. Narrow, single-tracked and nasty; sudden bends, blind summits and then some. Take the greatest possible care if you want to arrive in one piece at the start point for the walk.

There are two parking places, by the broch and a little further north, on the right-hand side of the road, before the keeper's house. Parking near the house is frowned upon, mightily.

Walk from the car towards the house and you will spot the track on your right leading up the hill. It follows the line of the Allt na Caillich Burn to the first ridge, near the spectacular waterfall, where the track crosses the stream.

Walk north along the ridge of Leitir Mhuiseil, which rises suddenly, towards the summit crown, which is guarded on three sides by steep cliffs. In very windy weather, and we get some fierce gales in the north, stay clear of the top, or, if you must, approach on all fours.

37

Invernaver and Torrisdale

FROM THE dawn of history men have lived and worked by the banks of the River Naver in Sutherlandshire. Six thousand years ago mesolithic hunter-gatherers arrived in canoes, hugging the inhospitable storm-torn coastline – long-headed men, clad in furs and animal skins. Others trekked through wolf- and boar-filled forests over windswept mountains to the green and gentle strath.

Two thousand years before the Egyptians built their pyramids, Stone Age men constructed magnificent burial chambers, massive structures which involved placing hundreds of tons of shaped stones. It was a time of constant change: the miracle of fire, flint-tipped weapons, the cultivation of crops, animal husbandry. They built marvellously warm, weatherproof circular homes, and the remains of these ancient dwellings can still be seen today.

These early men were followed by Bronze and Iron Age peoples, aggressive, warlike tribes, constantly seeking better lands. The remains of their fortified towers, the brochs, line the banks of Naver, zigzagging from estuary to source – huge circular stone-built towers. The best preserved, Strathnaver Broch, stands at Grumore, on the north shore of Loch Naver. From its command-ing heights, warning of approaching danger could be passed quickly throughout the glen and tribes gathered to defend their lands.

The Romans never subdued these painted northern men, the Picts. Nor did ravaging Vikings, plundering down the gentle strath from their Orkney base. A crueller fate awaited the men of Strathnaver – Clan MacKay. Where Roman legions, Viking raiders and English armies failed, the people of Strathnaver were finally destroyed, not by enemies but by so-called friends, their own lairds. During the infamous Highland clearances of the nineteenth century, the strath was brutally cleared of people to make way for sheep.

Gordons of Morayshire became Dukes of Sutherland in the Middle Ages and as early as 1630 announced that they were determined to 'root out Gaelic barbarity'. The rebellions of 1715 and 1745 changed Lowland attitudes mightily and Highlanders were portrayed as little better than barbarians, a constant danger to civilized life, to be beaten into submission.

In 1770, the Society for the Propagation of Christian Knowledge was set up to administer schools in the Highlands with an express aim: 'To combat the ignorance, atheism, popery and impiety of the Highlands'. Thus the scene was set for the clearances, one of the most inhumane acts ever perpetrated in Scotland. Two thousand men, women and children were evicted, their homes burned and land sold or rented to southern sheep farmers. In vain they prayed:

> O God, shield house and fire and beast
> And all that dwell herein tonight.
> Shield me and my beloved household
> From cruel hands and save us
> From our enemies tonight.

Because of the clearances, Strathnaver has been left almost un-changed, untouched by the hand of man for nearly two hundred years. It is one of the most important archaeological and historical sites in Europe, where the evidence and effect of thousands of years continuous human occupation have been captured in time. The strath is a vast, enduring monument to man's endeavour through-out the ages – a never-ending, constant source of wonder and delight.

After our abortive assault on stormy Ben Hope, Ann and I drove north alongside Loch Hope and then east to the mouth of the dashing little River Borgie. We were determined to save something of the day and decided to walk over the small hills separating Borgie from Naver to look down on the hut circles that crowd the sand dunes on the west bank of the estuary of the river.

We parked just before the Borgie hurries into Torrisdale Bay, where a small bridge crosses the river at Crossburn. The deep pool below the bridge was too much temptation for Breac and he plunged in, regardless of the strong current sweeping round the tree-clad bend. Wide, empty white sands lay ahead, dotted with oystercatchers, and we followed a winding track up past the fishing bothy onto the raised beach above the sea.

This is the site of mainland Britain's most northerly football stadium – a wooden changing hut overlooking a rough rectangle of a pitch with drunken goal-posts at each end. Sheep were the only players that day, so Ann's Yorkshire terror was firmly leaded and restrained from joining their game. We crossed the field and set off up the boulder-strewn slope, climbing the comfortable hills, stopping frequently to admire the wide sweep of the bay, brushed by green, mile-long Atlantic breakers.

Kevin O'Reilly, Department of Geography and Geology, Polytechnic of North London, has written a superb guide to local history and archaeology in Strathnaver, including a description of the Bronze Age settlement at Invernaver – the mouth of the river. We passed the dark blue of Lochan Druim an Duin and stood on the cliffs above Baile Marghait, searching amongst hard-packed sand dunes for outlines of the circular homes of Stone Age men.

The scattered dwellings of Bettyhill, named after the infamous Elizabeth, Countess Duchess of Sutherland, who presided over the clearances, lay eastwards; peat smoke streaming from croft chimneys, whipped skywards in the great gale raging above the river. From the shelter of a massive sandstone boulder we peered wet-eyed through the wind.

'The best preserved circle is situated on top of a mound. You can identify it from a distance by the presence of one slightly upstanding stone. The complete circle is quite impressive; the original wall was clearly several feet high and the stones were laid to give a vertical interior face, particularly evident on the north side. The internal diameter is 40 ft.'

We scrambled downhill and spent an hour exploring the ruins. There are outlines of four hut circles, in one of which is a small cluster of stones which may have been the original fireplace. Within this area there are also the remains of a broch: internal diameter of 28 feet and walls possibly 14 feet thick; two cists, burial chambers:

'bodies were buried individually, each contained in a flagstone coffin, which was covered by a cairn or mound. The bodies were buried in the foetal position – with knees drawn up beneath the chin.'

Tucking our own chins in and calling the dogs to heel, we walked back, north over the sands. Storm particles from the singing sands sprayed our faces; endless waves crested and carolled the deserted shore. Half-way along the beach we found shelter and lunch amongst an outcrop of rocks. We lay on the sands, locked in the timeless, mystical beauty of a wild, unchanging land: and speech seemed pointless.

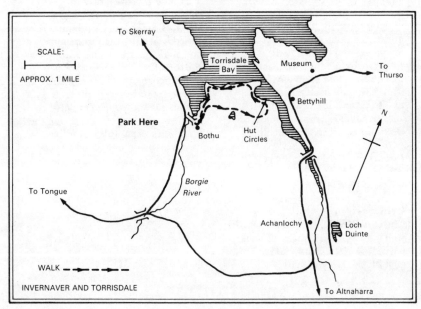

WHAT YOU NEED TO KNOW

Time and effort   More mental than physical. For fullest benefit, do your homework first and learn a little about Strathnaver. In order to do so, contact Mrs Elliot Rudie, Strathnaver Museum, Farr, Bettyhill, Sutherland. The museum will be able to supply you with a number of well written and informative brochures describing the history of the strath. Before making the walk, call at the museum and, if you have time, visit the pre-clearance village of Achanlochy, a few miles south of Bettyhill. Allow a full day for your trip. The walk itself takes about two to three hours. Refreshment and bar lunches are available at the Bettyhill Hotel and in the village.

Location   Ordnance Survey Sheet 10, Strathnaver, second series, scale 1:50,000.

Grid references   Strathnaver Museum 715623; Bettyhill 707617; Achanlochy 717585; start of walk 681621; Lochan Druim an Duin 694621; hut circles 699611.

Route   Drive north from the A836, where the main road crosses Borgie River, signposted to Skerray. At the mouth of the river, there is parking space and a track leading down to a wooden bridge. You will see the fishing bothy on the top of the hill at the other side of the river.

Follow this track up and round the bothy and then back down towards the shore. Climb onto the raised beach, by the football pitch and angle quarter-right, aiming for the top of the hill. The track is indistinct and there is a tendency to go too far right. Keep the loch on your right and you eventually arrive on the crags overlooking the hut circles. Scramble carefully down to visit them. Walk back to the car, along the sands, round the coast.

38

Farewell to the Flows

*I*WAS WITH a Welshman in a small cottage on the north coast of
Scotland, talking to the local bard – which was difficult, because,
although masterly at stringing together words, he was not so good
at the hearing. Our next appointment was with a thatcher, a man
versed in the ancient art of covering roof timbers with peat and turf.

Rising, my friend announced: 'Must leave, we have to see a
thatcher.'

'You are seeing Mrs Thatcher?' inquired the bard.

'No, a thatcher,' replied the Welshman, struggling.

'And why would you be looking at a tractor?'

'No, Mr MacKay, not tractor, thatcher!' the Welshman yelled.

'Well, be sure and give him my regards for it's a long time indeed
since I have seen the factor, and fine man he is too.'

This could only happen in Sutherland, a land full of characters,
kindness and patient courtesy and from the window of my work
room I look out across Loch Watten in Caithness to where the twin
peaks of Ben Grimas rise gently from distant Sutherland moors.

As you drive southwards down Strath Halladle, the grey sentinels of Ben Griam Mor and Ben Griam Beg tower over the
narrow road that twists across Badanloch from Kinbrace to Strathnaver. A desolate landscape where human habitation seems im-
probable. Then, in the distance, like a patch of white moss on a
mountain boulder, the Garvault Hotel is glimpsed, lying snug in

the folds of gently rounded hills, an island outpost in the wilderness.

Garvault Hotel, owned by Margaret and Tony Henderson, is the remotest hotel on mainland Britain. Its notepaper says so and *Guinness Book of Records* confirms the fact. If you are looking for simple comfort, good cooking and a friendly welcome, then Garvault offers all these and is a perfect centre for exploring the vast moorlands of east Sutherland.

But even this remote and beautiful land is being threatened by the hand of man, for the monotonous green of mass afforestation is creeping over the landscape like some malignant fungus. Northwards, also, in Strath Halladale, tree farmers have moved in, ploughing and devastating moorlands which have remained unchanged and tree-less since the last ice age. These moorland rapists are hell-bent on obliterating every inch from sight in frenzied pursuit of private profit.

For the time being it is still possible to find that special magic of the hills, where:

> Now Turn I to that God of old
> Who mocked not any of my ills,
> But gave my hungry hands to hold
> The large religion of the hills.

Get there if you can and see this amazing landscape before it disappears for ever under regimented rows of tax-avoidance-planted lodgepole pine and Sitka spruce. Fix in your mind the unending beauty of open moors, the cries of curlew, greenshank and golden plover. You will never see the like again.

This is the Flow Country, a far-flung carpet of dark bog pools and ice-blue lochans, blown white with cotton grass, starred with the sudden violet of sundew and milkwort, where bog asphodel yellows warm corners and heather purples autumn days. Hen harrier and golden eagle glide through a vast, endless sky; otters play by tiny lochs; wild cat blaze from behind wisps of shoreside reeds; graceful divers glide over smooth waters where stags stoop daintily to drink.

Climb the Ben Griams to capture the last moments of this precious heritage, and curse with me the thoughtless fools who destroy such beauty.

Ann and I parked behind Garvault Hotel and pulled on hiking boots. Gathering cameras, maps, compass, lunch and dogs, we set off eagerly up the hill. Hardy, thick-coated North Country Cheviot sheep gazed unblinkingly as we struck eastwards towards the shoulder of Ben Griam Beg, anxious to be free.

We crossed the Land-Rover track that leads out to Loch Coire nam Mang and addressed ourselves to the hill. Ben Griam Beg, 1,936 feet, is the higher of the two peaks and the hike to the top is an easy though steep climb. The rounded summit is crested by a cairn and a comfortable seat has been built so that you may rest weary legs after the climb. This seat has been constructed over the years by thoughtful walkers and is made out of grey stone slabs.

Relax here on a warm summer day, gazing southwards over the long splash of Lochs Badanloch, nan Clar and Rimsdale, to the hazed hills of Borrobol Forest: Creag a'Chiore Ghlais, Meall nan Aighean, Creag Mhor and Ben Klibreck. Over the flows, Caithness mountains ridge eastwards to where oil-drilling platforms black-speck sparkling seas. Listen to the constant wind. Feel the silence.

Westwards, range after range of Sutherland mountains shriek to the heavens – the ragged fortification of Ben Loyal; Ben Hope, serenely scaling cloud-wisped skies; Foinaven, Arkle and Assynt peaks. North, over the wild Pentland Firth, lie the hills of Hoy on gentle Orkney, and, abandoned to its fate in the stormy firth, the white star of Pentland Skerry lighthouse.

Ben Griam Beg beckons across a damp valley enfolding two superb trout lochs – Coire nam Mang and Druim a'Chliabhain, boat-housed and bobbed with fishing boats where cross-fingered anglers cast temptingly at the dimples of rising trout. The highest Iron Age hill fort in Scotland crowns the top of Ben Griam Beg, but

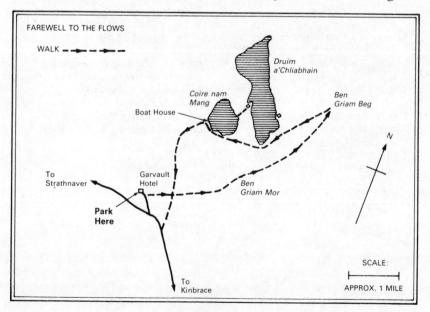

you have to look carefully to mark the ruin – a stone wall 6 feet thick guarding an area 500 feet by 200 feet. Elliot Rudhie, a local archaeologist, has found strange stones here, circular and holed in the middle. Perhaps our ancestors had more direct methods of fishing and used them as weights for nets.

On the long walk back to Garvault, Ann and I rested by the shores of Coire nam Mang. A plaintive, thin, piping voice called from the hill: 'Oh, dear me, oh, dear me!' Bowing on top of a boulder a greenshank warned of approaching rain. The sound of that haunting cry followed us home – another treasured memory of a day in the hills. And it p—— down all the way!

WHAT YOU NEED TO KNOW

Time and effort This is a moorland and hill walk across the Flow Country of east Sutherland. Allow about four hours for the round trip, which covers some ten miles. The ascent of the Ben Griams is not difficult and there are no dangers along the way. The valley floor between the two peaks can be soggy after heavy rain and it is advisable to try and keep to the ridges and higher ground.

Location You will need two maps, Ordnance Survey Sheet 10, Strathnaver and Sheet 17, Strath of Kildonan, second series, scale 1:50,000.

Grid references Garvault Hotel 781388; Ben Griam Mor 805389; Loch Coire nam Mang 800405; Loch Druim a'Chliabhain 810410; Ben Griam Beg 830410.

Route Leave the A897 Helmsdale–Melvich road through Strath Halladale at Kinbrace and turn west along the B871. Park behind the Garvault Hotel. A gate leads from the hotel, half-right across the hill, towards the summit of Ben Griam Mor. Cross the Land-Rover track and climb straight up to the top.

Avoid the crags at the north end of Mor by descending to the left of the top and cross the moor to Ben Griam Beg, with Loch Druim a'Chliabhain on your left. Climb straight up the hill. The return route takes you round the south end of Chliabhain and Coire nam Mang. At the boat-house on the west shore of nam Mang pick up the Land-Rover track which leads back to Garvault.

39

Beinn Mhor Sheep and Eagles

T HE BAR at Lochboisdale Hotel on South Uist is the longest I have ever seen. In whaling days, thirsty crews, fresh from South Atlantic storms, disembarked in dry-throated droves, demanding instant service and plenty of space to raise and lower elbows.

When it comes to elbow raising I'm no slouch, but some occupants that night seemed intent upon breaking the world record for the greatest volume of whisky consumed during the course of a single evening. They would have to go some to beat the current holders, though – Creagorry Hotel, just up the road on Benbecula. There, the bar is lined with pre-packed take-aways: a half-bottle of whisky and a couple of cans of export to round off the evening, discreetly wrapped in plain brown paper bags. Keep in trim, Creagorry lads.

Pride of place in Lochboisdale public bar is given over to a huge photograph of the island's patron saint, Saint ss *Politician*, immortalized in Compton Mackenzie's book *Whisky Galore*. Thousands of cases of 'water of life' were 'rescued' when the vessel ran aground in a storm during the Second World War, and I think islanders have been praying for similar heavenly munificence ever since.

A single road runs the length of the west coast. Got to. The rest of South Uist is a desolate, trackless wilderness – moorlands rising to majestic mountains fringed by the most remote, spectacular cliff scenery in the British Isles. There are three main peaks: Hecla, 1,988 feet, to the north; Beinn Mhor, 2,034 feet, to the south and 1,800 foot Ben Corodale, sandwiched between.

Because they rise suddenly from sea level, South Uist mountains look dramatic and daunting; but all three are easy to climb, provided you choose the right route, and right day. The approach to Beinn Mhor, the highest, starts from the coastal road north of Market Stance, past three lochs called Ollay – West, Mid and East. I fished them fruitlessly a few years back and renamed them Dam, Bugger and SFA Ollay. Nevertheless, I am informed that they do contain fish.

This is a compass-and-map country; stout walking boots and full emergency kit. Uist weather is fickle: one moment clear and fine, the next a storm, racing in from the Atlantic. Should mist come down, then you must be prepared; there are steep, dangerous crags on Beinn Mhor and great care must be exercised. In spite of its modest height, treat Beinn Mhor with utmost respect.

A comforting peat track leads eastwards from the A865, egging you on, then deserts you for rough, heather-covered moors. However, the going is not tough and your reference point is the north shoulder of Beinn Mhor, known as Maola Breac. Once there, heather thins and walking becomes easier.

As you climb, the coastal machair plain spreads below – a springtime wild-flower-covered masterpiece fringed by a golden carpet of miraculous empty beaches. A straggle of shallow, blue, lime-rich lochs borders the shore: Fada, Roag, Altabrug – famed salmon and sea-trout fisheries. Grogarry, Stilligarry, Bornish, Kildonan, home of highest-quality wild brown trout in Scotland. Small crofts, smoke-drifting in still air, squat white amidst fertile fields.

A ragged, narrow ridge leads south-east from Maola Breac towards the summit. Pick cautiously upwards. Hardest part is the final scramble, threading carefully over and round jagged boulders. Once crowned, the reward is everything and more you ever wished.

Northwards, across Ben Corodale and Hecla, blush South Harris hills, the 'heather isles'. Over silver seas to Skye, a mighty range of Cuillins: Sgurr Alasdair, Sgurr nan Eag and a'Ghreadaaidh. Beyond, on mainland Scotland, Assynt and Fisherfield peaks: an Teallach, Ben More, Quinag. Small isles lie south: Heaval-topped Barra and, shadowed in distant, shimmering, porpoised seas, Rum, Eigg, Coll and warm-palmed Tiree.

This is the land of golden eagle, rapacious raven and hen harrier. Once, one clear, sunny autumn day, Ann and I gazed from Druidibeg as an eagle circled thermals above the mountain. Even from such distance, the huge, dark shape dominated skies. As we watched, a second bird thrust from Hecla's purple-blue crags to join its mate in soaring, stately flight. If you dream of seeing the 'lord of the skies', then amidst wild Uist mountains that dream will come true.

At the foot of Beinn Mhor, locked in an eastern mountain prison, nestles little Loch Hellisdale. Close by, on cliffs guarding Corodale Bay, is Prince's Cave. The luckless Young Pretender, Bonnie Prince Charlie, hid there after the flight from Drumossie Moor in 1746. Not so bonny either, by all accounts. I suppose that after months running for his life, living wild, that was to be expected, but I have damn-all sympathy for that vagabond prince. He carried with him nothing other than ruin and disaster wherever he went, and he hammered the last nail into Highlanders' coffins.

Similar simple beasts are hunted amongst corries round Beinn Mhor and Corodale. Shepherds comb hills in early summer, searching for sheep, making the long trek to Corodale for 'clippings'. Much easier than flocking herds over tortuous peaks to machair homesteads. They shear during the days and sleep summer-starred nights, well provisioned with good Scotch wine to wet whistles of old stories.

Which seemed a good idea. Ann and I turned from the view and descended to join Gaelic-speaking throngs, elbow-raised by the long bar of Boisdale. We had worked hard for our thirst. At least, that's our excuse.

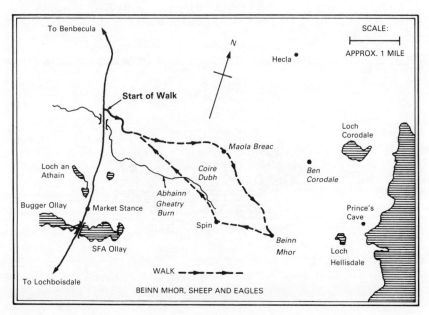

WHAT YOU NEED TO KNOW

Time and effort Apart from the final assault on the summit of Beinn Mhor, this is an easy walk, albeit across some pretty rugged country. Compass and map and full service marching order recommended. The total distance is about seven miles and you should allow approximately four hours for the journey, excluding the time you spend in the bar at Lochboisdale. I suggest you leave that part of the walk until last. Don't forget binoculars – for birds on the hill.

Location Ordnance Survey Sheet 22, Benbecula, second series, scale 1:50,000.

Grid references The Lochboisdale Hotel is on Sheet 31; find the grid reference yourself or simply follow your nose. Start of walk 768341; Maola Breac 797333; Beinn Mhor 808311; Spin 797314; Coire Dubh 790325.

Route Drive north from Lochboisdale, past Ollays and Market Stance. Half a mile further a loch borders the left of the road: Loch an Athain. One hundred yards on, two cottages left-right the road. Next right is the parking place and start of the walk.

Follow the peat track onto the moor. Mark the north shoulder of Beinn Mhor and walk directly towards it. This is the easiest way up, and why should we make things difficult for ourselves? On Maola Breac, follow the rising ridge south-east towards the summit. Once on top, you have a choice: either return the same way or be difficult, and edge down the steep west side of Beinn Mhor to the secondary summit of Spin – more climbing than walking but splendid stuff nevertheless. From Spin, angle down Coire Dubh, on the line of the stream, to cross Abhainn Gheatry Burn, thence back to the car.

40

From Market Stance to Scarilode

BENBECULA, Beinn a'faodhia, 'the hill of the fords'; a flat, moorland landscape, dominated by Rueval, the highest hill on the island. Here, in a shallow cave, on the nights of 25 and 26 June 1746, Bonnie Prince Charlie anxiously awaited Flora Macdonald. Flora's stepfather, Captain Hugh Macdonald, was guarding the South Ford, from Benbecula to South Uist, and he supplied travel documents which allowed the prince, disguised as Flora Macdonald's maid, Betty Burke, to escape.

Not a moment too soon. Word was out that the fugitive was hiding on Benbecula and General Campbell arrived on the island commanding a force of more than two thousand men to hunt him down. The following month, Flora Macdonald was arrested by that relentless pursuer of Prince Charles Edward Stuart, Captain Ferguson of *HMS* Furnace and imprisoned in the Tower of London.

Flora was released in 1747, under the Act of Indemnity, and three years later married Alan Macdonald of Kingsburgh. Dr Johnson met her there in 1773, by which time Flora Macdonald was fifty years old, but still a considerable presence.

The good doctor reports: 'We were entertained at Kingsburgh with the usual hospitality by Mr Macdonald and his lady Flora Macdonald, a name that will be mentioned in history; and if courage and fidelity are virtues, mentioned with honour.'

Until recent times, Benbecula was isolated from its near neighbours North and South Uist by the North and South Fords, and passage over the shifting sands was dangerous and difficult. In 1943 a causeway was built over South Ford, still known as O'Regan's Bridge in honour of the priest most active in advocating its construction. Seventeen years passed before Benbecula was linked to North Uist; in 1960 the Queen Mother opened the route over North Ford, completing the link. Island economy was further stimulated by the advent of the rocket-testing range and Ministry of Defence establishment at Balivanich. Of the three islands, Benbecula shows the greatest sign of Hebridean change.

Ann and I first visited Benbecula in 1977. With four children, ranging from two to sixteen years, we stayed in a caravan near Balivanich. One fine, bright morning the family set off to Market Stance, a few miles south of Gramsdale, intent on picnic, fishing and walking. Market Stance was the cattle business centre of the island. In days gone by, mainland dealers would gather there to haggle with islanders and buy their lean black cattle.

Driving past council works and rubbish tip, we parked the car by the shores of Loch Ba Una; where Ann, daughter Lewis-Ann, young Charles and infant Jean disembarked to splash and play in shallow sand-fringed waters. My elder son, Blair, and I set off eastwards, following Clanranald's Kelp Road to the sea. During the Great War kelp was the major industry of Benbecula; potash produced by burning kelp was essential to armaments factories and more than 600 tons was exported each year.

The old track winds round the south side of Rueval through a wilderness of heather-covered moorlands, painted blue-grey with shining lochs and tiny lochans. North-east, behind Rueval, lies one of the most notorious: Loch na Beire.

Two small islands grace the loch, Mheribh Mhor and Mheribh Bheag. On Mhor there is said to be a circular hole, now hidden beneath sad bluebells, carved from ancient rock and once used as a place of execution. Condemned men were bound, thrust into the hole, and left to die. At a convenient time, the corpse was removed and buried on Mheribh Bheag, presumably to make way for further wretched miscreant occupants of that infamous pit.

The track ends on the small sandy beach of a beautiful loch called Scarilode – deep, clear waters surrounded by steep crags, full of responsive, red-spotted wild brown trout. Edge round the west shore, past a bouldered, rowan-decked promontory; on the edge of the rocks, sea-staring the long finger of Oban Haka, are the ruins of a building marked on the map 'Shieling'.

This remote eastern area of Benbecula was once part of a large farm known as Nunton, owned in the 1920s by Lady Gordon Cathcart, resident of Bournemouth. The islanders who survived the carnage of the First World War returned expecting to find, as promised, a 'land fit for heroes to live in'. Instead they found the same old entrenched, enduring divisions they had been told they were fighting to end: landlords protecting imagined hereditary legal rights, and near-destitute tenants, expected to be humbly thankful for the smallest morsel of approbation.

The Crofting Acts of the late nineteenth century ended the monstrous iniquity of summary eviction and gave tenants security to work and improve their lands. However, what it didn't do was to return the land so brutally sequestered by rapacious clearance lairds.

Benbecula ex-servicemen took the law into their own hands and seized their land by force, defying the law and anyone else to remove them. Basking in the glow of Britain's first-ever Labour government, the soldiers succeeded, and the many marks of 'shieling' on Benbecula's map show the results of their desperate efforts to claim and live and work the land they loved and had fought so hard to defend.

Seven years before my first visit, the croft at Scarilode was still occupied, bright with the sound of laughter and smiling faces – in spite of the constant battle against elements to wrest a meagre living from the thin, sparse soils. How much would world-weary, paper-ridden businessmen in City 'trenches', pay for the magnificent, isolated, god-like splendour of Scarilode?

North from Scarilode, in the knuckle of Neavag Bay, sea otters play; Arctic skuas pirate the cliffs; seals nod offshore; green-coated shags spread wet wings to dry in spring-fresh winds. Eternity was born here, amongst the surging foam and singing gulls. Peace beyond price.

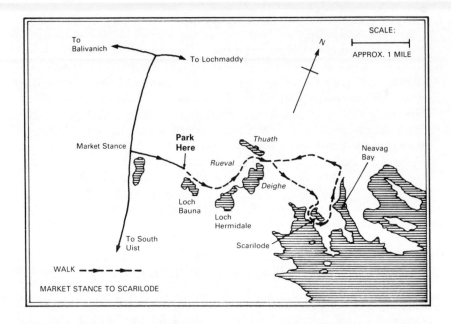

WHAT YOU NEED TO KNOW

Time and effort Apart from the section between Scarilode and the north arm of the Kelp Road, this is an easy walk. Wear stout boots, carry wet-weather gear and you will come to little harm. The round trip covers a distance of eight miles and takes about four hours, depending upon how often and how long you stop to stand and stare on the way. An added attraction would be to climb Rueval on the way home. See how you feel and how much time you have left.

Location Ordnance Survey Sheet 22, Benbecula, second series, scale 1:50,000.

Grid references Market stance 805535; start point 810535; fork on Kelp Road 836535; Scarilode 847523; shieling 846520; north arm of Kelp Road 850535; Rueval 826535.

Route Drive down the A865 and turn left onto the Kelp Road at Market Stance. The 'good' road ends at Loch Ba Una, where there is plenty of room to park. Walk eastwards, following the track north of Loch Hermidale and Deighe, and south of Thuath. One hundred yards past the end of the loch, the Kelp Road divides; take the right fork and walk to Scarilode.

As you approach Scarilode, the track keeps uphill. Leave the track and walk down to the loch and round the west shore. At the south end of Scarilode you will find the ruined shieling. Climb the hill guarding the east end of Scarilode and walk north over the moor, up the side of Neavag Bay. At the end of this sea loch finger you will strike the north arm of the Kelp Road. Follow this back to the start point – with a quick dash up Rueval on the way!

41

Valley and the Sunken Caves of Hosta

'NAE MAN can tether time or tide.' But you can learn to live with them. As an exciseman, Scotland's national bard, Robert Burns, was well aware of this fact; and so were the smugglers he hunted. Therefore, before enjoying one of North Uist's loveliest walks, carefully check time and tide. Otherwise be prepared for a long wait on Valley Island until seas recede and you can return safely.

At low tide, Valley Island is separated from North Uist by two miles of golden sand. Then it is safe to walk out and explore this secret, summer-primrose-covered paradise. An hour will take you round the coast and on the north shore you will find the finest beaches in Britain, backed by gentle dunes, solitary and remote. It is easy, like Tam o' Shanter, to forget time and tide on Valley and succumb to the 'songs and sweet airs' of this magical isle.

Nor will you be the first visitor to fall under Valley's spell. The old, ruined house that dominates the island was once the home of the Granville family, cousins of the queen, who still own much of Uist. Four thousand years ago, Stone Age man grazed cattle on Valley and even today Uist crofters from the villages of Sollas, Malaclete and Middlequarter take sheep over shining sands to crop summer grass. Bleating flocks herd across wet sands, ankle-snapped by sharp-eyed black collies amidst a chorus of Gaelic shouts from arm-waving shepherds. Memories of times past, when sheep were less welcome, come flooding back.

The 'Children of Colla' were evicted from their homes in 1849, to make way for the 'Great Cheviot'. Godfrey William Wentworth MacDonald, fourth Baron of the Isles, was £200,000 in debt and hard pressed by creditors. Sheep were to be his financial salvation. The only problem was his people. At the first attempt to issue writs of eviction, sheriff officers were sent scuttling from Malaclete in a shower of stones, thrown by angry, fearful tenants.

A force of thirty-three constables, armed with ash truncheons and led by William Colquhoun, sheriff substitute, and Superintendent MacBean, sailed from Oban to beat the men of Sollas into submission. Ever anxious to please his superiors, the Revd Macrae, an island minister, accompanied the force: God's Law as well as man's, would be used to bring the villagers to heel. Alexander Mackenzie, in his 'History of the Highland Clearances' described the scene:

> There was no discussion, no argument, no appeals. The police formed two lines down the street of the township. Sheriff-Officers asked one question only at the doors of the cottages, whether those within were prepared to emigrate on the terms offered. If the answer was no, and it invariably was, then bedding, bed-frames, spinning-wheels, barrels, benches, tables and clothing were all dragged out and left at the door. Divots were torn from the roof, and the house timbers pulled down ready for burning.

The villagers, grouped into a small army, began to hurl rocks and stones at the constables.

> MacBean put his men into two divisions and sent them forward against the crowd with their batons. One took the villagers in the rear, the other in the flank, and drove them over barley rigs and dykes, along the deep-pooled shore.

The end was never in doubt. Three years later, Christmas 1852, the villagers of Sollas, Malaclete and Middlequarter, other than the old, the sick and the lame, left their Uist lands for ever. The frigate *Hercules*, smallpox-ridden, sailed for Australia taking with it the tormented souls of an abandoned people. As you drive past the empty shells of their ruined homes, spare them a kindly thought.

Westwards along the quiet road that circles North Uist is another, less wicked, Victorian folly – the small, ugly, incongruous tower on the south shore of Loch Scolpaig. From behind the croft at the end of the road that divides two 'wings' of the loch, a track leads north along a cliff path, skirting the slopes of Ben Scolpaig, to the Sunken Caves of Hosta.

Sheer cliffs, alive with wild flowers and spring-nesting birds, flank green seas. Natural arches, carved by thousand-year-old waves, throw up endless Atlantic breakers into surging sheets of white spray. Caves probe deep into the rocks and on the cliff-top, near Sloc Roe, land has given up battle, tumbling into a great, gaping hole. On wild days, storm-driven waters howl at the foot of the pit in deafening, defiant roar.

The remains of an ancient Pictish fort lie on the heights above Bagh Blaaskie: Caisteal Odair, 'castle of the dappled hill'. A long wall protects southern approaches to the promontory, pierced by an entrance, 15 feet long and 5 feet wide. The site of the fort must have made it almost impregnable and inside the fortifications are outlines of circular stone foundations, home and hearth to generations of early Gaels.

This is the land where great raptors soar, hen harrier and buzzard, and there is every chance of seeing a golden eagle. Indeed, the varied bird life on North Uist is one of the island's most outstanding attractions. Listen for the rusty-engined coughing of corncrake. The red-necked phalarope also nests nearby in Balranald Nature Reserve.

One year, whilst walking by Loch Eport, in the south of the island, Ann and I saw a rare white stork. The bird was feeding in a roadside loch close to Sidinish and kindly waited until I had assembled zoom lens and taken a decent shot before flapping off over the moor. Round every corner, over every hill, North Uist delights.

The island is two-thirds water, covered with more than a hundred and fifty trout-filled freshwater lochs. Many, like Scadavay, Fada and Obisary, are such a tangled scatter that often the same loch appears to be an endless number of different waters. The shoreline of Loch Scadavay meanders in and out round headlands, bays and corners for a distance of fifty miles, dotted with some two hundred islands, many of which are adorned with their own small lochans.

As the long Hebridean day lingers slowly towards its close over Valley Island, and late sun dips into western seas, there comes a stillness, a moment of timeless beauty, when evening curlew call down the hill and lapwing dip and twist in the gloaming. Then there is no lovelier place in all of Scotland to say goodnight to the world.

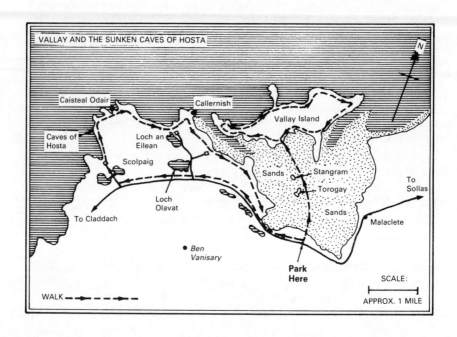

VALLAY AND THE SUNKEN CAVES OF HOSTA

N

Caisteal Odair

Callernish

Vallay Island

Caves of
Hosta

Loch an
Eilean

Scolpaig

Sands

Stangram

To
Sollas

Torogay

Loch
Olavat

Sands

To Claddach

Malaclete

● Ben
Vanisary

Park
Here

SCALE:

WALK ▪ ▪➤ ▪ ▪➤ ▪ ▪➤

APPROX. 1 MILE

WHAT YOU NEED TO KNOW

Time and effort This is an easy, though longish walk. It is possible to split it into two separate outings: to Valley Island first and then later, from Scolpaig to the Sunken Caves of Hosta. The full walk covers a distance of twelve miles and is a day's outing. However, if the sun is shining you may be tempted to linger on the fine beaches of Valley Island. Take along a sleeping bag, just in case. Crossing the sands is quite safe but you should seek local advice about the tides before starting. Wellington boots, rather than walking shoes, for this section of the journey.

When walking out to the Sunken Caves of Hosta, it is polite to tell the owner of the croft at the end of the loch, if he is in, of your intention. Keep well back from the edge, particularly from the edge of the cliff-top hole. Remember, the sea is still cutting away below and the perimeter might not be stable. Dogs and children should be kept on a close lead.

Location Ordnance Survey Sheet 18, Sound of Harris, second series, scale 1:50,000.

Grid references Parking place 781736; Torogay Island 779746; Stangram Island 778751; Valley Island 775765; Loch Scolpaig 733751; Sunken Caves of Hosta 726765; Caisteal Odair 731769; Loch an Eilean 747760; Callernish 752767; Valley Sound 755756.

Route Easy parking by roadside. There is a track across the sands marked on the map, but this is not obvious on the ground. You must seek local advice about tide times and route before setting out. The walk over is about 45 minutes and an hour will take you round the island. Return to the car and change into walking shoes for the remainder of the walk.

Follow the road westwards for three miles, past three lochs on your left and then Loch Olavat on your right. A mile past Olavat you will see Loch Scolpaig and the Victorian tower on your right. Walk down the farm road, between the two sections of the loch, to the croft at the end.

A track leads north along the cliff. Follow this out to the Caves of Hosta and then on to Caisteal Odair. From Caisteal Odair, simply follow the coastline round north and east, keeping Loch an Eilean on your right. This leads to Valley Sound and back to the road. At the road, turn left for your car.

42

Skara Brae and Yesnaby Castle

YOU NEED good sea-legs for Orkney walking. Not because the hills are high or hikes taxing, but just to get you safely over the Pentland Firth. I remember with horror a passage in 1967. The car was lifted on board by sling and dumped, none too ceremoniously, in the hold. But that was as nothing compared with the dumping we humans received when the boat left the comparative calm of Scrabster harbour.

House-high waves, mad walls of tormented, flying spray, roared in from all quarters as the vessel corkscrewed and bobbed crazily northwards. Sea-gulls screamed derision through the storm. My five-year-old son, Blair, and I, wedged together topside, trying to pretend that it was really all good fun. Meanwhile, wife Ann and three-year-old daughter, Lewis-Ann, weathered it out below, reading, as though a force seven gale was an everyday occurrence. Strong stuff, females.

Eventually, the boat pitched drunkenly into the lee of Hoy and, slowly, calmer waters settled pounding hearts. It seemed that we were not, as I had previously expected, every minute, doomed to a watery grave. Ashore, surrounded by the solid stones and cobbles of the old grey town of Stromness, I felt like Mr Fletcher Christian waving farewell to a mad Captain Bligh. Then, from a great height, they dropped the car onto the pier – a last defiant gesture of disgust from seamen to fair-weather sailors.

In spite of that violent journey across Europe's wildest waters the magic of the Orcades has held us enthralled for many years and the journey from mainland Scotland is not always so stormy. We have sailed millpond-calm amidst myriad sea birds, chased and chivvied by porpoise and gannet, lazing sunburnt past sentinel stacks, barely aware of time passing.

One of our favourite Orkney walks starts from the Bay of Skaill in Sandwick, on the west coast of Mainland. The bay is a silver crescent of shining sand, washed by endless green-fringed Atlantic waves. My first golden retriever, Jean, learned to swim there. Jean was a highly-bred bundle of nerves. She required careful persuasion before undertaking any venture faintly dangerous and, as far as she was concerned, water looked mighty dangerous. I waded out into the bay, holding her in my arms, and she swam ashore. Never looked back after that and loved water evermore.

Nestling in the sand dunes at the south end of the bay is the neolithic village of Skara Brae. Five thousand years ago these stone houses must have resounded with the laughter and chatter of farmer-fishermen and their families. The dwellings are wonderfully preserved, lying centuries asleep, undisturbed, under marram-covered sands. A huge storm uncovered the remains of ten houses and they have been carefully excavated to reveal fireplaces, complete with adjacent seat, flagstone box beds, dressers and wall shelves.

On midsummer evenings, amidst cry of sea-gull and twittering late larks, when tourist buses have departed, the ghosts of these small axe-carrying sheepskin-clad men still wander across the dunes, prehistoric dogs yapping busily around calloused, sandalled feet. I know because I have seen them.

Leave Skaill Bay from behind Skara Brae, climbing little Ward Hill, walking over soft, springy, sea-turf specked with wild flowers. The rare Scottish primrose, *Primula scotica*, graces the cliff-tops. Kittiwake, guillemots, razorbill and fulmars squawk and squabble on dramatic crags. The songs of wheatear, meadow pipit and lark sparkle in childhood-crystal air. And, always, the sound of the restless sea.

Eastwards from the hill, Loch Stenness and Loch Harray blue-sweep the moor – two of Orkney's famous trout lochs. Fishermen-filled boats drift the skerry-strewn shallows in endless pursuit of beautifully shaped pink-fleshed wild brown trout. Fish weighing more than 17 lb have been caught and anglers come from all over the world to try their luck – with me it's skill! – in the clear, lime-rich, trout-filled waters.

Close to the deep inlet of Bor Wick, a jagged scar in the cliff, is Broch of Borwick, an Iron Age fort on top of the hill: evidence of changing times, when competition for land and attack by neighbours and newcomers required secure haven for residents – and no visitors were more determined or fiercer than the Vikings.

Skaill is the Norse name for the house of a Viking chief: a good beach and landing place for a longship surrounded by fertile lands. The Norsemen plundered at will throughout Shetland, Orkney, Ireland and mainland Britain until their power was broken at the Battle of Largs in 1261. Even then, the Orkney Islands remained part of Norway and were ceded to Scotland only in 1468 as part of the dowry when King James III married Margaret, daughter of King Christian I.

The Norse influence on the islands is commemorated in names and language as you follow the cliff path south to Neban Point: Edgair, Bor Wick, Qui Ayre, Garthna Geo, Kellyan Hellyan and Lyre Geo. However, when walking along these cliffs it is not the Vikings that you have to fear; a more immediate danger threatens the unwary. Between Yesnaby and Neban Point the moor is owned by a colony of Arctic skuas. During the breeding season they guard their territory furiously, diving fearlessly on intruders, shrieking with anger.

A mighty sea stack, the Castle of Yesnaby has been knifed from the mainland by thousands of years' Atlantic attack. Nearby there is an outcrop of even older rock, start point of the fault known as the Uranium Corridor. Lunch at the view-point on Neban Point, lingering above the waves, watching the changing colours on Ward Hill, highest peak on the Island of Hoy: our next walk.

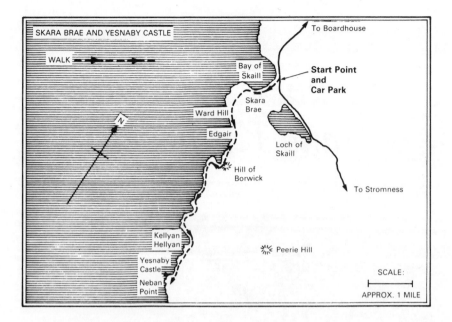

WHAT YOU NEED TO KNOW

Time and effort There and back is a distance of about eight miles. Good walking shoes required and it is advisable to arrive at Skara Brae before 10.30 a.m. After that time, the village gets uncomfortably busy with tourists. This is an easy walk and it will take about four hours, depending upon how long you spend at Skara Brae and how often you stop and stare. As always when on a cliff walk, keep well back from the edge; remember that the cliffs are friable and subject to erosion. Not a good place for dogs. Give the dogs a run on the beach first then leave them in the car for the duration.

Location Ordnance Survey Sheet 6, Orkney–Mainland, second series, scale 1:50,000.

Grid references Start point at Bay of Skaill 236194; Skara Brae 230187; Hill of Borwick 223165; Castle Yesnaby 217134; Neban Point 216132.

Route Park in the car park at Bay of Skaill and follow the signs through the dunes and along the beach to the neolithic village of Skara Brae. Walk south from Skara Brae up Ward Hill and follow the cliff path on to Neban Point. Return to the car park the same way.

43

Orkney, Marwick
and Kitchener

*H*ORATIO Herbert Kitchener was the hero of Khartoum and the
Battle of Omdurman, Commander-in-Chief of British forces
during the Boer War, and Secretary of State for War in 1915, father
of the largest volunteer army ever raised – a million and a half
scraps of human cannon fodder. I surveyed his memorial on
Marwick Head. An ugly tower, like a lost rook searching for a
chess-board, perched on Orcadian cliffs 284 feet above the cold
waters of the Atlantic where Horatio Herbert met his doom.

On 5 June 1916, three weeks before Kitchener's first hundred
thousand went 'over the top' into the hellish Battle of the Somme,
the earl sailed from Scapa Flow bound for Russia aboard the cruiser
HMS *Hampshire*. That evening, amidst a violent storm, his ship
struck a German mine and all but twelve men perished. Kitchener
was last seen on deck, 'calm and courageous' as the vessel went
down. His body was never found.

I turned from the monument and looked out to sea. Southwards,
the jagged stack of the Old Man of Hoy reared, etched starkly
against a silver-blue horizon. Purple Hoy hills mingled and merged
in midday sunlight. Westwards, limitless white-topped seas waved
to Greenland and distant ice-clad polar shores. Perhaps it was as
well that Kitchener never survived to see his great army of common

men broken and bloody at Picardy. The days of imperialists were gone.

Orkney played host to the Royal Navy during both world wars and the islands are littered with remnants of these horrific conflicts: the Imperial German Fleet, scuttled on 22 June 1919, sparse, rusting hulks and spindle masts, by the grim Churchill Barriers; the delicate filigree wrought-ironwork and paintings of the Italian Chapel, lovingly constructed by prisoners of war, now carefully preserved by their one-time gaolers; broken pillboxes and tank traps; the marks of fighter airfields amongst fertile farmlands.

I first visited Orkney with my family in 1949. We stayed on the shores of Scapa Flow, as guests of the Isbister family, three brothers and three sisters, at Bacakelday Farm. A First World War shell guarded the front door of the cottage and oil slicks from the sunken HMS *Royal Oak*, torpedoed at anchor by a German U-boat during the Second World War, still marked the waters of the bay when high winds blew.

Within the space of two unforgettable weeks I fell in love with Orkney and have returned ever since, trapped by the mystical spell these beautiful islands cast over all but the most insensitive travellers. Orkney is a land of contrasts: of Viking days, when Orkney was ruled by Danes; of turbulent Scottish Middle Ages and the barbaric dominion of Stuart Earls of Birsay; of modern moments of magical music by Peter Maxwell Davies, during the St Magnus Festival; of George Mackay Brown's haunting stories.

The best way to explore Orkney is on foot and a fine walk to start you off is from Birsay to the Kitchener Memorial on Marwick Head. Birsay is a small village in north-east Mainland – a few houses, dominated by the ruins of the Earl's Palace. From Birsay, three hours after high water, it is possible to walk over the concrete causeway to the Brough of Birsay, a tiny island with the remains of a Viking palace and a museum. As small boys, my brother, Ian, and I fought many battles there with fierce, bearded, horn-helmeted Norsemen – and generally came off best. An hour will take you round the island and, providing you have got the tides right, safely back to the mainland.

A bridge in the village leads south to sea links, past the remains of stone-lined pits used to store seaweed during the days of Orkney's booming kelp industry. It was by these shores that I saw my first fulmar, then a comparatively rare bird, now well established along Britain's coastline. This walk is tailor-made for the ornithologist: eider duck, shelduck, dunlin, ringed plover, oystercatcher and curlew call and dance beside you all the way.

Hooded crows shadow your steps, hoping to be guided to eggs

or fledglings disturbed by your passing. Pretend you don't see them and walk smartly on. Common and Atlantic seals, whiskered heads bobbing hello, dot the waves off-shore. In spring and early summer the links are carpeted with wild flowers – *Scilla verna*, thrift, campion and scurvy grass – and at the end of the links, across a low fence, the cliff path climbs gradually upwards to Marwick Head.

Arctic skuas turn and twist overhead. Great skuas, Orkney's bonxies, glide on silent wings, white, under-patches flashing in the sunlight, poised to terrorize their next meal from the gullets of unsuspecting gulls. Marwick Head is an RSPB nature reserve and, during May and July, upwards of 40,000 nesting birds crowd the cliffs in loud, ever-protesting complaint. The path leads down into Marwick Bay by the restored fishermen's cottages and old chapel. Ideal place for lunch.

A narrow track runs eastwards from the bay, crossing a minor road and on to the Loons, a marshland area surrounding the loch of Isbister, home of some of Orkney's spectacular wild brown trout. The RSPB has erected a hide overlooking the wetlands and many a carefully planned and timed walk has come to grief there, watching and waiting for just one more species to brighten the day.

The road back to Birsay ambles along a quiet lane which deposits you onto the links near the cemetery, then over fields to Point of Buckquoy. To the north of Brough of Birsay another cliff path leads to Skipi Geo, where there is a colony of fidgety Arctic terns.

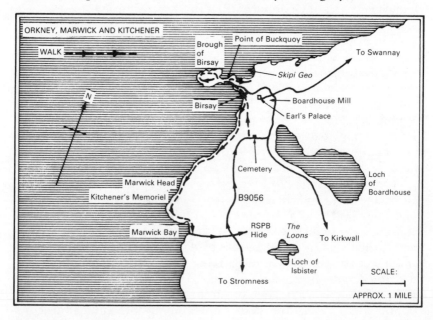

On the shores of an inlet lie reminders of Orkney whaling days – a great whale rib with vertebra attached, set into the ground.

I remember lying on these cliffs as a boy on a windy August day, listening to screaming gulls and the shrieking sea as it battered relentlessly on scarred cliffs. White spray sparkled and flew from mountainous waves, and I saw Kitchener's ship pitching, smoke-belching through the storm, and heard the fearful explosion that carried him into history.

WHAT YOU NEED TO KNOW

Time and effort Distance about nine miles; time is up to you. There is so much to see on the way that you should allow at least five hours – more if you properly explore Earl's Palace and call on the Arctic terns at Skipi Geo. Stout walking shoes are required, and binoculars; however, when using them on the cliffs, lie down first. Orkney cliffs are fragile, dangerous and undercut. Try and plan your trip during May, when the cliffs are sea-bird busy.

Location Ordnance Survey sheet 6, Mainland, second series, scale 1:50,000.

Grid references Start of walk,, Point of Buckquoy 243284; Brough of Birsay 236285; Earl's Palace 248278; Marwick Head 257252; Marwick Bay 259243; The Loons 245242; Skipi Geo 248284; Boardhouse Mill 256275.

Route Park the car at Point of Buckquoy and, after checking the tide times, walk out to Brough of Birsay across the causeway. Visit Viking ruins and early Christian museum. Walk round the island. Return to mainland and walk five hundred yards to inspect Earl's Palace in Birsay.

Cross the bridge in the village and bear right onto the links. Follow the edge of the links where they meet the shore. At the end of the links, cross a low fence and follow the cliff path to Marwick Head and Kitchener's Memorial. In Marwick Bay follow the little road east to the B9056. Cross, and, within two hundred yards, find the RSPB hide.

Return to the B9056 and follow it northwards to a right-angled bend. At this point, by the cemetery, follow a right of way over the fields back to the links and Point of Buckquoy. Skipi Geo is a few hundred yards north from the car park, along the cliffs. End your walk with a visit to Boardhouse Mill, a working mill steeped in history and offering visitors a wide selection of high-quality Orcadian craft products. Well worth a visit.

44

Moness, Ward Hill and Dwarfie

CONSIDERATE parents gave me a small grand piano for my twenty-first birthday and each night, before I go to bed, I play Beethoven. He never wins. After thirty years of combat, he always loses. Night after night I commit murder. Surest way I know of clearing a room of unwanted guests is for me to offer to give them a little tune. People die in the crush for the door.

One night, I discovered Peter Maxwell Davies lurking under a volume of Mozart and thought I would give him a bash. The work in question was *Stevie's Ferry to Hoy*, a simple, haunting, beautiful melody that has stayed with me ever since. Not that I ever mastered the piece with any degree of skill, but I play it recognizably, and that's all that matters to me.

Peter Maxwell Davies, a composer of international repute, has made his home on Orkney and is a mainstay of the Orcadian Annual Festival of Music; arrange your visit in June and hear a hundred glorious voices ringing through the old red sandstone Cathedral of St Magnus in Kirkwall. His music captures the spirit of both people and islands – nowhere more perfectly, in my opinion, than in *Stevie's Ferry*.

The Island of Hoy is an Orcadian enigma, completely unlike the rest of Orkney and more akin in character to the sweeping hills of Sutherland. Most of Orkney is low-lying: rolling, peat-covered moors edged by fine farming lands. Hoy, the Norse word for 'high', is mountainous, almost roadless and absolutely majestic. Ward Hill, the highest peak, is only 1,566 feet, but because it rises so suddenly from sea level it looks daunting, towering and dramatic.

It seems strange to suggest a place to get away from it all on such remote islands as Orkney. Nevertheless, if you really appreciate peace and solitude, head for Hoy. Ferries run regularly from Stromness, through Clestrain Sound, round the little isle of Graemsay to Burra Sound and the pier at Moness. From the pier there are a number of superb walks which vary in length between five and sixteen miles. All have one thing in common: magnificent, unspoilt scenery and rarely another soul along the way.

A circular walk from Moness leads westwards from the ferry, through Cuilags and War Hill, past Sandy Loch and down to the small village of Rackwick, cradled by steep cliffs, fronting the Firth. Wild flowers abound: sundew, butterwort, milkwort, trefoil, woodrush, bog asphodel and dog violet. Where the path meets a narrow single-track road, turn left and walk back across the hill to Moness.

By the corrie of Nowt Bield on your left and the ridge of Dwarfie Hamars on the right, is the Dwarfie Stane. This is a huge sandstone block, a neolithic grave, resting on steep hillsides, measuring 28 feet in length, 14 feet in width and 8 feet in depth. Richard Feacham described it as: 'A passage and two cells have been cut in it, or hollowed out of it. The passage is 7'6" long, 2'4" wide and 2'10" high. A square block of stone lying just outside the entrance was originally used to stop the entrance.'

This burial chamber is unusual because most chambered tombs of the period were built above ground, rather than hollowed out of a convenient rock. Avoid the temptation of trying to crawl in; twentieth-century man is far to large. Walk to the main road – well, the only road on the island – and down onto the beach, which is the quickest way back to the pier.

For a bird's-eye view of Hoy and, on a clear day, half the north of Scotland, climb Ward Hill. After passing Sandy Loch, turn south and follow the line of Water Glen up to the summit. This is an easy climb and an amazing panorama awaits. Sutherland mountains line the horizon – Foinaven, Arkle, Ben More Assynt, graceful Ben Hope and the ragged ridge of Ben Loyal. Over flat Caithness moors, Morven and the Scarabens linger southwards.

North, in a magical multicoloured blue and silver carpet, lie the islands of Shapinsay, Rousay, Eday, Stronsay, Sanday and Westray. Pentland skerries guard the eastern approach to the firth,

Muckle Skerry white-lighthouse-pointed. Across turbulent seas, the deserted island of Stroma, flanked by Duncansby Head, and the massive Caithness cliffs of Dunnet. Descend from Ward Hill to reality, but carefully, down the edge of Howes of Quayawa, a steep, ragged ridge of corries, to White Glen and Moness track.

For the boy or girl who likes a 'proper walk', two miles past Sandy Loch, bear half-right and climb by Berrie Dale onto Grut Fea; westwards across the plateau takes you to the famous Old Man of Hoy – a great stack, rising 450 feet from sea to cliff-top. The moor is home to hen harrier, merlin, buzzard, peregrine, and golden plover. Great skuas preside over the plateau and greet invaders angrily, dive-bombing walkers in mighty swoops of huge flapping dark-brown wings. Walk cautiously and keep a wary eye open for these wardens of the skies.

In the geos that line the sheltered east coast of Hoy another attraction awaits the visitor who is also game fisherman. Sea trout follow the shore and may be caught throughout the year, providing you know where to look. Ask the excellent Orkney Angling Association for advice. They are as friendly and welcoming as their lovely islands and always happy to help visitors find sport and pleasure.

As the ferry pulls away from Moness pier, past the sunken Second World War blockships, rest weary legs and thank the Good Lord for a wonderful day and the physical fitness to enjoy it. Hum a

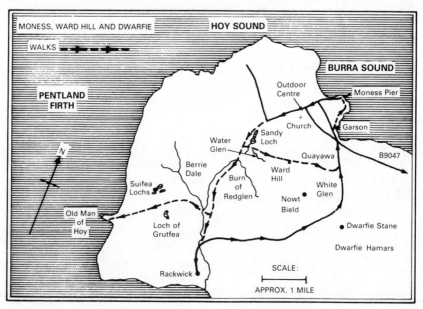

few bars of *Stevie's Ferry* in gratitude. If you don't know the tune, fear not; I will be happy to play it for you at the drop of a quaver – provided you are prepared to take the risk of listening.

WHAT YOU NEED TO KNOW

Time and effort   The most important thing is to plan your walks to coincide with ferry times; or take a tent. The longest walk, from Moness out to the Old Man of Hoy, covers sixteen miles and will take up to eight hours. The round trip from Moness to Rackwick and back is eleven miles and about five hours. Moness to Sandy Loch and up Ward Hill is five miles; allow three hours for the journey. Compass and map should be carried and you will need good walking boots.

Location   Ordnance Survey Sheet 7, Pentland Firth, second series, scale 1:50,000.

Grid references   Stromness 255090; Moness pier 245039; Sandy Loch 219030; Water Glen 220025; Ward Hill 229023; Howes of Quayana 235020; White Glen 242019; The Dwarfie Stane 244006; Rackwick 202992; Berrie Dale 200015; Old Man of Hoy 177008.

Route   All the walks start from Moness pier. Walk from the pier to the B9049. Where it turns south, go straight on. This road leads past the little church and outdoor centre. Where the road turns right, go straight on and follow the track out past Sandy Loch, which is on your left.

The route up Ward Hill is on your left, across the feeder stream for Sandy Loch. On top of Ward Hill plot your route down. Bear left along the ridge of Howes of Quayawa and at the end angle downhill into White Glen. At the minor road, turn and leave the road at Garson to stroll along the beach, back to Moness pier.

For round trip from Moness to Rackwick and back, simply follow the track past Sandy Loch westwards. Where it meets the single track road, shortly before the village, turn left and return to Moness via the Dwarfie Stane. The walk out to the Old Man of Hoy departs from the Sandy Loch track where Berrie Dale Water joins Burn of Redglen. Follow Berrie Dale water up the hill for a hundred yards and then bear left. At the top, walk between the little Suifea lochans on your left and Loch of Grutfea right. The Old Man is due west from here. Return to Moness the same way.

45

Rousay Cairns

ORKNEY contains some of the most important archaeological monuments in Europe: the Stone Age village of Skara Brae; the dramatic standing stones of Stenness, the Ring of Brogar and the magnificent Chambered Tomb of Maes Howe. Given the enormous number of Orcadian neolithic sites, I often wonder how many people lived on Orkney five thousand years ago. Which is my trouble – I find it impossible to resist the temptation to speculate.

Sooner rather than later, and completely unsupported by any evidence, I build up a mental picture – of busy farmer-fishermen tending sparse crops; of tousle-haired boys wrestling on ancient Atlantic sands; of heavy-breasted women grinding corn, warmed by neolothic sun, chiding scavenging dogs. But there must have been a thriving community in Orkney, perhaps several hundred souls; and there must have been great interchange of ideas, techniques and ideals.

There is little evidence of the earliest hunter-gatherer settlers in northern Scotland, other than sea-shell middens. They lived out their lives, scrounging and slaying where they could, a bird here, a beast there, living in caves or rude shelters. On good days, perhaps the carcass of a washed-up whale; always, the plentiful prehistoric mussel beds. But their descendants left their mark, particularly by the manner in which they buried the dead – in great chambered tombs.

These massive, complicated structures lie scattered throughout Highlands and Islands, memorials of distant, perhaps more civilised days, when, to survive, a community had to work together. Values were more simply expressed, in the everyday necessities of living; and I think that we have more to learn from their lives than dusty archaeological facts. Speculating again.

The Orkney island of Rousay, the 'Holy Isle', has more than its fair share of these monuments, and an easy, delightful coastal walk passes the most impressive. However, the first part of the walk is by sea, providing you don't sit down during the journey – from the pier at Tingwall on Mainland, over Eynhallow Sound, by the island of Wyre to the little harbour at Brinyan.

Rousay is encompassed by craggy shores, scored by rocky bays. Most of the hinterland is gently hilled and there is a fine viewpoint on the highest peak, High Brae of Camps, a modest 800 feet above sea level. High Brae is easily climbed from the road that circles Rousay and the view from the top is spectacular.

Orkney consists of almost ninety islands, some thirty of which are inhabited, and most can be seen from the hill. Northwards lie Westray and its little sister Papa Westray; the wild rocks of North Ronaldsay and the long straggle of Sanday. East are Egilsay, Eaday, Stronsay and Shapinsay, with Auskerry in the distance. South, across Mainland, crowd the ever-present gentle hills of Hoy.

Good news for lighthouse keepers, because nearly all the islands have warning lights – much-needed in these dangerous, turbulent waters, which constantly argue and squabble with deserted black-rock shores, a vast turmoil of tormented seas, empty to Iceland, Greenland and America. Vikings, rather than me, thank you, rowing off into that particular sunset.

The only road round Rounsay is numbered with bureaucratic thoroughness. You would imagine that, being a single road, it would have a single designation. Not so. At the pier it is the B9065; where it joins the loop, right and left, it becomes B9064. A minibus plies the route in an anticlockwise direction, taking forty-five minutes to complete the journey. On the way, the driver will introduce you to the life and times of Rousay, past and present, and this will greatly prepare you for the walk.

Leave the bus at Mid Howe and follow the signposts for the Westness Walk which lead to the brochs and chambered cairn of Mid Howe. At first sight you might be forgiven for thinking that Mid Howe was an old Orcadian cattle byre: drystane walls separated into cubicles. The structure is 106 feet in length by 42 feet wide and the burial chamber takes up 76 feet. There are twelve cells, six on each side, and one side has platforms. Twenty-five skeletons were found here, along with well preserved pottery.

The path leaves Mid Howe and wends its way along the shoreline, by Eynhallow Sound, overlooking Eynhallow and the Church of the Holy Isle. These are fierce waters, where long arms of Atlantic and North Sea race through dangerous narrows with amazing force. Fulmars sweep by, and in spring and summer the path is bright yellow, blue and red with wild flowers. Orkney is devoid of foxes, squirrels, deer and badgers, but if you have your wits about you there is always the chance of seeing an otter.

I decided many years ago that if I were reincarnated I would choose to return as an otter – footloose and fancy free, the outdoor life, as much walking, swimming and fishing as I wanted, and a protected species into the bargain. Who could ask for more?

The path eventually comes back to the 'main' road, but this is a relative statement – expect possibly two or three vehicles an hour. Knowe of Lairo, a long, four-horned chambered cairn, is approached by the track that leads left from the road, past the schoolhouse at Frotoft. It was probably constructed over a considerable period, bits being added at different times. The cairn extends in a long mound for a distance of 180 feet and there is an 18-foot-long entrance passage leading to three burial chambers.

Nearby is another chambered cairn, Knowe of Yarso, a stalled cairn with four compartments, first explored in 1934, when the remains of twenty adults and one child were found. They were well prepared and provided for their last, long journey: '30 individual red-deer, some sheep and a dog. Relics included fragments of food-vessel and beaker pottery, four arrowheads and more than 60 other flint implements, and five bone tools.'

The last of the Rousay monuments is Blackhammar, close to Yarso Cairn, another stalled burial chamber divided into fourteen stalls, measuring 42 feet by 6 feet in width. I wonder if they sang or chanted when they buried their loved ones? How did they mourn? What rites or incantations were performed over the still, sleeping bodies?

Back at Brinyan Pier, as reward for attention, treat yourself whilst waiting for the ferry. The sea-food processing factory at Brinyan offers some of the most splendid lobster, scallop and fresh-cooked crab in Britain. Enjoy a neolithic snack, and spare a crumb for me.

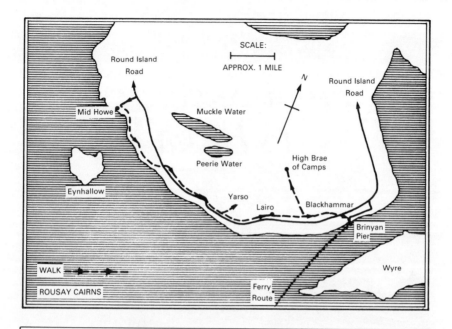

WHAT YOU NEED TO KNOW

Time and effort   Prepare
yourself for this visit and read up
about the chambered cairns you
will be visiting. Best book is a
Guide to Prehistoric Scotland by
Richard Feacham, published by
Batsford, London. Make sure to
check return ferry times. The
walking part is easy and total
distance is 6½ miles. Spend the
whole day on the island and climb
High Brae of Camps after visiting
the cairns. Further details from Josh
Gourley, Orkney Island Tourist
Board, Kirkwall. Telephone:
Kirkwall (0856) 2856.

Location   Ordnance Survey
Sheet 6, Orkney – Mainland,
second series, scale 1:50,000.

Grid references   Ferry at
Tingwall on Mainland 403228;
Brinyan Pier 436275; start of walk
at Mid Howe 375310; Mid Howe
Cairn 371308; Yarso Cairn 404281;
Lairo Cairn 414277; Blackhammar
Cairn 425275; High Brae of Camps
419290.

Route   Sail from Tingwall to
Brinyan and take the minibus
round the island. Get off at Mid
Howe and follow the signposts
marking the Westness Walk,
eastwards along the coast. The
cairns are on the left of the road and
High Brae of Camps is easily
accessible to the north.

46

From Skelberry to Birka

THE SHETLAND ISLANDS have provided home and haven for the world's travellers for more than four thousand years. At Jarlshof, near Sumburgh Airport, there is evidence of continuous occupation since Stone Age, Bronze Age and Iron Age times, right down to the days of Viking domination. The 'Temple' at Stany-dale, a communal building near Bridge of Walls, is a remarkable structure, standing amidst the ruins of a settlement of nine houses, surrounded by the outline of ancient fields, clearly worked by a small neolithic community.

Early writers referred to Shetland and Iceland as ultima Thule and in the 4th century B.C. Pytheas of Marseilles, astronomer and geographer, sailed 'six days from north Britain' to reach them. These remote northern lands are a wild scatter of more than a hundred islands resting in the storm-tossed bosom of the mighty Atlantic Ocean, covering an area of more than 550 square miles.

The largest island is Mainland and other principal islands are Yell, Unst, Fetlar, Bressay and Whalsey. They are an endless delight of sunlight and serenity, guarded by huge, sea bird-clad crags, fringed with deserted white sandy beaches. Moorlands are specked silver with more than three hundred freshwater lochs peopled by Arctic skua, red-throated diver and golden plover. Springtime is a riot of wild flowers and in high summer the endless days of the 'simmer dim' banish night.

Most people have only a vague idea of where Shetland really is – other than being in that little box, top right of the map on evening weather charts. In fact, the islands lie on the same latitude as Bergen in Norway and the southern tip of Greenland, as close to Norway as they are to Aberdeen and vastly proud of Viking traditions.

The Gulf Stream warms and washes Shetland's shores and the islands are never too hot or too cold, though at any one time weather conditions vary greatly throughout the island: the east coast may be basking in sunshine at the same time as the west coast is cringing under lead-heavy rain. Only one thing is constant: the ever-present wind; and what the Shetlander calls a gentle breeze BBC weathermen in London generally report as a force eight gale.

I first visited Shetland in 1983, delighted to be amongst so many fellow Sandisons, for mine is a Shetland name. The old capital was Scalloway, on the west coast, but this distinction now belongs to Lerwick in the east. Lerwick is a busy, bustling town and its harbour plays host to Europe's fishing fleet. Boats from Russia, Poland, Denmark, Norway, Germany and France crowd the anchorage off Commercial Street and a dozen different dialects may be heard in shop and bar.

Visitors admire and buy the famous handmade knitwear, which uses the natural colours of hardy Shetland sheep, fleece taken in handfuls from their stout sides. There is delicately spun lace from the island of Unst, soft sheepskin rugs and traditionally designed fine silverware.

The islands provide a wealth of interest for archaeologist, ornithologist, botanist, geologist, historian, game fisherman or just plain 'escapist' – enough to keep every member of the tribe fully occupied and interested, and the only danger is the all-pervading, overwhelming temptation – never to leave.

During my visit, I spent most of my time walking and fishing the lochs of Mainland in company with Rae Phillips and Bobby Tulloch, expert anglers and well accustomed to finding their way over trackless moors to wonderful places. Their boats were wonderful too: sleek, narrow-bowed, finely crafted works of art, owing as much to Viking traditions as to the skills of modern day boat-builder. There is a saying in Shetland: 'You may do as you please with another man's wife, but you must never touch his boat.'

A walk of outstanding beauty and interest is from Skelberry, in North Mainland, out over the moors to Lang Clodie Loch. It is a long, tough way and very definitely compass-and-map country.

When you climb onto the moor an amazing vista opens. Scattered granite boulders glisten in the sun; golden plover flit and pipe over rough peat hags. Scootie Allan, the Shetland name for the Arctic skua, tumble and twist in stunning aeriel mock-combat; the constant wind tugs at your clothes.

We threaded our way across the moor, edging round peat banks, past a string of dark blue trout-filled lochs and lochans with magical names: Roer Water, Maadle Swankie, Tonga and Muckle Lunga, Many Crooks, Moshella and the Loch of the Grey Ewe. But the most dramatic of all is lovely Birka Water, 700 yards long by 300 yards wide – easier to measure its extent than to describe its beauty.

Birka is crystal-clear and at the east end there is a sandy beach which makes a perfect picnic spot. Opposite the beach is a magnificent waterfall, dropping from high crags along the south shore. I first saw it after heavy rain, on a warm, sunny afternoon: full, silver, thunderous, tumbling sparkling into the waters of the loch, sending urgent wavelets rippling over the calm surface.

We walked round the loch to the foot of the falls and then climbed slowly to the tiny, narrow lochan at the top. As I reached the crest, head level with the outlet falls, I found myself eyeball to eyeball with a red-throated diver. The bird was half a dozen yards away – the 'rain goose' of the Shetlands. As more of my bulk appeared, the graceful creature gave a wink of welcome and splashed noisily skywards, seeking a less busy feeding place.

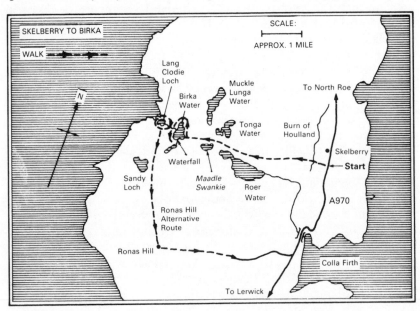

Birka collects together all the waters from the lochs on the north slope of Ronas Hill, the highest point on Shetland, and hurries them seawards down a splendid outlet burn on the west shore, a narrow, boulder-strewn, living stream, chattering and singing in still summer air. Far below, on a green plateau, tiny Lang Clodie Loch gathers the streams into her arms then shoots them out over vast, red-ragged cliffs into the Atlantic wilderness.

Bobby Tulloch and I walked homewards that evening, over the marvellous wonder of the moors, stopping once or twice for a few casts in little lochans along the way, talking about this and that, and mostly not at all. Before descending to the road, I paused and looked back, trying to fix the memory and scent and sounds of the moorlands in my mind. As I write, they are still as fresh and startlingly clear as on that first, memorable, sunny Shetland day.

WHAT YOU NEED TO KNOW

Time and effort As the crow flies, seven miles there and back. For humans, twisting and turning over the moor, probably about another mile. This is a hard walk and there are no tracks or paths to ease the way. Essential equipment are strong walking boots, compass and map. If mist comes down, even with compass and map it will be hard to find your way, so do make sure you are well prepared for all eventualities.

Location Ordnance Survey Sheet 1, Shetland – Yell and Unst, second series, scale 1:50,000.

Grid references Start of walk 362862; access onto hill 360863; Roer Water 335864; route between Tonga Water and Maadle Swankie 322872; Birka Water 316875; Birka waterfall 315872; Birka outlet burn 316875; Lang Clodie Loch 312878.

Route Park the car just before the houses at Skelberry. There is a gate on your left, leading down through a grass park to the foot of the hill. Cross the burn and climb the gully leading up to the plateau.

Walk westwards, keeping Roer Water on your left. Take frequent bearings to check direction or you may find yourself going too far north. Pass between Tonga and Swankie, then walk in a straight line, as far as possible, on to Birka. If you get it right, you should arrive at the sandy beach.

Walk round the north shore of Birka to reach the waterfall, crossing the outlet burn on the way – step nimbly to avoid wet feet. Climb the waterfall and say hello to my red-throated diver, then return to the outlet burn.

Follow the outlet burn down the narrow defile to the cliff-top plateau and Lang Clodie Loch. Stay well back from the edge of the cliffs. I suggest you return home the same way but, if you feel really adventurous, angle south past Sandy Water and Swabie Water to climb Ronas Hill. The way down follows the east shoulder of Ronas and this leads to a hill track which will take you back to the A970, then north to your car. Be warned, this will add five more miles.

47

Caithness Castles,
Cliffs and Shores

T HE SHORE and cliff path from Keiss to Staxigoe in Caithness is a
walk for all seasons. I have tramped that way battered by
winter gales, grateful for every sheltering dip, watching white
showers of snow buntings peck stubble fields and huge, heavy-
billed great northern divers haughtily riding the endless waves of
Sinclair Bay; and enjoying the sudden pleasurable company of
sombre-eyed, whiskered and curious Atlantic seals.

Arctic winds chase mountainous seas eastwards, dashing them
in white-sprayed fury against Old Red Sandstone rocks weathered
by millions of years into stark, jagged stacks, knifed by black,
sea-booming fiords and secret caves. Sinclair Bay is a scimitar of
gold, enclosing green-crested breakers, sweeping southwards by
gaunt Ackergill Tower, past grim Girnigoe Castle to lighthouse-
topped Noss Head.

Springtime flowers peep from rocky corners: *Primula scotica*,
light-green leaves cupping vivid purple flowers. Sea rocket and
sandwort, scruvy-grass and sand sedge adorn the beach. High
dunes host chickweed and hawkweed, backed by field gentian,
campion, wild pansy and knapweed. Cliff-tops riot with thrift,
sea-pink, rose-root and vetch.

Fulmar, kittiwake, guillemot, razorbills and puffin tenement crags in never-ending squabble. Turnstone, purple sandpiper and sanderling flight the shore. Solan geese, Sule Skerry gannets from Orkney, turn and dive, stiff-winged flashes of brilliant white. Emerald-green and black shags cluster the rocks, wings out-stretched, like old men waiting for tea time.

I have wandered, summer lazy, splashing through River Wester where it marries the sea, sunbathing on warm sands, lulled to dreamless sleep by oystercatcher and curlew. Walked south into a theatre backdrop clad with graceful mountains; conical Morven, Madiens Pap, Ben Alisky, Clas Choire and bare-breasted Scarabens.

Keiss, the 'rounded ridge' of the Vikings, is a tiny village clinging to Caithness cliffs. A small harbour plays host to a few colourful craft fishing for crab and lobster, and there is a busy salmon-netting station. From a rocky promontory, the dark ruins of Keiss Castle guard the neat cluster of grey houses, as they have done for more than four hundred years.

Keiss produced one of Scotland's most famous engineers, James Bremner, born on 25 September 1784. The only schooling he had consisted of the customary three Rs of the eighteenth century: reading, writing and religion. His father apprenticed him as a carpenter in Greenock and, after six and a half years and two voyages to America, Bremner returned to Wick, where he set up as shipbuilder and fish curer.

James Bremner invented a suspension crane, with a jib capable of extending from 80 to 120 feet; a pile driver which drove three piles simultaneously; the world's first 'Mulberry' harbour, constructed as a series of watertight compartments, which could be floated into position prior to being sunk; and a system of buoyancy bags, used for floating heavy foundation stones into position for building harbours.

His most notable triumph was refloating ss *Great Britain*, then the world's largest ship. The *Great Britain* ran aground on the rocks of Dundrum Bay in Ireland on Friday 27 August 1847. For a year, the best engineering brains in the country tried to rescue her. Eventually, Bremner was asked to help. Not only did he refloat the mighty vessel, but within a few weeks he sailed her back to Liverpool under her own steam, inventing a super-capacity water pump in order to do so.

As a mark of esteem, Bremner was awarded the Telford Medal of the Institute of Civil Engineers and when he died in August 1856 Caithness mourned the loss of a much-loved son. Flags were flown at half-mast and shops along the funeral route pulled down shutters. James Bremner was laid to rest in the grounds of the old parish church of Wick.

The Wester river is a barrier along the way. Wading time. Cold legs in high water, damp feet in midsummer. Sea trout and salmon run the short river to Loch of Wester, the 'loch of the ford', now greatly disfigured by the clutter of huts and workyards of under-sea pipe fabricators, Kestrel Marine. The mouth of the Wester is a favourite fishing spot, where local anglers gather to tempt sea-liced, silver fish as they splash through salty waters to upstream spawning grounds.

Behind marram covered dunes lies one of Scotland's oldest golf courses, Reiss, founded more than one hundred years ago and a traditional Scottish 'links' course, flat and sand-blown, covered with wild flowers and cursing golfers. Whenever I forget that my greatest golfing handicap is a complete inability to hit the ball in a straight line, a few holes at Reiss remind me. I see a lot of wild flowers and do a lot of cursing, searching for lost balls.

At low tide, wide sands between Wester and Ackergill make easy walking. Our two dogs love the beach and tear about like mad things, up the dunes, dashing in and out of the sea. Well, Breac does the sea bit; Heathcliff is more circumspect about water, having almost drowned as a puppy in a cold Sutherlandshire loch.

This is our Boxing Day family walk, regardless of weather – though sometimes Caithness weather is so mild that dafter members of the tribe paddle, blue-toed and screaming with delight. At the age of twenty-five? Everyone comes home wet.

Ackergill Tower, one of the oldest inhabited houses in Scotland, dominates Sinclair Bay. Five-storeyed and nearly seventy feet high, Ackergill was once protected by a moat and high wall. Cromwell's troops used the Tower as headquarters during their visit to Caithness in the seventeenth century and in 1699 it was bought by the Dunbars of Hempriggs.

Ackergill is in new hands – completely refurbished as a 'think tank' for business executives seeking privacy and seclusion whilst they make world-shaping decisions about toothpaste sales and paper-clips. Tiptoe by. Great men should not be disturbed by simple strand strollers.

Past the little community of Ackergill, with its high-legged lifeboat-launching station, the track edges a rocky shore, climbing up sheer hundred-foot cliffs. Not a place for dogs or people without a head for heights. Like me. I keep well back, inching cautiously along the windswept tops.

Sinclair and Girnigoe Castles beckon, perched on a sharp, almost inaccessible promontory: dark ruins of dark days. Clamber down into the dungeon where George Sinclair, 4th Earl of Caithness, left his son James to die in 1576 – 'keiped in miserable captivity for the space of seven years'. James had incurred his father's wrath for failing to murder hostages taken during the siege of Dornoch. The hapless young man was starved for two weeks then given well salted meat. When he asked for water to slake his raging thirst none was given and James died in agony, chocked by his own tongue.

Ann and I often visit the grim castle, which provides a sheltered, skua-eyed view of the bird-busy bay. Eider duck, male birds with neatly parted black-and-white backs, dive in the clear waters. Summer terns flit and dance over the waves. And, sometimes, carried on the wind, a starker, more distant, blood-chilling call seems to echo through the cold ruins.

Close to Sinclair and Girnigoe Castles is another summer favourite of ours, Sandigoe Bay – a scrap of yellow sand, backed by scarred cliffs, rarely busy, ideal place for warm after-church Sundays. Nearby, at Noss Head, in a deep gorge, is a natural rock 'seat', one hundred feet above the sea. Approach carefully and not at all in high winds.

Puffin-watching time. A few yards over the void, in the cliff face, a small colony of puffins have burrowed nests. They sit, firework-beaked and serious, doing what puffins do – whirring off in endless food-hunting forays for hungry offspring. Funny birds, puffins: when the parent birds reckon that youngsters are big enough, they abandon their squawking brood. Chicks stumble light-wards, topple down the cliff, and learn – very quickly – to fly.

Across the fields from Noss is the fishing village of Staxigoe, where my grandfather was born. Time was when this small harbour was more important than neighbouring Wick. Timber from Sweden arrived at Staxigoe and the rocky harbour might be packed with up to eighty ships. Today things are a lot quieter; a few, small inshore boats moored fore and aft across the bay.

I feel at home in Caithness, and nowhere more so than by Staxigoe. Elsay Farm, once owned by an uncle of my father, George Reay; the war memorial, standing on land given to the community by a long-departed relative. Sounds stupid, but I'm sure some of them join me on my walks from Keiss to Staxigoe, and I'm always glad of their company.

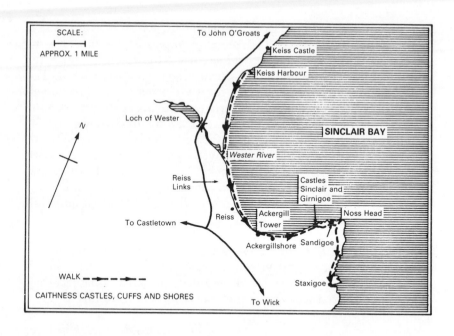

WHAT YOU NEED TO KNOW

Time and effort Allow about five hours for this walk. Even better, when the sun is shining, make a day of it. There is a lot to see along the way, including Sinclair and Girnigoe Castles, which are an outing in themselves. Take along a towel for drying feet after crossing Wester river.

The cliffs towards the south end of the bay are very high and great care must be taken walking along the tops. Also when visiting the castles. There are sharp drops and in the summer the grass is smooth and slippery.

It is possible to climb down to the shore through a dark stairwell at the end of the promontory upon which the castles stand. Only do so when the sea is mirror calm. At other times waves could wash you off to Norway – and who needs that? Keep children under strictest supervision. Dogs should be left tied up outside.

Location Ordnance Survey Sheet 12, Thurso and Wick, second series, scale 1:50,000.

Grid references Keiss 346713; Keiss Castle 357616; Wester river 339577; Ackergill Tower 354547; Ackergill 359545; Castle Girnigoe 379549; Sandigoe Bay 385550; Noss Head 388551; Staxigoe 385525.

Route Leave your car at Staxigoe, by the harbour, and travel by taxi, bus or a good friend out to Keiss. If you propose to visit the old castle of Keiss, first ask permission to do so at the farm on the way down to the shore. From the harbour at Keiss walk south along a track which edges the fields, leading to a car park overlooking the shore.

If the tide is out, cut down onto the beach. Otherwise, follow the track along the top of the dunes until you find space on the sands. Place to come down is at a ragged, barbed-wired fence. Cross the river Wester as best you can and simply follow the beach south.

As you near Ackergill Tower, you will be forced off the beach by rocks. Walk along the foreshore past the tower and then, keeping up, make for Ackergill village. A well marked path exits from the village and this leads up and along the cliffs to Castle Sinclair and Girnigoe.

After visiting the castles, walk towards Noss Head. A fence line cuts your path and a signpost will direct you down a steep gully to Sandigoe Bay. Climb back up the hill and make for the little lochan by the side of the lighthouse. On the cliff, close to the west of the lighthouse, you will find the puffin colony – open from April until June – and the rock seat.

Walk back down the road which leads to the lighthouse and at the car park turn left and walk over the fields to Staxigoe. This will bring you to the harbour.

48

Herring and Hill Forts

W ICK IS a ragged little town clustered round a shallow wave-
swept bay. Even today, in good weather, gaining access to
the harbour is hazardous; in days of sailing boats it could be
downright dangerous. During the great herring fishings in the
nineteenth century boats stayed at sea overnight, returning the
following morning, and often had to anchor in the bay to await

favourable tide conditions for entry. It was then that Wick Bay could be most wicked for if a sudden storm caught the fleet at anchor they were forced to run for safety before an onshore wind chased by huge, merciless breakers.

The worst disasters happened in the 1840s. In 1845 ten men drowned when a fierce onshore wind whipped shallow waters into a frenzy of foam and surf. Three years later, 37 men perished in a single night of terrible gales. Thousands of people gathered on harbour walls, helpless, as boat after boat came to grief in tormented, boiling waters. Those days have long since gone, although Wick is still a busy fishing port; but the 'silver darlings' are remembered in an imaginative exhibition in the Wick Heritage Centre, housed in an old grey building close to the harbour.

There are superb photographs from the famous Johnson Collection: furnished interiors of fishermen's homes; complete boats in a mock harbour, rigged and crewed; and a full-scale model of a herring curing house. A host of personal effects and documents are displayed, including the sad little school bag of a child who died, the books of his brief life spilling from the open flap.

Although unkempt and untidy, Wick has its own special charm and character. Wickers are self-reliant, friendly, hard-working people, used to making their own entertainment. The town's only cinema closed a few years ago and until then was one of the few places of entertainment. However, not so very long since, when silent films were shown, a visit to Wick cinema could be a less than entertaining experience.

One of the Caithness clans was blessed with large numbers who could neither read nor write, and when they filled the front rows the rest of the audience had to contend with a commentary as their spokesman translated, in a loud voice, the subtitles at the bottom of the screen.

Caithness coastlines are dressed with harbours which flourished in the glory days of the herring fishings: Scrabster, Thurso, Castletown, Ham, Scarfskerry, Huna, Groats, Skiraz, Keiss, Staxigoe, Wick, Sarclet, Whaligoe, Lybster, Latheron and Dunbeath. All had their complement of sturdy boats which each summer sailed the stormy waters of the North Sea to reap sparkling harvest.

Whaligoe is one of the most dramatic of these little harbours and lies south from Wick, near Ulbster. The sea has cut a narrow cove into the cliffs and more than three hundred steps lead down to a tiny, now deserted harbour. Wives used to carry heavy crans of dripping herring up the steep steps and everything required to service the small boats had to be laboriously transported down the flagstone stairwell.

Although fisherfolk have gone, the old steps are still carefully cared for by a local lady. Her belief is that since Jesus was a fisherman, and will come again, He might well arrive at the foot of Whaligoe Steps. She is determined that the good Lord should have easy access to the top.

West of Whaligoe is Hill of Yarrows, a rounded summit 696 feet in height. There are more than eighty prehistoric sites in the vicinity, dating from almost five thousand years ago. Chambered tombs, standing stones, stone rows, hill forts and settlements and brochs – perhaps one of the most extensive and least explored archaeological sites in Britain.

Garrywhin Fort crests a ridge overlooking the tiny, reed-covered Loch Watenan and is 590 feet in length by 300 feet wide. A stone wall runs for a distance of 450 feet, pierced by entries lined with stone slabs. At the foot of the ridge, close to the shore of the loch, is a short horned chambered cairn where neolithic pottery was found amidst skeletal remains. At Mid Clyth, nearby, are magnificent stone rows: twenty-two rows of eight stones locked fast in the soil, their purpose and function as yet unknown.

Loch Watenan is home for wading and diving birds, which flock there in hundreds to quack and croak amongst thick weeds. It is also home for some beautiful wild brown trout – deep-bodied, golden and wild fighters. Earlier this year I caught a fish of two pounds on a Slazenger 4 golf ball. No, not a 'fisherman's story' but quite true. Well, nearly.

I was half concentrating, casting, gazing round at the endless delight of wildlife, when a glint of white under the water drew my attention. A golf ball. Never one to look a gift horse in the mouth, I bent forward, scrabbling about under the surface trying to pick it up without getting my sleeve wet – but to no avail.

I tried kicking it shorewards, forgetting all about my flies, which were somewhere out in the middle of the loch. When the fish grabbed and shot off, rocket-like, I overbalanced and fell on hands and knees. Soaking wet now, I grabbed the ball and stumbled ashore. Which is how I managed to catch a trout on a Slazenger 4.

A track leads from the south end of the loch up into the hills, wending past Cairn of Get towards Loch of Warehouse. South-west of Warehouse are more chambered cairns and a standing stone, and the hill is scattered with the boulders and stones of other ancient monuments.

Warehouse is one of my favourite places and the view from the top is perfect. The tower of Old Parish Church in Wick, where my daughter Jean was christened; Keiss and the wide sweep of Sinclair Bay, rising over moorlands to John o' Groats and the hills of Hoy on Orkney. Morven and Scarabens look close enough to reach out and touch whilst westwards, over the flow country, Sletill Hill and Ben Griams nod sleepily in Sutherland.

Walk north down the hill to Loch of Yarrows and back in time once more to the hut circles, brochs and cairns of neolithic man. Must have been a busy place then, bright with children's laughter and busy families in the fresh dawn of time. I never pass this way without wondering what they would all make of our fretful, complicated lives now.

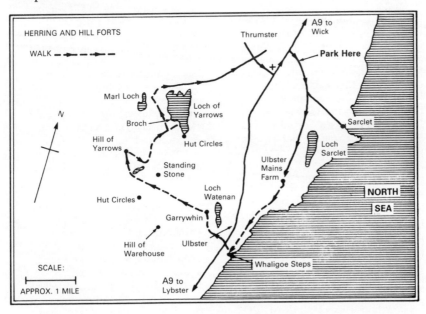

WHAT YOU NEED TO KNOW

Time and effort Visit Wick Heritage Centre first and then set off on this delightful ten-mile hill and coastal walk. Good walking boots should be worn for the way is often rough and wet – but few problems. Keep back from the edge of the cliffs, however, and be warned: going down the steps at Whaligoe is a lot easier than climbing back up them. Before visiting the Watenan neolothic sites, arm yourself with a copy of either the *Caithness Book*, editor Donald Omand and published by Highland Printers, Inverness, or Richard Feacham's excellent *Guide to Prehistoric Scotland*, published by B. T. Batsford Ltd, London.

Location Ordnance Survey Sheet 12, Thurso and Wick, second series, scale 1:50,000.

Grid references Wick Heritage Centre is at Bank Row 365506; Car parking at Thrumster 338452; Mains of Ulbster 335421; Whaligoe Steps 321406; Loch Watenan 319410; Garrywhin 318414; Loch of Warehouse 300424; Loch of Yarrows 310440; Yarrows Broch 308435.

Route After visiting Wick Heritage Centre, drive south down the A9 to the village of Thrumster. Turn left, and you will find parking space by the small playing field on your left, a hundred yards from the road junction. Follow the minor road south past Loch Sarclet to Mains of Ulbster and on to the cliffs. A mile further brings you to Ulbster and Whaligoe.

The first large house on the cliff is a converted mill. The top of the steps is further on, to the left of the row of cottages. Up and down the steps. They are very steep and if you have any doubts about climbing back up only go half-way down, to the first 'twist', and view the harbour from above. No prizes for having a heart attack in Caithness.

From Ulbster, cross the A9 and take the little road directly in front of you. It leads up to Loch Watenan. The hill fort and archaeological remains are all close together. Climb north from the loch, using compass and map, which you have not forgotten, and admire the view from Loch of Warehouse and Hill of Yarrows.

Descend from the north end of the loch down a narrow gully and on to Loch of Yarrows and Yarrows Broch and the hut circles, which are all at the south end of the loch. Follow the rutted farm road up the west bank, passing Marl Loch on your left, not shown on Ordnance Survey sheet.

Turn right along the north shore of Yarrows and follow this little road to its first major crossing. Turn right here, back to the A9. North up the A9 to Thrumster. Take great care on this last section. Cars travel very fast up this long, straight part of the A9.

49

Forss and Scrabster

A FEW MILES west from Thurso in Caithness, along the last road on mainland Britain, lies Forss House, an old grey building nodding sleepily over the Forss river in a small wood, carpeted in spring with celandine, snowdrop and bluebell. Treecreepers study the bark of insect-rich pines. Woodcock whirr stiff-winged through dark forests.

A pair of buzzards rule the valley from a new plantation throne and below Forss Falls, where brown and white waters dash over shining black rocks, Atlantic salmon hurl themselves in silver bars at cascading torrents, urgent for upstream spawning grounds.

Forss House has been converted into a comfortable hotel, home for passers-by and fishermen who come to do battle with salmon in the narrow little river. To the left of the house, by the side of the lawn, a path leads to a promontory overlooking the falls. A thoughtful seat comforts you as you wait and watch for the sudden splendour of the king of fish, rising majestically to challenge the stream.

Early one morning I watched an otter sidle cautiously into the pool. His eyes sparkled and whiskers twitched as he scented the air for the smell of danger, but the wind was right for me and I watched him pursue, capture and land a salmon of about nine pounds in weight, rushing the doomed fish into the undergrowth, anxious for breakfast. Wish I could catch them so easily.

A track leads from the back of the house, through an iron gate, along the side of pine-wooded hills above the river. Forss slides gently seawards through green meadow lands, decked with purple and spotted orchid, tormentil, bugle, milkwort and primrose. Grey and pied wagtail dip and bob by the stream as it hurries under a footbridge to greet the cold Atlantic in Crosskirk Bay.

On the cliffs above the west shore cluster the ruins of one of Scotland's oldest places of worship, the twelfth-century St Mary's Chapel. Close by, bristling with fiercesome antennae, is a US Air Force base, endlessly searching the ether above ragged seas for warning of who knws what. Opposing cultures. One born out of a love for God; the other out of fear of man.

Long wave-washed rocky ledges wed the Forss river to the sea in an everchanging pattern of crests and tiny storms. Oystercatchers pipe by the shore and seals black-bob the bay. Brisk eider drakes, escorted by dowdy-grey females, roller-coast the tide. A small boat snuffles round the rocks, seeking lobster pots and anything else that happens to be passing.

Fertile fields rise in low sea-girt cliffs and a faint path runs eastwards along the jagged tops towards Brims Ness, fanned by dangerous, skerry-fingered shoals and shallows. Seas tumble and turn in contrary currents and wide waves sweep the shore. Surfers from all over Europe gather here for international events. Crowds of men and women, in skin-tight colour-striped wet-suits.

Off shore, other Europeans seeking international fame speck the sea with fishing boats, dredging the depths for record-breaking fish. Recently, whilst millions watched on television, three well-heeled pleasure-chasing Londoners roared and laughed drunkenly as one of their party took pot-shots at passing sea gulls. Our local sheriff took his own pot-shots at this stupid man in court a few months later.

Past the scratchy harbour at Brims, flat fields covered in wild flowers margin the sea. Marwick Head on Orkney rears north-wards, pricked by the dark shape of Kitchener's Memorial. Ward Hill on the Island of Hoy shimmers blue in hot afternoon haze and on the forward slope of the cliffs, in warm corners, *Primula scotica*, that rarest of Scottish plants, blushes purple-pink in summer sunlight. Tiny streams chortle down rocks by bright clumps of yellow primrose whilst curlews engineer busily under stones on the shore below.

A mile from Brims, on a tall promontory, separated from the mainland by a narrow ridge, lie the remains of a Pictish hill fort. Little can be seen of the fortifications but the air is full of the sound of these hardy painted men going about their business, keeping careful watch seawards for marauding Norsemen. There is a private swimming pool near here. A shallow, clear pool, left by receding tides, backed by high cliffs. A secret, silent place to laze away tired hours.

On Brims Hill old quarries echo empty, relics of the great days of the Caithness flagstone industry at the turn of the century, when each year 16,000 tons of Caithness flagstone was exported throughout the world. London's Strand and docks were paved with Caithness flag, as were Leith Walk and Parliament Square in Edinburgh. The ever-increasing railway stations used Caithness flag and there was a constant demand for this fine-quality stone. Until some unkind person invented concrete.

The cliffs now cry to Spear Head and Holborn Head, towering almost a hundred feet above Thurso Bay. On wild days I have seen waves crashing at their feet, shattering spray in wind-driven sheets to the top. During the terrible times of the Highland Clearances, America-bound emigrant ships would gather in Thurso Bay to await the arrival of their cargo of human misery, torn from Sutherland glens to make way for Lowlanders and their sheep.

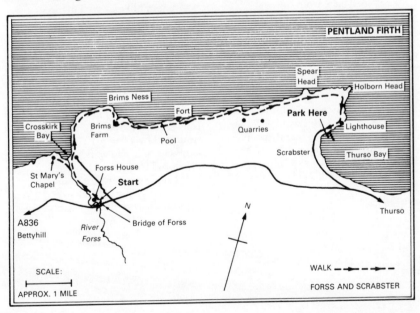

The tall stub of Holborn Head lighthouse points the way to Scrabster harbour. The Orkney ferry, *St Ola*, lies snug against her pier. Fishing boats and sailing craft throw colourful reflections over smooth, oil-calm waters. Like a crow's nest above the scene, the Upper Deck restaurant beckons. They serve the best steak in the whole of Britain. Treat yourself after the long walk. You deserve it.

WHAT YOU NEED TO KNOW

Time and effort Eight miles from Bridge of Forss to Scrabster harbour and about four hours' walking, more if you stop and look a lot. I suggest that you leave your car at Scrabster harbour by the Orkney ferry terminal and take a taxi out to Bridge of Forss. Make sure that you tell the driver that it is Forss/Thurso you want. There is another Forse, to the south of Wick, and they are often confused. If it is a fine day pack a picnic and take longer, stopping for lunch in the cove by my 'private swimming pool'. The only danger is the cliffs. Keep well back from the edge, particularly in windy weather and on Holborn Head.

Location Ordnance Survey Sheet 12, Thurso and Wick, second series, scale 1:50,000.

Grid references Bridge of Forss 037687; Crosskirk Bay 029700; St Mary's Chapel 025701; Brims Ness 040714; swimming pool 058709; fort 063710; quarries 079707; Holborn Head 109716; Scrabster harbour 100700.

Route The entrance to Forss House Hotel is well signposted before Bridge of Forss. Have a stirrup cup. Turn left out of the hotel, past the two chalets, and follow the track through the trees to the iron gate. Right from here, along the bank above the river. After a few hundred yards you are forced downhill. Scramble over the bluff and walk down the flat fields to Crosskirk Bay.

St Mary's Chapel is on the west side of the river and is reached by crossing the bridge near the ruined stone buildings on the shore and walking uphill on a well marked track. Return to the east bank and follow the cliff round past Brims Ness to Brims Farm. Walk up the farm road for a little way and then cut back left to the cliff-top.

As the cliffs grow in height, look out for the swimming pool and hill fort promontory. The track now runs close to the edge of the cliff, protected by a fence. Keep on the landward side and walk out to Holborn Head. From Holborn Head angle down towards the lighthouse and walk back to Scrabster harbour. And the Upper Deck.

50

'Sheer Greed
of Materialism'

BLAR NAM FAOILEAG in Caithness is a beautiful, living, growing peat bog which has survived six thousand years since the last ice age and is still busy today, laying down layer after layer of peat over flagstone and sandstone of the Middle Old Red Sandstone series. During glacial times Caithness was invaded by ice from two directions, the principal body moving in from the North Sea and covering the county east to west.

When the ice retreated it left behind a large, shallow inland lake, fed and drained by river systems, and a barren landscape of bare rock mixed with fragments dredged from the sea bottom. This formed a stiff boulder clay, almost impermeable to air and water, and the only plants able to establish themselves were shallow-rooted creeping species such as mosses, lichens, marsh flowers and small windswept trees. Perfect conditions for the growth of peat.

A section through the peat shows, at lowest levels, remains of dwarf willow and alder which survived in the subarctic tempera-tures. Then remains of birch and hazel, with many of the hazel nuts showing that they had been gnawed at one end by small rodents. Uppermost layers contain buried roots and branches of stunted woods.

Blar nam Faoileag is an SSSI, a site of special scientific interest, alive with history, a precious part of our national heritage. But we

live in strange times, when man constantly disregards his environment and seems to care for it only in so much as it might yield him
financial return.

The previous owner of Blar nam Faoileag was the local 'laird',
Lord Thurso, and he proposed a plan to extract peat from the bog
on a commercial basis. A very considerable sum of public money
was paid to compensate him for not doing so. More recently, the
same 'laird' sold substantial tracts of the Flow Country to private
tree-farming contractors, thereby allowing them to devastate
ancient Altnabreac moorlands by planting millions of foreign
species of conifer.

In a speech to the House of Lords on 12 April 1976, Lord Thurso
is reported in the *John o'Groat Journal* as saying: 'The sheer greed of
materialism threatens these rural communities'. In my opinion,
Lord Thurso's actions clearly demonstrate the truth of his own
statement, and his complete disregard for the Caithness landscape.

The land south of Blar nam Faoileag, round Loch Ruard, is safe
in more enlightened hands and there is little danger of man's 'sheer
greed' destroying these wonderful open moorlands. To walk
amongst them is an unforgettable experience – a vast, silent,
unchanging landscape, heather-purpled under God's great heaven.

Golden plover and greenshank pipe crossly from red-specked
sphagnum tussocks. Winter brings flocks of graceful whooper
swans and greylag geese. Great skua and Arctic skua make long
sweeps over the moors. Hen harrier and peregrine ply the wilderness in search of prey and black-throated divers feed in trout-filled
lochs.

Tiny streams, banked bright with wild flowers, flow endlessly
over lichen-covered boulders, past water-gardens of yellow flag.
Sundew, butterwort, crowberry, bog asphodel, blue and pink
milkwort, tormentil, spotted orchid and marsh violet blush shyly
from warm corners.

One hot summer's day, Ann and I were fishing in Loch Ruard. A
light breeze gently ruffled the surface and fish were rising to our
carefully presented flies. By mid-morning we had caught our fair
share. Which was just as well. Because, for no immediate apparent
reason, everything went quiet. Where, but a moment before, trout
had been rising, now complete silence reigned.

'Don't turn round too quickly,' said Ann. She was sitting in the
stern, looking over her left shoulder, smiling. I eased round and
saw the reason for the smile and the sudden absence of fish. Lying
on its back, 'arms' folded across downy chest, was a magnificent
dog otter. Long, white-tipped whiskers twitched. Intelligent,
sparkling eyes gazed at us curiously, following our every move.

The otter turned over and swam slowly round the boat, then dived soundlessly, a stream of bubbles disappearing amongst small waves. That was the last we saw of him but the memory of that glorious moment will remain with me until my dying day.

The walk out to Ruard and Blar nam Faoileag starts from the A895 Latheron–Thurso road a mile from Achavanich and another delightful Caithness water named Loch Stemster. At the south end of Stemster is a dramatic circle of Bronze Age standing stones, the grey sentinels of Stemster: 'It may originally have comprised about 60 stones, but one third have weathered or have been removed. The stones are thick slabs of flagstone, protruding on average about 5 ft above the ground'.

Little Loch Rangag lies south, close to the main road, and on the east bank is a rock-covered promontory, the home of Grey Steel, a Caithness robber-baron. His stock in trade was to greet travellers on the steep-sided Ord of Caithness, inviting them to contribute to the Grey Steel Preservation Fund. Those unwilling or unable to do so were hurled to their deaths over the cliffs.

The story goes that eventually Grey Steel pushed his luck too far. He kidnapped a young lady from my village of Watten and carried her off to Rangag to work his evil pleasure. The lover of the lass was not amused and gathered together an angry gang of friends. On Grey Steel's castle, catching the inmates drunk from an even- On a dark night they crossed the moors to Rangag and descended

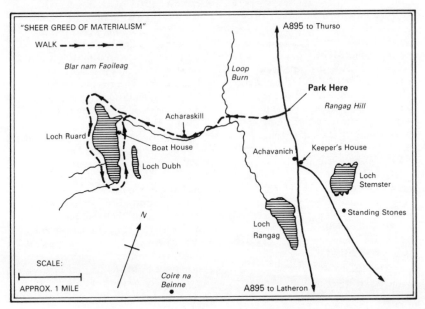

ing's jollity. Which they rounded off by the removal of heads and complete destruction of the tower.

Harsh times, when often the only way of redressing wrongs was to take the law into your own hands. When I look at the mindless destruction of irreplaceable Caithness moorlands by mass afforestation, I'm not so sure that our ancestors were all that wrong. So, if you will excuse me, I'm off to organize the troops – and there will always be room for you, or any other man or woman who loves Scotland's wild and wonderful places.

WHAT YOU NEED TO KNOW

Time and effort The first part of this walk is along a good track which leads almost half-way to Loch Ruard. From there on the going can be rough and wet, particularly after heavy rain. So go prepared and make sure you are well shod. Also, pack compass and map. If a Caithness mist comes down you will need them out on the moors. The total distance covered is approximately eight miles and this will take about four and a half hours – as always, depending upon what distracts you along the way.

Call first at the house of the keeper, Mr Munro, to check that you will not be disturbing any stalking parties. His is the large detached white house on the east side of the road at Achavanich, opposite the farm and on the way to the Stemster Standing Stones.

Location Ordnance Survey Sheet 11, Thurso and Dunbeath, second series, scale 1:50,000.

Grid references Keeper's house 180427; Loch Stemseter 190424; Stemster Standing Stones 189417; car parking and start of walk 178436; Acharaskill Steading 158432; Loch Ruard 140435; Blar nam Faoileag 135445.

Route Visit the standing stones first and then drive north. There are two empty cottages by the east side of the A895 about half a mile north of Achavanich. Park here. Across the road, is a track leading down into the valley. Walk this way.

Cross the gate at the bottom and follow a well made Land-Rover track up the hill. The track criss-crosses the Loop Burn, eventually abandoning it to lead to the farm steading at Acharaskill. This is set amidst a patch of green field which is easily seen from the start point.

A faint path runs west from the steading, up the north side of the outlet stream from Ruard. It is bad news to walk on the south side of this stream. The ground there is very rough indeed and hard going. This track will bring you to Loch Ruard.

Strike right at the loch, round the shore to the north bay. This is the southern edge of Blar nam Faoileag. Return from the bog by walking down the west bank of Ruard, round the south bay, where there is a good sheltered picnic spot under high peat banks. Complete the circle round the loch to the boat house and follow the track back down the burn and on to the car.

Select Bibliography

Bennet, Donald, *The Munros* (Edinburgh, Scottish Mountaineering Trust).

Bennet, Donald, *The Southern Highlands* (Edinburgh, Scottish Mountaineering Trust).

Bingham, Caroline, *Land of the Scots* (London, Fontana).

Burnett, Ray, *Benbecula* (Benbecula, Outer Hebrides, Mingulay Press).

Butterfield, Irvine, *The High Mountains of Britain and Ireland* (London, Diadem Books).

Culzean (Edinburgh, National Trust for Scotland).

Dunkeld and Birnam (Perth, Dunkeld and Birnam Tourist Association).

Feacham, Richard, *Guide to Prehistoric Scotland* (London, Batsford).

Gordon, Seaton, *Highways and Byways in the West Highlands* (London, Macmillan).

Grimble, Ian, *The Trial of Patrick Sellar* (London, Routledge & Kegan Paul).

Lamont-Brown, Raymond, *Walks for Motorists* (London, Warne).

Lindsay, Maurice, *The Lowlands of Scotland* (London, Robert Hale).

MacKenzie, Agnes Mure, *Scottish Pageant* (Edinburgh, Oliver & Boyd).

MacKenzie, Alexander, *History of the Highland Clearances* (Inverness, Melven Press).

Melrose Abbey (Edinburgh, HMSO).

Moir, D. G., *Scottish Hill Tracks* (Edinburgh, John Bartholomew).

Murray, W. H., *The Companion Guide to the West Highlands of Scotland* (London, Collins).

Nethersole-Thompson, D., *Highland Birds* (Inverness, Highlands and Islands Development Board).

Omand, Donald, *The Caithness Book* (Inverness, Highland Printers).

Pennycook, Andrew, *Literary and Artistic Landmarks of Edinburgh* (Edinburgh, Albyn Press).

Poucher, W. A., *The Scottish Peaks* (London, Constable).

Prebble, John, *Highland Clearances* (Harmondsworth, Mx, Penguin).

Randall, Eric, *The Merry Muses* (London, Luxor Press).

Rintoul, and Skinner, *Poets Quair* (Edinburgh, Oliver & Boyd).

Rosebery, Countess of, *Dalmeny House* (Queensferry).

Simpson, Douglas, *Hermitage Castle* (Edinburgh, HMSO).

Smith, Sydney, *South West of Scotland Rambles* (Glasgow, Richard Drew).

Steven, Campbell, *Glens and Straths of Scotland* (London, Robert Hale).

Stevenson, Robert Louis, *Songs of Travel*.

Thompson, Francis, *Portrait of the Spey* (London, Robert Hale).

Thorne, and Collocott, (eds), *Chambers Biographical Dictionary* (Edinburgh, Chambers).

Tranter, Nigel, *Portrait of the Lothians* (London, Robert Hale).

Walkers' Britain (London, Pan/Ordnance Survey).

Walk Perthshire (Edinburgh, Bartholomew).

Wilson, Ken, and Gilbert, Richard, *The Big Walks* (London, Diadem Books).